FOUNDATIONS OF UNDERSTANDING

ADVANCES IN CONSCIOUSNESS RESEARCH

ADVANCES IN CONSCIOUSNESS RESEARCH provides a forum for scholars from different scientific disciplines and fields of knowledge who study consciousness in its multifaceted aspects. Thus the Series will include (but not be limited to) the various areas of cognitive science, including cognitive psychology, linguistics, brain science and philosophy. The orientation of the Series is toward developing new interdisciplinary and integrative approaches for the investigation, description and theory of consciousness, as well as the practical consequences of this research for the individual and society.

Volume 10

Natika Newton

Foundations of Understanding

FOUNDATIONS OF UNDERSTANDING

NATIKA NEWTON
New York Institute of Technology, New York

JOHN BENJAMINS PUBLISHING COMPANY
AMSTERDAM/PHILADELPHIA

TM The paper used in this publication meets the minimum requirements of American National Standard for Information Sciences — Permanence of Paper for Printed Library Materials, ANSI Z39.48-1984.

Library of Congress Cataloging-in-Publication Data

Newton, Natika.
    Foundations of understanding / Natika Newton.
       p.   cm. -- (Advances in consciousness research, ISSN 1381-589X ; v. 10)
    Includes bibliographical references and index.
      1. Comprehension. 2. Comprehension (Theory of knowledge) 3. Cognition. 4. Communication--Psychological aspects. 5. Human information processing. I. Title. II. Series.
BF325.N48   1996
153.4--dc20   96-28754
ISBN 90 272 5130 4 (Eur.) / 1-55619-190-1 (US) (Pb; alk. paper)   CIP

John Benjamins Publishing Co. • P.O.Box 75577 • 1070 AN Amsterdam • The Netherlands
John Benjamins North America • P.O.Box 27519 • Philadelphia PA 19118-0519 • USA

Contents

CONTENTS

vii

Acknowledgements

The ideas in this book have been developing since the late 1970's, when I first began to wonder what it is that we actually *do* when we consciously think about something. Many people, therefore, have been influential. In particular, I have benefitted enormously from four NEH Summer Seminars. Gilbert Harman helped me organize my early views about mental imagery at his Princeton seminar in 1982. Sydney Shoemaker focussed my thinking on self-consciousness at his seminar at Cornell in 1985, and introduced me to the work of Gareth Evans and other influential writers. Michael Bratman, in a 1992 seminar at Stanford, gave me crucial guidance in developing what is now Chapter Three, the core of the foundationalist theory of understanding. Stephen Stich, at San Diego in 1988, let me see clearly what is wrong with an approach to intentionality that is modelled on language use.

In 1993 I was awarded a Faculty Research Grant by the AAUP Joint Council, New York Institute of Technology. This grant allowed me time to complete Chapters Four and Five.

Two philosophers, Ralph Ellis and Kathleen Wider, have been particularly inspirational to me in the more recent stages of my work. Both have developed accounts of consciousness that intersect, in different ways, with my own. I have benefitted immensely both from their own work and from their kind and insightful attention to mine.

Among many others who have helped me at various times are Marcelo Dascal, Willem DeVries, George Graham, Asa Kasher, Thane Maginnis, Al Mele, Erika Newton, Joel Newton, Peter Smith, Lynn Stephens, Susan Wood, and Tony Zador. I am indebted to Maxim Stamenov and Gordon Globus for strengthening and polishing the final version of the book, as well as to an anonymous referee for several useful suggestions.

I am grateful to Lawrence Erlbaum Associates for permission to use the illustrations in Chapter Four, and to the Cambridge Center for Behavioral

Studies for permission to use previously published material in Chapter Eight. The five paragraphs beginning at the bottom of page 13 are used with permission of the Philosophy Documentation Center, publisher of the *Philosophy Research Archives.*

Finally, I owe an incalculable debt to my husband, Marshall D. Newton, for his steadfast patience in sustaining, encouraging and advising me (whether I wanted him to or not) throughout this long project.

CHAPTER ONE

Introduction

A few aspects of life are still widely believed to be true mysteries — in principle inaccessible by the physical sciences. One of them is phenomenal consciousness. The qualitative properties of sensed objects, their colors, sounds, smells as *subjectively experienced by the perceiver,* seem to some philosophers and scientists impossible to reduce to brain mechanisms that human minds can comprehend (e.g. Penrose 1989; Chalmers, 1995). Flanagan (1992) has called such thinkers the New Mysterians. At the same time, however, some cognitive neuroscientists such as Crick (1994) are working to resolve the apparent mystery. The main focus of their work has been the visual system, which yields the bulk of examples of these qualitative properties or qualia. If an physical explanation can be found for our knowledge of, e.g. 'what the experience of red *is like,*' then other such experiences, it is hoped, will fall into place.

A few writers discuss a broader range of qualia — subjective experiences of mental states other than purely sensory ones, such as beliefs, desires, or decisions (e.g. Goldman 1991). Such 'intentional' mental states, like purely sensory ones, are recognized by their subjects through conscious experiences. Common examples are the 'tip-of-the-tongue' phenomenon and the 'Aha!' experience. Writers interested in consciousness, however, whether or not they are Mysterians, seldom explore these experiences in detail (cf. Metcalfe and Shimamura 1994). Such an exploration is the aim of the present study. I believe that an examination of the conscious experiences of these cognitive mental states will help unravel certain entrenched philosophical puzzles concerning both consciousness and intentionality, or representational thought, and show that our experience of intentionality can be explained in terms of familiar, nonmysterious physical mechanisms.

By *intentionality* I mean the ability of a thought to mean or refer to another thing, to be 'about' something other than itself. (A narrower sense of the term applies to actions: intentional actions are those done deliberately. Unless otherwise specified, I will use 'intentionality' in the broader sense applying to mental states in general. As I hope to show, however, the broader sense is closely related to the narrower.) Intentionality has for many years been considered, along with consciousness, an essential property of the human mind. Human mental states have been widely and almost uncontroversially treated by philosophers as possessing both consciousness and intentionality, while the possession of these properties by other things, such as nonhuman minds or computers, is a matter of debate. Among philosophers they are usually examined independently, rather than as interdependent components of mentality, or in terms of a common mechanism.

The term *'consciousness'* has many different senses, and in nonphilosophical contexts is often treated as synonymous with 'awareness' simply to refer to perception or knowledge (e.g. 'He was conscious of a cool breeze;' 'He was conscious that someone had entered the room'). The mysterious sort of consciousness is a *reflexive* mental state that somehow perceives or knows *itself* as a mental state of the subject, along with other qualitative phenomena that the subject concurrently senses.

Intentionality and consciousness are normally treated in terms of quite different paradigms. Phenomenal consciousness has been viewed primarily as a passive phenomenon: as a mental state in which a unique type of information, inaccessible by objective means, is somehow received. Intentionality has also been treated as a passive condition. The dominant approach to intentionality in recent years has been to discuss it in terms that are used for symbol systems like natural language. Mental states such as beliefs or desires are viewed as *'having* meaning' analogously to the way sentences in natural language 'have meaning;' they are spoken of as representing other things — as being 'about' or being 'of' things other than themselves (their *content*) — in the way that stories or pictures represent other things. Mental states, or mental representations, are viewed as constituting a type of language (Fodor 1978). On these two models, in principle, language-using systems could have intentionality without having conscious states (e.g. computers); nonlanguage-using systems (e.g., animals) could have conscious states but not intentional ones.

It is the goal of the present book to offer an alternative to the above approaches, which in my view lead to dead ends. I believe that both consciousness and intentionality can be understood in terms of a complex but unified type of psychological *activity*, that they are realized in interacting brain mechanisms and share a common origin in experience. By their nature, I will argue, all intentional states are potentially or actually conscious states; the linguistic model obscures this important fact. While I believe that the paradigms described above are misleading, however, I also believe that the popularity of these approaches themselves, as well as the psychological phenomena they purport to describe, can be explained in terms of our conscious experiences of intentionality. While consciousness is not usefully thought of as a type of perception, and intentionality is not usefully thought of as the property of representing or having meaning in the way that language has meaning, part of thinking of them correctly is understanding why they appear to fit those descriptions.

In my analysis of consciousness and intentionality, two other phenomena play crucial roles. The first is *understanding*. While sentences in natural language and mental states are both said to have meaning, in the former the possessing of meaning is obviously dependent on an understander — a language user — to recognize and interpret the meaning. In the case of mental states, such understanding may be built in as a part of intentionality. In either case intentionality is closely related to understanding, and, I shall argue, is best defined in terms of understanding.

The other phenomenon is *basic goal-directed action*. This may seem remote from the three mental properties introduced above, in that basic goal-directed action can more readily be described in terms of nonintentional physical mechanisms. But if that is true, it is a positive feature of my proposal. I shall argue that all conscious intentional states can be reduced to nonintentional sensorimotor states associated with the basic goal-directed action abilities that humans share with simpler organisms and, conceivably, with inorganic machines.

The reduction is not a smooth one, particularly in the case of intentionality. That concept as defined in philosophy is, I argue, the result of a metaphor; this metaphor is derived from the experience of goal-directed action. Consciousness, including the consciousness of understanding meaning, is a phenomenon associated with the brain's sensory and motor mechanisms that make such experience possible. Thus the account is a complicated one. The present chapter is devoted to laying out the components of the account and offering a preliminary sketch of the way they fit together. In the following section, the relation between intentionality and conscious understanding is introduced.

1.   Intentionality

Two aspects of the traditional concept of intentionality are important for the present theory. The one most commonly acknowledged stems from Brentano's characterization of mental states such as desires or beliefs. A desire is a desire *for* an object; a belief is a belief *about* some state of affairs. But while mental states are related in this way to objects, the relations are different from any physical relations. They are distinguished, said Brentano,

> by what the scholastics of the Middle Ages referred to as the intentional (also the mental) inexistence of the object, and what we, although with not quite unambiguous expressions, would call relation to a content, direction upon an object (which is not here to be understood as a reality), or immanent objectivity. (Brentano, quoted in Chisholm 1957: 168-9)

As Chisholm (1957) points out, the intentionality of a mental state is a peculiar sort of relation to a content: neither a sentence asserting the relation — e.g. 'Diogenes looked for an honest man' — nor its contradictory implies that the object exists. Statements asserting nonintentional physical relations, on the other hand — e.g. 'Diogenes sat in his tub' — do imply the existence of both relata.

How can such a property be explained within a materialist framework? The most prominent effort to do so during the past twenty years has involved the language of thought hypothesis, or 'mentalese' (Fodor 1978). On this account, thinking is a process in which brain states interact computationally by means of their physical structures. The result is thought that is purely syntactic in its mechanism, but that has a semantic aspect in that its 'sentences' are isomorphic with the sentences of natural language, which refer to the world. It is thus possible to say that mental states are intentional (have meaning) in the way that natural language sentences are intentional. Just as one can *say* 'Scientists are searching for Bigfoot' without implying the existence of Bigfoot, one can think about Bigfoot in the 'language of thought' without implying the creature's existence. In this way psychology merges with philosophy of language.

The theory that mental content is in part determined by environmental conditions, originating with Putnam (1975), also precludes direct consciousness of the intentional properties of thought. The Twin Earth example is well-known: a person who while on Earth uses the term 'water' to refer to H_2O, is transported without his knowledge to Twin Earth, a planet just like Earth except that unbeknownst to him 'water' there refers to XYZ rather than H_2O. On Twin Earth his use of 'water' will refer to XYZ, but he will have no way of knowing that. As Putnam says, meanings are not just in the head; hence they could not be directly accessible by introspective consciousness.

If the intentionality of thought is similar in this way to the intentionality of natural language, then one would not expect to derive an understanding of consciousness from an account of intentionality. Language of thought proponents do not claim that a subject has conscious access to internal syntactic computations. Introspection cannot be trusted to reveal the nature of the mind's cognitive mechanisms. Consciousness is discussed in philosophical contexts primarily in relation to the experience of phenomenal qualities, rather than in relation to meaning-bearing states of the mind.

Ironically, however, an implicit connection to consciousness is the second aspect of the traditional concept of intentionality that is important in the present context. While a close relation between intentionality and consciousness is not widely and explicitly recognized and is often denied, it is sometimes acknowledged that we can be, at times at least, introspectively aware of the intentionality of our mental states. For example Millikan rejects what she calls "meaning rationalism," or the ability to be infallibly aware of the intentionality of one's thoughts, in an unmediated way. She notes, however, that one could "admit that people are (sometimes) aware of the intentionality of their thoughts, just as they are sometimes aware of others looking at them or aware that it is raining" (Millikan 1984: 91).

Another much discussed example of the consciousness of intentionality is provided by Searle (1980) in his argument that a purely syntactic device could not understand any 'sentences' it computes, and hence would not be intentional. Searle's 'Chinese Room' example asks the reader to imagine playing the role of a computer in manipulating Chinese symbols that in fact represent coherent questions and answers. If the manipulator does not read Chinese then he will not understand the questions and answers that he nevertheless processes correctly. The purpose of the Chinese Room example was to make this fact vivid to the reader:

> The aim of the Chinese Room example was to try to show this by showing that
> as soon as we put something into the system which really does have intention-
> ality, a man, and we program the man with the formal program, you can see
> that the formal program carries no additional intentionality. It adds nothing,
> for example, to a man's ability to understand Chinese. (Searle 1980: 422)

Searle's example indirectly raises the issue of consciousness because it appeals to the reader's ability to be *aware of what she does and does not understand.* If understanding were not the sort of thing of which one could be aware in oneself, then the example would have no force, a supposition clearly contra- dicted by the degree of discussion it has generated. Thus many philosophers appear to agree that it is possible at least sometimes to be conscious of the intentionality of one's mental states, and hence that intentionality is the sort of thing that can in some way present itself to awareness.

But this admission does not sit easily with the view that the intentionality of mental states is their ability to bear meaning analogously to sentences in natural language. The meaning carried by sentences of English is a function of the ways they are used, and is an external relation; intrinsically, they are meaningless. Some hold that the intentionality of mental states is similarly external, and is a function of the role played by the states in the subject's psychology. For example, that a mental state is a desire *that Clinton will be re- elected President* is the fact that it was caused by certain sensory input and that it in turn causes certain other mental states and certain verbal and nonverbal behavior under certain circumstances (the ways these causes and effects can be objectively determined has never been specified). If this is the nature of intentionality, how can we be conscious of that intentionality simply by having the mental state? It may seem that I can be conscious of my desire that Clinton will be re-elected President, but in the absence of a simultaneous awareness of the entire causal nexus of that desire, which determines its content, what mechanism could mediate my consciousness of that content? If, on the other hand, intentionality is internal or intrinsic to the states, then a comparison with language cannot help us to understand this property.

A hint to a solution can be found in the Chinese Room example. Searle's emphasis in his general argument is upon the impossibility of deriving seman- tics from syntax, and it is this aspect of his argument that is usually discussed. But an equally important issue he raises concerns one's *consciousness of understanding,* or of not understanding, the meanings of symbols that one manipulates. The force of the example lies in the certainty with which the man in the room can say that he does not understand Chinese. No one who has discussed this example has attempted to argue that the man in the room understands Chinese *in the usual sense* — in the sense, that is, that he understands the English instructions — even though he believes he does not. A kind of privileged access to one's understanding of a symbol appears to be widely acknowledged among Searle's critics. It is this sort of understanding that Searle identifies with intentionality, in his argument that syntactic computation could not produce intentionality.

2.   Understanding

I believe that the phenomenon of conscious understanding is particularly suited for getting a handle on intentionality, for two reasons. First, while other intentional states may have phenomenological aspects, that associated with understanding is, we might say, *closer to the content, or meaning, of the state.* By this I mean that the way it feels to understand something is directly and entirely a function of what is understood, whereas the way it feels to desire something is not directly and entirely a function of what is desired. Consider an example. As Flanagan notes, "beliefs (when they are experienced) are experienced differently from desires, and desires differently from expectations" (Flanagan 1992: 67). Now suppose that while on Earth I desire to drink a glass of water that I see, and believe that what I desire is H_2O. Then, unbeknownst to me, I am transported to Twin-Earth where I desire to drink a glass of what appears to me to be water, and believe that what I desire is H_2O. According to the Putnamian account of this case, what I believe on Earth is true, and what I believe on Twin-Earth, where what is called 'water' is XYZ, is false. But this difference will be undetectable to me, since the content of my intentional states is not determined by just what is in my head. On the other hand, the difference between my desire and my belief on Earth, and the difference between my desire and my belief on Twin-Earth, *will* be detectable to me. Thus the phenomenology of beliefs and desires need not be a function of their content. Perhaps all beliefs feel different from all desires because of nonintentional properties they may possess (e.g. a desire may manifest itself by a sense of restlessness or dissatisfaction lacking in a belief).

The content, however, does play some role in the way specific desires and beliefs are experienced. While in the Twin-Earth case I do not experience the difference between desiring water and desiring XYZ, I *would* experience the difference between desiring water and desiring bread. While I may have no access to the real referents of 'water' or 'bread,' or to the chemical nature of substances I desire, I do have access to what 'water' and 'bread' *mean to me.* This is because when I think of water I think of certain sensorimotor experiences, and my conscious desire for water is a desire for something that causes *those experiences.* My thoughts about bread are thoughts of phenomenally quite different experiences. In the same way, my beliefs about water and bread are beliefs about something causing those experiences, whether or not that something is H_2O, XYZ, or yeast and flour.

We might say that thinking about a type of thing in terms of certain sensorimotor experiences is having *an understanding* of that type of thing. The sort of understanding we have of something determines the way our thoughts of that thing are experienced. The distinction between having *an understanding* of a term and knowing its correct meaning is similar in some ways to Frege's distinction between sense and reference in linguistic contexts. Unlike Frege, however, I want to say that we can have a similar kind of understanding of *anything* we can encounter or think about, not only linguistic entities. For example, a very young child could desire water without having a word for it. Her desire for the water takes the form of a desire for something causing the very same sensations as in our above example. When she learns to say 'water' she will have gained much power, but her mental experience when she says 'I want water' need be no different from that in her nonverbal state of wanting water. It is this mental experience that I am calling her 'understanding' of 'water.' In saying that understanding is 'closer to the content' of an intentional state than is its status as a belief or a desire, I mean that the mental experience that constitutes one's understanding of some stimulus, linguistic or otherwise, is a specific response to that stimulus, and serves as one of the subject's ways of thinking about that stimulus. Desires and beliefs *as such*, on the other hand, may be characterized more generally. An immediate implication is that any conscious intentional state — a mental state that is about an object — is accompanied by an understanding of that object. I cannot consciously desire water without having some understanding — some way of thinking about — water.

This fact constitutes the second reason that the experience of understanding can provide a clue to the nature of intentionality. In most debates about the existence of intentionality in some system or other, the issue comes down to whether or not the system can be said to understand what it is doing. We have seen that it does so for Searle. Haugeland makes the same point:

> To put it bluntly: computers themselves don't mean anything by their tokens (any more than books do) — they mean only what we say they do. Genuine understanding, on the other hand, is intentional 'in its own right' and not derivatively from something else. (Haugeland 1981: 32-33)

As Haugeland suggests, the way that truly intentional things 'have meaning' is active: *they mean* something by their own efforts; they are not simply *used* to mean something by some other agent. To mean something in this active way, one's own understanding of what one means is essential. The notion that there is this kind of 'intrinsic intentionality' is derided by Dennett and others (Dennett 1987). Nevertheless, it is clearly possible *to mean,* and we know that it is because we know the experience of understanding what we mean. Whether or not the experience is 'mistaken,' or the understanding 'illusory,' or what we mean confused or erroneous in a given context is irrelevant; it is the experience itself that makes it so difficult to deny the existence of intentionality — the act of meaning — in our mental states.

3. The experience of understanding

For the above reasons, the experience of understanding is uniquely suited to give access to the nature of intentionality. Before I outline the theory of intentionality that will be developed in this book, however, further clarifications of the experience of understanding as it is discussed here are necessary.

First, understanding is not here used as a normative concept. One may understand *incorrectly*; understanding is sometimes misunderstanding. The 'Aha!' experience may be mistaken; what seemed to be a solution may not work after all (just as pain experience may inaccurately signal bodily damage). My claim is not that the experience of understanding is *reliable*; it is that this experience provides a window to the nature of our intentionality, which is likewise not a normative concept. Misrepresentation, like representation, is an intentional property. Partly for this reason, arguments against consciousness of intentionality based upon the theory that meaning is widely determined do not address the issue I raise. Those arguments may show that we lack access to the *actual* referents of our thoughts, but not that we lack access to any intrinsic meaningfulness *for us* that they may have. Moreover, while the mental entities studied here as bearers of intentionality are what are commonly called 'representations,' these are viewed as intentional not because they represent the world but because they are experiences that are meaningful to the subject.

Gordon Globus expresses the postmodern rejection of representations as traditionally understood:

> We do not know reality, according to postmodernism, by means of any representations of that reality. We know reality directly and immediately; there is nothing that gets between us and the reality we always and already find ourselves in.
>
> Modernity, in contrast, relies on representations of the world — mental and neural re-presentations that mediate between us and the world. (Globus 1995: 127)

The view of representations taken in this book is compatible with the postmodern position. Indeed, the source of our understanding of the representation/reality dichotomy is addressed explicitly in Chapter Five.

An objection might arise here. There seems to be a large degree of variation among experiences of understanding that I have described, from the very specific 'Aha!' and 'tip-of-the-tongue' (TOT) experiences to the seemingly infinite variety of vague imagery aroused by stimuli of all types. What justifies grouping these together as a single phenomenon?

The answer is that in spite of the variability of the experiences, they do form a single category if one thinks about them as follows. The 'Aha!' and TOT experiences are close to one end of a spectrum that ranges from complete bewilderment to complete enlightenment. At one end is confusion, puzzlement, mystification: the absence of understanding. Next come feelings like TOT, which signal glimmers of understanding. The 'Aha!' feeling arises when the understanding that has been at the tip-of-the-tongue finally emerges. After that comes the subject of this book: the vast range of specific sensorimotor images and sensations that constitute one's ongoing, undramatic understanding of one's environment.

Puzzlement may be more salient to us than understanding. Puzzlement, like pain, requires remedial attention, while understanding allows us to proceed uninterrupted. For that reason, TOT and 'AHA!' experiences are labeled, but not the ordinary states in which we understand what is going on around us. But while understanding *as such* may not attract our attention, the mental experiences that we have when we understand are consciously accessible, in the same way as are our pain-free bodies if we choose to notice them while we are occupied with the world. We know, and can say, when we understand something completely (have an understanding of it that satisfies us); this ability is based upon conscious experiences, however widely they may vary.

Thus the topic of this study can be categorized as: the conscious experiences upon we base our beliefs that we understand.

Second, it should be noted that one's understanding of a kind of thing can change from occasion to occasion, and can be more or less adequate. I may use different sensorimotor experiences to think about water in different contexts; and I might think about water by means of some experience that was not originally connected with water at all, such as the sight of vodka in a glass. As I have said, my concern is not with the *adequacy* of the experience of understanding, but with the nature of the experience itself. I am, moreover, not claiming that there is *one specific* experience that is essential to the understanding of a concept whenever an instance is encountered, such as certain particular images that are evoked by the term 'water.' The experience may change with every new encounter. What makes them all instances of understanding 'water' is that they are all used by the subject to respond to 'water.' in such a way that their occurrence leads the subject to believe that she understands the term. How this process works is, of course, the subject of this book.

I must also stress that as I am using 'understanding,' it applies to more than just language. We can understand objects and states of affairs as well. It is true that normally we do not speak of understanding objects; instead we say that we 'know what an object is.' We also say, however, that we 'know what a word means,' and that phrase is equivalent to saying that we understand the word. Objects and words are different in that words have referents; objects, unless they are playing a symbolic role, do not. Thus we most often demonstrate our understanding of a word by identifying its referent, whereas we demonstrate our understanding of an object in other ways, such as by explaining its use. I shall argue, however, that these two ways of understanding are at root similar in that both of them involve use, and the two ways of understanding are manifested by similar mental experiences: experiences derived from past occasions when we used the word or the object.

Similarly, it may sound odd to say that we *understand a state of affairs*. While we might say that we understand *why* the water is in the glass, we don't say that we understand the water's being in the glass; we just know *that* it is. Ordinary locution, however, cannot be allowed complete authority over our subject matter. When we say that we know the water is in the glass, we certainly understand what we mean by those words. Independently of language, moreover, we understand from our own experience *what it is* for the water to be in the glass: the glass contains the water, the water is surrounded by the glass, it can be drunk from the glass, and so forth. Ultimately, all knowledge requires some sort of understanding to the extent that we understand what it is that we know.

Finally, how close a relation am I claiming between conscious experience and understanding? I have stipulated that as I am using the term 'understanding,' all conscious intentional states are states of understanding. I have also claimed that having an understanding of something is being able to think about it in terms of some sensorimotor experience. Can there be unconscious understanding? Can one understand something in ways other than through the mental evocation of sensorimotor experiences?

The answer to both questions is affirmative. There are many ways of understanding what we encounter. For example, one can understand a glass of water (or, less oddly, understand what a glass of water is) in being able to drink from the glass, and one can drink inattentively, without being conscious of what one is doing and without remembering the act afterwards. This behavior manifests some understanding. One can converse about abstract subjects like mathematics without evoking any sensorimotor experiences in connection with the mathematical terms, and still exhibit understanding of them. As Ryle says, "Understanding is part of knowing *how* " (Ryle 1948: 54). My claim is not that one is always conscious of understanding but that, normally, one *can* be. One can be aware, under normal circumstances, that one is drinking from a glass of water. And while one can understand an abstract term by being able to use it in relation to other abstract terms, as in a mathematical discussion, the ability to do this sort of thing depends upon sensorimotor experience and is understood ultimately in those terms. The way such conceptual activities are understood in terms of basic sensorimotor experiences has been examined at length in Johnson (1987).

It is useful once again to compare the experience of understanding with the experience of pain. Whether or not pain can be unconscious, clearly it can be conscious. While individual pains differ widely, moreover, all pain experiences form a recognizable type. In the same way, I shall argue that there is a *type* of experience associated with understanding something, even though individual instances are very different. A pain sensation can be burning or throbbing, but what makes it pain is not the burning or the throbbing aspects alone, since those properties can also be associated with painless sensations. Likewise, my understanding that Pat Buchanan could be elected President may fill me with dread, but the dread itself does not constitute my understanding of that possibility. I can dread other things in the same way, and I can experience vague sensations of dread associated with no particular event that I understand.

The absence of understanding is equally obvious, as is the absence of pain. When understanding arrives suddenly it is the 'Aha!' experience; when it is absent we usually feel puzzled, confused, at a loss. Like pain, moreover, the experience is treated as self-verifying. If you think you feel pain then you do, whether or not there is a physical source. If you think you are puzzled then you are puzzled, even if for some reason you ought not to be — as when the solution is actually before your eyes. And if you think something is meaningful, then you do have an understanding of it, even if it is a misunderstanding.

It is difficult to say what makes a sensation a pain, and it is difficult to define the experience of understanding with a set of necessary and sufficient conditions. I do not believe that it is useful to try. Instead, I propose to begin from the fact that just as there do exist unmistakable cases of conscious pain, there also exist unmistakable cases of conscious understanding. My plan is to analyze these, and to discover the mechanisms that make them possible. The hope is that this method will cast light on both consciousness and intentionality in general.

4.   A foundationalist theory of conscious understanding

The account of intentionality and conscious understanding proposed here consists of five primary theses, as follows:

(A)   The apparent 'direction upon an object' that characterizes intentionality as traditionally conceived is not an intrinsic property of mental states themselves, but is a *metaphor*. Its source is the experience of embodied action.

The proposal that mental terminology is metaphorical is not a new one. Jaynes (1976) and Johnson (1987) are two prominent examples of writers who point to the dependence of mentalistic and even more abstract concepts upon terminology referring to sensorimotor experiences of bodily events. Let us look at some specific examples.

First, there are both mental and physical 'acts.' Most mental events, like some physical ones, involve objects. Physical acts of approaching or avoiding objects, manipulating them, making and altering them, or just focusing one's eyes on them, have counterparts in the mental acts of concentrating on or repressing thoughts of objects, analyzing them, creating or developing them, or just attending to them. Mental acts can be occurrent or dispositional, as can physical acts. I can take a mental, as well as a physical 'attitude' or 'stance' with respect to something.

Second, like physical acts, mental acts have a goal or 'target,' and are often said to be directed at 'intentional objects.' The object in this sense might be the idea I am trying to recapture or the fountain of youth I am looking for. While in these cases the being of these 'objects' is to be thought about, other objects of mental acts can have independent existence: I can read a book or taste an apple.

Third, there is said to be mental, as well as physical, perception. The most common mental metaphors describe consciousness and knowledge as a form of seeing. Mentally as well as visually we can consciously 'focus' only on one thing at a time; distractions interfere with one's conscious deliberation about a problem. Also common are mental 'feelings' and 'sensings.'

Finally, mental and physical objects are given values, and these values motivate action. Propositions are true or false; arguments valid or invalid; social views good or evil. These values motivate or are offered as justification for the respective mental acts (or propositional attitudes) of affirmation or denial, acceptance or rejection, approval or disapproval.

Thus, as they have been traditionally described, mental events parallel bodily ones. Mentally we perform instances of the same abstract action patterns and enter into the same types of relations to objects as we do physically. We have mental goals, suffer mental pain (sorrow) and pleasure (joy), experience chronic mental conditions (moods), have special mental abilities (intelligence or talent), and can be mentally tired (depressed) or energetic (manic).[1]

The popularity of such metaphors could be explained in various ways. Perhaps our minds are in fact functionally similar to our bodies, and operate analogously — the metaphors are literally correct. This explanation is implausible, and probably incoherent, if only because of the difficulty in explaining intentional *inexistence* by this route. Another way is historical: the metaphor originated with Plato and has become entrenched simply by tradition. While there is probably some truth to this explanation, it is incomplete: it fails to explain why the metaphor has worked as well as it has, both for Plato and for later thinkers and writers, if the mind is not actually functionally similar to the body. A more promising approach is to hypothesize merely that the basis for the metaphors lies in our *conscious experience* of our intentional mental states, while remaining uncommitted about the intrinsic nature of these states. If we then make that *conscious experience itself* the object of study, we avoid at least some of the risk of question-begging metaphysical assumptions about the nature of mind. That is the approach taken in this book. Thus one question this book addresses, stemming from the metaphorical nature of mentalistic terminology, is: how is our experience of intentionality related to the experience of embodied action? The second thesis summarizes the proposed answer:

(B)   The mental states that are described as intentional are in fact images or memories of episodes of goal-directed action, and are generated in response to sensory stimuli.

This claim is also not a completely original one. Cognitive neuroscientists and neuropsychologists like Damasio (1994) and Edelman (1989, 1992) have argued that all thinking involves the activation of sensorimotor images; that even 'talking to oneself' in natural language requires linguistic imagery. If the claim is correct, then it points to a partial answer to the above question. The basis for the metaphors of embodiment in descriptions of mental states is the fact that these mental states are constructed of images or memory traces of embodiment — of sensorimotor activities that the agent has performed.

The answer is only partial because it does not mention the crucial link between the mental states and the metaphors. A metaphor reflects a conscious recognition that features of something one experiences are similar to something else — the source of the metaphor. Thus the present theory specifies that it is our *conscious experience of the images of embodiment,* activated during cognitive processes, that ground our concepts of intentionality. Such conscious experiences are qualitative; they are occasions in which we imagine or remember the way it *feels* to use our bodies in various ways. The 'directedness upon an object' that appears to characterize intentional mental states is the experienced directedness of a physical action toward a goal. Thus the third thesis is as follows:

(C)   Our apparent introspective awareness of the intentionality of mental states is our conscious experience of the sensorimotor imagery that constitutes these states.

As noted above, our ability to be conscious of the intentionality of our mental states is far from uncontroversial. The theory that intentionality originates in the computations of a language of thought, and the theory that intentional content is determined in part by environmental conditions beyond the subject's awareness, both preclude direct consciousness of intentionality.

It is because consciousness of intentionality is a difficulty for the dominant theories of intentionality that the focus of the present study is upon *conscious understanding.* While understanding is undeniably intentional, understanding as I have characterized it is also undeniably a state of which we are aware. When I speak of conscious understanding, I have in mind the type of experience that enables us to affirm with some authority that we understand something (independently of the *objective correctness* of the understanding), and the lack of which leads to expressions of puzzlement. Hence, the fourth thesis:

(D)   Conscious understanding is based upon the experience of the sensorimotor imagery used when we interpret and reason about perceived objects and events.

The bulk of the present book is devoted to elaboration of the above thesis.

The theory that intentionality, and understanding in particular, is entirely based upon sensorimotor imagery is a far-reaching one. It applies to language understanding as well as to the understanding of nonlinguistic states of affairs. The basis of language understanding in experiences of embodiment, however, has recently been extensively covered (e.g. Lakoff 1987; Johnson 1987), while our conscious ability to understand nonlinguistic events is rarely discussed (cf. Cussins 1993; Nemirow 1995). Nonlinguistic understanding is therefore the primary focus of this book.

The present theory might be called a *foundationalist theory of understanding.* The idea is that the understanding of any content, conceptual or nonconceptual, is based upon a primitive sort of understanding that an agent, human or not, has of its own voluntary actions. Unlike a foundationalist theory of knowledge, the present theory is not a normative one. It is not a claim about *justification,* but a claim that our experience, when we understand something, *in fact* comes from our experience of understanding our own basic voluntary actions. This is shown in three stages: through discussions of our understanding of actions, of physical objects, and of persons. Understanding these three are essential components of understanding language. Thus the present study should be seen as providing the groundwork for related theories about language understanding.

Finally, there is the issue of consciousness itself. It may appear overly ambitious to attempt to resolve two mysteries in one short book. My discussion of consciousness itself, however, will be brief; my goal is to point toward a way that an account of phenomenal consciousness can be combined with a theory of intentionality, rather than to embark on an elaborate defense of the account or to shine light on every dark corner. Nevertheless, I am convinced that the direction I shall discuss will eventually lead to a demystification of conscious experience.

As noted above, brain researchers in the 1990's have begun to address the difficult issue of phenomenal conscious in the context of visual awareness. Crick (1994) and Crick and Koch (1991) have argued that visual awareness involves cortico-thalamic loops that mediate attentional processes. Others emphasize short-term or working memory systems that retain processed sensory input for extended on-line processing (Baddeley 1992a and 1992b; Damasio 1994; Edelman 1987, 1992). The common view appears to be that phenomenal consciousness can be explained by sensory mechanisms in a way that involves a blending of memory images with novel sensory input.

Ralph Ellis (1995) has offered a theory of consciousness that is highly compatible with that proposed here. In order for consciousness to occur, the organism must attend to sensory input and look for a particular pattern of data. Incoming stimuli will not produce conscious states in a passively receptive organism:

> Only after the organism purposely chooses to focus attention in a certain way can the 'looking-for' consciousness occur in the form of the consciousness of an image or possibility. And only after this imaginal consciousness develops … does perceptual consciousness occur corresponding to the perceptual object whose input is activating the primary projection area. (Ellis 1995: 55)

On Ellis's account, a mental image of the object is matched to a pattern of sensory input; the result is perceptual consciousness. Imagery is thus essential to perceptual consciousness.

What does this have to do with conscious understanding? Very briefly my hypothesis is the following. If the conscious understanding or interpretation of sensory stimuli involves, as claimed in Thesis D, the activation of imagery, and if this imagery is combined with current sensory and somatosensory input, the result would be the familiar experience of making sense out of ongoing events by incorporating them into a unified world-view that includes our embodied selves. The fact that this experience is conscious is not an additional fact about understanding; it is the result of the sensory and memory systems that are activated when we respond fully — that is, with understanding — to sensory stimuli. The fifth thesis is thus the following:

(E)   Conscious understanding occurs when sensorimotor imagery in working memory is blended with current sensory and somato-sensory input.

Two aspects of this claim will be defended. First, the mechanism itself will be described, on the basis of the work of the researchers mentioned above. Second, it will be argued that this mechanism alone is sufficient to account for all conscious experience, and that no additional mental properties need be postulated.

5.   Plan of the book

In this introduction I have frequently cited work of other writers that reflects the orientation of this study. In general, there is a movement in philosophy and cognitive psychology to explain cognitive activities in terms of embodiment. Thinking does not occur in a vacuum; it is a central activity of bodies in the world, interacting with other bodies. The present work focuses on one aspect of this activity, but the wider context is important. Thus before beginning specific discussions of the origins of understanding, I devote Chapter Two to what I call the 'Sensorimotor Theory of Cognition.' In this chapter I look at a variety of studies of the relation between embodiment and cognitive activity. In addition, I discuss recent work in the neurosciences that provides empirical support for this theory.

Chapter Three presents the core of the foundationalist thesis of un-derstanding: that basic actions are understood in their own terms, in a way that requires no prior understanding. The goal of this chapter is to develop a set of minimal sufficient conditions for understanding one's basic actions. This foundational type of understanding can then be seen to underlie the un-derstanding of objects and of other persons. In Chapter Four I argue that the understanding of objects is based upon the understanding of actions in which they play a role. Chapter Five takes up the issue of how we understand objectivity, or the idea of an external world existing independent of our actions. It is argued that objectivity is understood in terms of our experience of error in goal-directed action. In Chapter Six, the understanding of persons is examined. Infants come to understand what a person is, on this account, with the aid of a built-in imitative mechanism, along lines suggested by recent work on the development of a 'theory of mind' in the child. In Chapter Seven I show how the understanding of actions, objects and persons combine in language understanding. The analysis in this chapter is a general one. Lakoff, Johnson and others have provided detailed accounts of how particular concepts and linguistic structures are based upon our experiences of embodied action. My purpose is to argue that the understanding of language and communication themselves as general features of the world are based upon the prior understanding of actions, objects and persons.

Finally, we turn to the question of conscious experience itself. The mechanisms of the conscious understanding of actions, objects and persons all centrally involve imagery: the reactivation of past sensorimotor experiences of the subject, blended with current sensory and proprioceptive input in response to novel stimuli. We must therefore ask about the mechanism of phenomenal consciousness of such a blend of sensations.

One difficulty with identifying brain mechanisms of conscious experience is that of characterizing the experience we seek to explain. Conscious experience is notoriously ineffable. But if we cannot describe it precisely, how can we hope to identify its mechanisms? What criterion can we use to associate this mechanism with *this* phenomenon? In Chapter Eight a solution is sketched. Four features of our experience of phenomenal consciousness are isolated and described. Then I examine specific brain mechanisms discussed in recent neuroscientific work, and argue that they can account for each of these four features. The apparent ineffability of conscious experience is shown to be an effect, perhaps an inevitable one, of our inability to distinguish these four elements in subjective experience.

Note

1.   The preceding six paragraphs are taken from Newton 1985: 408-409.

CHAPTER TWO

The Sensorimotor Theory of Cognition

1. Background

The belief that higher cognition makes use of the same structures as those involved in sensorimotor activity I call the sensorimotor theory of cognition. The theory holds that representations of sensory and motor experiences form the raw material for all types and levels of cognition; that no matter how abstract, every cognitive structure is built directly and entirely upon these representations. The central concept of this theory is that of a sensorimotor representation: an activated memory trace of sensory and motor experience. Different versions of the general theory have been proposed throughout this century (e.g., Washburn 1916; Werner and Kaplan 1952). Piaget (1954) held that abstract thought is a development out of sensorimotor skills; David McNeil (1979) argued that sensorimotor ideas are vehicles for signs that refer by 'semiotic extension' to nonsensorimotor objects. More recently Mark Johnson has argued that "we make use of patterns that obtain in our physical experience to organize our more abstract understanding" (Johnson 1987: xv). This chapter is a defense of one version of the theory.

The strong appeal of the sensorimotor theory for many people is based on two general considerations. First, the theory explains what Jackendoff calls 'cross-field generalizations' (1987: 156). Terminology belonging to spatial, kinetic and kinematic domains occurs in all semantic fields, including the most abstract. We speak of inclusion and exclusion, distance and proximity, operations upon entities, etc., in logic and mathematics as well as in concrete contexts. This terminology is not accidental. Abstract relations cannot be explained otherwise; they are isomorphic with physical relations and are naturally expressed in physical terms. Margaret Boden (1982) points out the paradox implicit in the Annunciation story, in which the Archangel Gabriel converses with Mary even though he lacks any embodiment or physical environment. Language comprehensible to Mary must have been meaningless to such a being:

> It is abundantly clear that many linguistic expressions of 'non-spatial' matters (*sic*) are parasitic on purely spatial notions. Familiar examples include the conceptualization of time as passing, as being of long or short duration . . . Similarly, we often express comparative degrees of abstract properties such as social status, intelligence, or moral worth by terms drawn from more concrete contexts, such as above, below, higher, lower, etc. . . . Since Gabriel as an essentially spiritual being can hardly be represented as having any orientation, nor any location relative to 'other objects in the external world' . . . it is difficult to see how he could have learnt these notions in the first place. And if he had not learnt them in the first place, how could he have used them so felicitously to talk of abstract matters to a human woman in the second place? (Boden 1982: 130)

The spatial nature of abstract concepts is also supported in McNeil's studies of gestures (1985, 1992). He argues that gestures are computed by the same psychological structures as the speech they accompany, and that they express the same types of spatial relations whether they accompany abstract or concrete sentences (1985: 357). This ubiquity of bodily and spatial reference is completely accounted for by the sensorimotor theory of cognition: abstract domains are structured on the basis of physical domains, and hence their fundamental elements — entities and their relations — are referred to in physical terms. For this reason the sensorimotor theory has had particular appeal for linguists (e.g. Lakoff and Johnson 1987; Langacker 1987).

The second consideration concerns a view of human experience with roots in phenomenology (e.g., Merleau-Ponty 1962); this view became focused during the development of artificial intelligence. The idea is that the study of intentionality in the form of cognitive activity, including linguistic activity, is the study of a realm of human experience which essentially involves embodiment. Therefore, to explain cognition and language without taking the experience of embodiment into account is not to explain a human activity. As Johnson (1987: xix) puts it:

> Our reality is shaped by the patterns of our bodily movement, the contours of our spatial and temporal orientation, and the forms of our interaction with objects. It is never merely a matter of abstract conceptualizations and propositional judgments.

Contemporary cognitive science purports to explain how humans reason and use language, but its focus is upon the relations between abstract symbol structures and the external world. Little recognition is granted to the question of how humans grasp these relations and make use of them in their lives (cf. Winograd 1972; Haugeland 1979). The sensorimotor theory takes an organic view of linguistic structures, and explains them as aspects of embodied activity in physical and social contexts. Abstract symbol structures can be understood and used because they are recursive isomorphic with the sensorimotor structures with which humans are primordially familiar, in a sense described by Polanyi (1958: 90):

> We may say in general that by acquiring a skill, whether muscular or intellectual, we achieve an understanding which we cannot put into words and which is continuous with the inarticulate faculties of animals.
> What I understand in this manner has a meaning for me, and it has this meaning in itself, and not as a sign has a meaning when denoting an object. I have called this earlier on an existential meaning.

In spite of these considerations the theory has had rough going against the dominant Western paradigm in cognitive science and philosophy of mind: that cognition is shaped primarily by language or language-like structures, which are discontinuous with more primitive sensorimotor structures, and which provide a unique, autonomous mapping of reality which subserves human reasoning ability. An advantage of the linguistic paradigm is its compatibility with computational formalism, allowing theories to be couched in the terminology of computer science and giving an air of technological sophistication to the theory. Complaints about neglect of experiential reality are often met with arguments that this 'reality' is an illusion explained by the computational structures; they are not significant when taken at face value (e.g., Dennett 1988).

As with the sensorimotor theory, two main strands of the linguistic view coexist (although less compatibly). One is computationalism, or computation-representation functionalism (Block 1980): the world is represented in a 'language of thought,' which functions like a computer language. Thinking is performing computations on the symbol strings of this language, which are purely formal but interpretable as referring to entities and states of the external world and which are translatable into natural language. The mechanisms performing these computations do not 'know' what the symbols represent; they 'understand' only syntax. This theory is primarily associated with Fodor

(1975), and is a development from computer science. The other strand does not involve claims about a language of thought underlying natural language; it is a claim about the direct determination of thought processes by natural language structures. Originally proposed by Whorf (1956), a version of it has recently been articulated by Dennett (1991), who argues that language structures determine our thoughts, since "of all the structures we become acquainted with in the course of our lives, certainly the most pervasive and powerful source of discipline in our minds is our native tongue," and that "the obligatory structures of sentences in our languages are like so many guides at our elbows, reminding us to check on this, to attend to that, requiring us to organize facts in certain ways" (1991: 300). Dennett expressly rejects the language of thought hypothesis (1991: 302). His account of the influence of language upon thought is more behavioristic; thinking, at the level he speaks of in the passages above, is analyzed as a form of covert language behavior. There is no deeper level at which the linguistic elements of this behavior have 'meaning' or 'intrinsic intentionality.'

The two strands of the linguistic theory differ on the mental organization underlying cognition, but both view cognition as language-like: as a matter of the referential relation of the elements of thought to their counterparts in the external world (Johnson refers to this shared view as Objectivism). Dennett, it is true, rejects any absolute mapping; for him, the fact that thinking is language-like means that thoughts, like words, have no determinate meanings (Quine 1960; Davidson 1984). I associate the two strands in negative terms: they are alike in rejecting an explanatory role for the experience of embodiment in intentionality and language comprehension. Linguistic comprehension consists in mastery of purely linguistic rules. Language is an autonomous representational medium.

How does the sensorimotor theory view the role of language in cognition? In the version I shall defend, language is itself a sensorimotor activity which has evolved for social interaction, specifically through communication; words and sentences are its tools. It is a type of volitional activity subject to the same action-planning mechanisms as any other activity. As Steven Pinker (1994: 229-230) notes, "Human communication is not just a transfer of information like two fax machines connected with a wire; it is a series of alternating displays of behavior by sensitive, scheming, second-guessing social animals." Thus, like any other activity, linguistic behavior can be mentally represented or imagined. We mentally rehearse conversations with others or philosophical arguments we intend to present, just as we mentally run through the stages of other potential actions.

Pinker argues forcefully against the linguistic determinism of writers like Whorf — the view that thinking is shaped by language:

> The idea that thought is the same thing as language is an example of what can be called a conventional absurdity: a statement that goes against all common sense but that everyone believes because they dimly recall having heard it somewhere. . . . Think about it. We have all had the experience of uttering or writing a sentence, then stopping and realizing that it wasn't exactly what we meant to say. To have that feeling, there has to be a 'what we meant to say' that is different from what we said. (Pinker 1994: 57)

On this view and that of the sensorimotor theory, linguistic entities are tools for implementing preformed social intentions, just as construction tools and methods are means of implementing one's intention to build a house. While in both cases the tools determine the form of the finished product, they were originally developed in response to human physical needs and abilities. Just as hammers and saws extend natural hand motions, language evolved to fit preexisting social and cognitive patterns. I suggest that while language has developed a complexity such that we now say things that our ancestors could not have thought, comprehending these things still occurs at the level of sensorimotor activity, where our basic motives and goals are formed. Hence the presence of sensorimotor terminology at all levels of abstraction.

2.   The sensorimotor theory and mental models

If the sensorimotor theory is to be defended adequately, it must be made more explicit. How, exactly, are sensorimotor structures used in cognition? How, indeed, are they used in sensorimotor activity? If we cannot be explicit about this more concrete level, claims about the abstract level must remain sketchy and programmatic. Therefore, I propose that the sensorimotor theory be combined with another account of human reasoning: the mental model theory.

The mental model approach to cognition holds that various problems in the use and comprehension of natural language can be solved by viewing understanding as a process carried out over analogical representational structures created in response to linguistic formulae (see, e.g., Johnson-Laird 1983; Gentner 1983; Fauconnier 1985; Ballim et al. 1991). The idea is that comprehension is 'constructive' rather than 'interpretive' (Johnson-Laird 1983: 243); in response to linguistic material one creates a mental model of what is described. The models may be mental images or unconscious representational structures of which conscious images are *views* (Johnson-Laird 1983: 157). In Fauconnier's theory, the mental 'spaces' used to represent objects and relations between them are not necessarily analogical models; Fauconnier's concern, as well as that of Ballim et.al., is with nested belief clusters structured so as to facilitate propositional attitude reasoning (see also Dinsmore 1987); such belief clusters may be represented in propositional form. The construction of models is constrained by the possibilities of relationships or interactions among the elements of the domain of discourse. One can think of these models as virtual spaces in which occupiers are manipulated according to rules. Reasoning about the entities in a domain is carried out by mental manipulation of the occupiers. Relationships among domains are represented by mapping rules applying to two or more mental spaces.

For example, suppose a friend says 'I have an office-mate, Fred, who believes that he was captured by space aliens, and tells me how he was subjected to strange experiments, and then returned to earth.' You may form various mental images associated with two 'spaces:' some involving a man in an office with your friend, and others involving a space ship and little green men. The imagery involving the office represents the real world, and is subject to the appropriate constraints; that involving the space aliens represents fictional events, and is subject to whatever constraints limit Fred's beliefs as you understand them. These images may be experienced vividly or faintly, and sequentially or simultaneously (for example, in the format of Fred and a 'dream bubble'). The relationship between the spaces is represented by the constraints governing how they are constructed and how their occupiers can behave.

How might these models be realized in the brain? One can hypothesize rule structures in the form of cell assemblies developed *ad hoc* for each new domain, but the value of the theory in explaining human cognition depends upon the compatibility of the spaces with normal reasoning mechanisms which operate across them, and which therefore must include universal constraints holding in any space. Among these are general knowledge structures and the basic rules of inference. This is where the sensorimotor theory comes in. Mental models are sensorimotor representations constructed by the same mechanisms as those involved in perception and action, and reasoning via mental models is similar to reasoning about possible actions — i.e. to constructing hypothetical motor plans in light of sensory information. Formally, the proposal is that sensory and motor information feeds a central representational system (consisting of sensory and motor association areas distributed about the cortex) from which multimodal representations of the external environment and the agent's body and spatial position are drawn. Via connections with the amygdala (LeDoux 1992), the sensory information includes emotional content. These representations serve purposes that range from the planning of immediate physical actions to mathematical reasoning. Representations of actions, when sufficiently activated and not inhibited (Norman and Shallice 1986), can trigger motor programs resulting in motor behavior. Language activity is a subspecialty of the motor system, with unique syntactic structures, which it shares the central representational system for semantic and planning purposes. With this proposal, in addition to accounting for human experience in our cognitive theory we can make some concrete empirical predictions.

It can be objected that sensorimotor structures and linguistic structures are not the only contenders for the role of the determinants of thought. There are other candidates, such as that offered by Jackendoff (1983, 1987), one of the linguists who takes seriously the use of spatial terminology in abstract semantic domains, and who draws conclusions which appear to favor the sensorimotor theory. He notes that logic:

> has formal parallels to a very concrete semantic field having to do with pushing objects around in space. Although radically at variance with the philosophical tradition, this result makes a great deal of sense in the context of a theory of meaning as conceptualization. One can begin to see the principles of logic as abstractions away from the general algebraic form implicit in our understanding of the physical world, and through this one can begin to envision the evolutionary channels by which they might have developed in the computational mind. (Jackendoff 1987: 157-158)

While Jackendoff recognizes that abstract reasoning depends upon nonlinguistic structures, he nevertheless does not commit himself completely to a sensorimotor theory of cognitive representation. Instead, he proposes what he calls the *conceptual structure hypothesis*: "There is a single level of mental representation, conceptual structure, at which linguistic, sensory, and motor information are compatible" (Jackendoff 1983: 17). Conceptual structure is governed by 'conceptual well-formedness rules,' which are universal and innate, and which dictate what concepts may be constructed in response to the subject's experience (1983: 17). In Jackendoff's view, the linguistic system is a subset of conceptual structure because "linguistic inference is but a special case of more general modality-independent principles that must be attributed even to nonverbal organisms" (1983: 19).

Jackendoff's views on the relation of linguistic inference to general cognitive principles are similar to those defended in this chapter; what, then, is the difference between conceptual structure and sensorimotor models? Jackendoff does not hold a true sensorimotor theory of cognition because he believes that certain concepts fundamental to cognition cannot be represented by sensory imagery alone. His theory is that conceptual structure works together with 3D model structures incorporating visual imagery, which "reflects the intuition that knowing the meaning of a word that denotes a physical object involves in part knowing what such an object looks like" (Jackendoff 1987: 201). Conceptual structure alone is not capable of representing, for example, the common understanding of the differences among ducks, geese, and swans. The 3D model is insufficient by itself, however, since an image used, for example, to represent walking, can also be used to represent a human being; the requisite distinction is not available in visual form. The role of conceptual structure is to provide concepts such as ACTION TYPE, OBJECT TYPE, or TYPE/TOKEN, to be applied to 3D models.

On the sensorimotor theory the level of conceptual structure is unnecessary since the requisite distinctions can be made within the structure of the image. Jackendoff, like many theorists, construes imagery in terms of a visual model. The term 'image' has traditionally been associated primarily with vision, but that association can be seriously misleading when one is constructing a theory of the relation of imagery to cognition. As with any modality — olfaction, audition, proprioception, kinesthesia — traces of visual experience can be stored and reactivated, giving rise to either categorical or episodic memories which we refer to as images. We can image tastes, sounds, stomach aches (Newton 1982). Jackendoff's 3D models need not be purely visual; in fact, it would be odd if all sensory modalities were not represented in them. If they are not purely visual, however, then they can easily represent conceptual distinctions such as HUMAN vs. WALKING. One need only specify that in addition to the visual component of the image, there are relevant kinesthetic and somatosensory components, highlighted by attentional focus, present when the image represents WALKING but not when it represents

HUMAN. These nonvisual aspects provide a context which spotlights the salient features of the image. This approach can provide a purely imagistic account of the difference, for example, between viewing Wittgenstein's (1953) duck-rabbit as a duck and as a rabbit (Jackendoff 1983: 25): one simply notes that if the figure is a duck it looks to one's left, and if it is a rabbit it looks to one's right. Noting this requires reference to one's own spatial orientation with respect to the figure, which entails a somatosensory representation along with the visual one. (We look in later chapters at theories of brain organization capable of subserving representational fractionalization and attentional spotlighting, which are necessary if these distinctions are to be represented imagistically.) If Jackendoff could thus get along without conceptual structure as a level of representation distinct from sensorimotor representation, then on his remaining arguments, as well as on my own, the sensorimotor theory of cognition is a major alternative to the linguistic theory. There may, of course, be still other alternatives; I shall not consider them here.

Jackendoff has proposed a formal structure for cognitive processing which includes separate modules for conceptual structure and the 3D model for visual representation. My proposal does not separate these functions into distinct modules, but it is an oversimplification to say that it simply combines them into a central representational system, for the following reasons.

First, the central representational system on the sensorimotor theory includes input from all modalities, not only the visual, and is distributed among all the primary and secondary cortical association areas. Somatosensory information is of central importance, since it provides orientation information which helps to distinguish different perspectives and saliencies in the same (objectively speaking) represented state of affairs. In addition, emotional coloration provides information crucial for the planning of action.

Second, on the sensorimotor theory the primary function of the central representational system is the planning and control of voluntary action. Hence all representations should be viewed as available for playing the functional role of action plans, which can lead to the development of motor programs that, when activated, trigger motor behavior. This means that representations would normally involve higher-level action planning regions in the frontal cortex. It also means that language production, a species of motor output, shares the action-planning representational system with nonverbal behavioral systems. We will examine neuroscientific evidence for both of these claims later in this chapter.

The key difference between the sensorimotor theory and most other proposals for cognitive structure is the central role given to the planning of voluntary action. In this way the theory is distinguished from those treating cognition as more purely intellectual — as the activity of structures of pure reason operating independently of pragmatic concerns. Very similar to the sensorimotor theory in this respect is Baars' Global Workspace theory (Baars 1988). On Baars' account, specialized, cognitively isolated modules or processors have access to a common working memory, through which they can share information and cooperate in providing input for decision-making. The information broadcast in the global workspace is conscious, unlike that in the individual modules. It is organized by *contexts*: "coalitions of unconscious specialized processors that are *already committed* to a certain way of processing their information, and which have ready access to the Global Workspace" (1988: 65). Goal contexts appear to be of widest application; they are intentions that guide the selection for conscious experience of information relevant to achievement of the goal: "The stream of consciousness can be considered as a flow of experiences created by the interplay of many goal contexts" (1988: 225). While Baars' theory is in agreement with the sensorimotor theory as regards the primary function of conscious experience, Baars is not willing to say that all conscious experiences are based upon sensorimotor experiences. Tip-of-the-tongue states, for example — the well-known experiences of almost, but not quite, being able to remember a word — are according to him not associated with any qualitative images. Baars does not, however, recognize motor imagery, and thus does not consider the possibility that partially-realized motor images of speech could underlie these states (Metcalfe and Shimamura 1994).

To summarize the above discussion: I propose that all higher cognitive activity makes use of the same structures as those involved in sensorimotor activity, and that these structures take the form of analog models of reality. These mental models are constructed and manipulated by representational systems subserving action planning in light of sensory information. This theory is held in explicit contrast to what I am calling the linguistic theory of cognition, according to which human thinking proceeds via manipulations of uniquely human syntactic structures (either of a language of thought or of natural language), and that sensorimotor experience is not an intrinsic or essential feature of human cognition and language comprehension.

In what follows we first look at three sources of empirical evidence for this theory: (1) behavioral evidence that analog models rather than formal inference rules are used in reasoning; (2) neuroscientific work on brain mechanisms for action, reasoning and language supporting the sensorimotor theory; and (3) evidence that human cognitive abilities evolved from sensorimotor abilities in our ancestors. Finally, in connection with common objections to the theory, we speculate briefly about the role of language in thought.

3.   Evidence from human reasoning

The traditional view of human reasoning is that it makes use of the rules of inference of formal logic. If it is also the case that cognition is structured by a syntactic language of thought, then human reasoning should be analogous to machine computation. It has become clear, however, that humans do not reason the way machines compute. The most obvious case: humans are good at pattern recognition, while machines are not; machines, on the other hand, unlike humans, are good at logical deduction. Active research programs are underway in alternative computational architecture — parallel distributed processing (McLelland and Rumelhart 1986) — as well as in the extension of traditional inference procedures with non-monotonic or defeasible reasoning models (Nute 1991). These efforts, however, have not yet produced a new paradigm within which difficulties with the traditional model can be resolved. In this section I review three of these difficulties, and proposals for handling them via the mental model approach.

The first difficulty concerns the use of logic in reasoning. If deductive logic determines human reasoning, then we would be expected to draw certain types of inferences, but we rarely do so. One of these concerns logical closure: deductive logic dictates that the logical implications of true beliefs are true. But no one believes all of the logical implications of his or her beliefs. Harman (1986: 14) points out that resorting to implicit beliefs will not help:

> One cannot be expected even implicitly to believe a logical consequence of one's beliefs if a complex proof would be needed to see the implication . . . It won't help to . . . say that one's beliefs should be closed under obvious logical implication . . . since any logical implication can eventually be demonstrated by a proof consisting entirely of obvious steps.

Another problem is illustrated by the well-known selection task, in which subjects are confronted with four cards, given a hypothesis about them, and asked to state which cards must be turned over to determine the truth of the hypothesis. The overwhelming majority of subjects fails to include the card that would falsify the hypothesis. Subjects are sensitive to content: if they are given the problem in realistic terms (for example, if it involves letters and stamps, or descriptions of modes of travel) the majority get it right. Even after success with realistic content, however, they fail to transfer the reasoning pattern to abstract problems (Johnson-Laird 1983: 29-34). This result is unexplained if people reason by logical inference rules, which apply in abstract as well as realistic situations.

Failure to transfer the reasoning pattern from concrete to abstract contexts could be interpreted as evidence against the sensorimotor theory, which holds that abstract concepts are developed out of concrete ones. The theory, however, maintains only that the concrete is a necessary condition for the abstract, not that it is sufficient. Abstract reasoning is difficult for human beings, particularly when negations are involved; there is no general agreement on why this is so. What is clear is that if reasoning were accomplished via formal inference rules, the discrepancy would be completely unexplained (Johnson-Laird 1983: 32-33).

Another peculiarity of the selection task, the 'matching bias,' has been discussed (Dascal 1987). Subjects are sensitive to the linguistic form of the instructions: the items on a card are considered relevant if they match the terms in the hypothesis. This suggests that language does play a role in thought. Dascal proposes that the field of psychopragmatics, which studies "the way in which the 'linguistic environment' of thought influences thought" (1987: 190), is the appropriate forum for the exploration of this role, and he points out the difficulties of acquiring evidence of purely noncommunicative uses of language. This point is an important one for the sensorimotor theory, which holds that thought is determined by familiar sensorimotor patterns; language, as a form of sensorimotor activity, cannot be without influence. The difference between the sensorimotor and the linguistic theory of cognition is that the latter sees language as the sole determinant of thought in its most fundamental forms, while the sensorimotor theory sees language as one part of the 'environment,' to use Dascal's term, in which thought can take place. In this case, the particular form of verbal instructions would be expected to influence the selection of mental models (see Langacker 1987: Ch. 3) which, however, remain fundamentally nonverbal in structure. Thus the linguistic sensitivity of subjects of the selection task is of great interest, but it does not count against the position that logical reasoning does not rely upon formal inference rules.

A third example concerns reasoning about inductive probability; while not an example of failure of deductive inference procedures it shows unexpectedly 'poor' reasoning in supposedly 'logical' creatures. Even though it is a fundamental truth that the probability of a conjunction of propositions is less than or equal to the probability of its components, people routinely judge compounds to be more probable than their components (Tversky and Kahneman 1983).

These sorts of findings are explained by Nisbett and Ross (1980) as the result of two types of extra logical reasoning methods: (1) the use in reasoning of certain 'judgmental heuristics' — nonlogical judgment strategies which are generally useful but which can lead to error; and (2) 'knowledge structures' involving theories and schemas which organize general knowledge. Johnson-Laird has been more detailed in accounting for human inference behavior in terms of mental models rather than rules of inference. The possibility of valid reasoning without logic, he argues, explains "the central paradox of how children learn to reason, namely, how they could acquire rules of inference before they were able to reason validly" (Johnson-Laird 1983: 145), and it accounts better for the sorts of reasoning phenomena described above. Reasoners "construct finite models of premises, formulate putative conclusions on the basis of them, and search for models of the premises that are counter-examples to such conclusions" (Johnson-Laird 1983: 133; see also Huttenlocher 1969). While this method can work perfectly for short and simple arguments, the limits of working memory lead to errors in more complex cases of the sort mentioned above; hence the motivation for the externalization of reasoning techniques into a formal system.

The second difficulty concerns propositional attitude attribution. We are able with great practical success to predict the behavior of others. Our predictions are generally formulated and justified in the language of 'folk psychology:' we say that Henry *desires* x and *believes* y; therefore he will do z. While we are often quite wrong about what Henry will do, in general our predictions come true. This social success is true of nonhuman animals as well; Cheney and Seyfarth (1990) describe in detail the apparent ability of vervet monkeys to predict the behavior of their conspecifics, an ability upon which their survival depends. There are two reasons why this ability poses a difficulty for theories of cognition. One is that on some eliminativist theories of cognition (e.g., Churchland 1984) it is unexplained how humans know about others' mental states. The 'beliefs' and 'desires' to which we advert in our predictions are not, it is held, the actual causes of human behavior, but rather elements in a common-sense theory of psychology which will ultimately be replaced by a more accurate scientific picture. If, however, commonsense psychology is scientifically inaccurate, why does it work in predicting human behavior? The second problem is that even if commonsense psychology is not inaccurate, the knowledge structures required to apply it appear unable to be modeled in formal systems such as AI programs. For such modeling a theory of psychology must be expressible by a set of formally describable causal regularities, such as 'If x desires p and believes q, then x will do r.' It is well known, however, that commonsense psychology is not formalizable in this way: there are too many exceptions to the rules. As Gordon (1986: 166) points out, one can build *ceteris paribus* clauses into the theory, but the question remains: "how does one know how to recognize atypical situations or to expand the *ceteris paribus* clause?"

Gordon's proposal is that psychological attribution and prediction make use of practical simulation: we imagine being in the other person's situation, and determine what we ourselves would do.[1] Gordon does not have a detailed theory about how we so reliably predict our own behavior, but offers a suggestion compatible with the sensorimotor theory:

> our declarations of immediate intention are causally tied to some actual precursor of behavior: perhaps tapping into the brain's updated behavioral 'plans' or into 'executive commands' that are about to guide the relevant motor sequences. (Gordon 1986: 159)

The mental model theory offers a mechanism for simulative reasoning: one models a possible reality (e.g., a reality as it appears to a person whose actions one is trying to predict) and applies one's own normal reasoning methods within it. For example, Dinsmore (1987) proposes a knowledge structuring system in which propositional attitude contexts are signaled by 'space builders' such as 'Henry believes . . .' What Henry believes is represented in a mental space which is distinct from 'real world' space, but whose occupants can be mapped onto occupants of the real world space in certain specified ways. More recently, Ballim et. al. (1991: 167) have argued that belief ascription, and cognition in general, are fundamentally dependent upon metaphor,[2] such that "one's ascriptional activities use one's states of mind as metaphors for other people's states of mind." They have developed a program, ViewGen, for the construction of nested topic 'environments' for representing the beliefs and viewpoints of individuals within wider contexts. ViewGen does not solve the problem of general commonsense knowledge representation, but it does suggest a structure for belief ascription and metaphor which would allow basic commonsense knowledge to be applied in novel reasoning tasks. With metaphors, knowledge from one domain is transferred to another; it need not be developed and represented separately in the second domain. Motor programs work similarly. If I learn how to write in script by holding a pen and using my hand muscles, I can then write in the same script by holding a piece of chalk and using my arm muscles; the abstract motor program is transferred from one context to the other (Pribram 1976). Haugeland makes a related point concerning images:

> The beauty of images is that (spatial) side effects take care of themselves. If I imagine myself astride a giraffe, my feet 'automatically' end up near its belly and my head near the middle of its neck. . . I don't have to arrange for these results deliberately or figure them out; they just happen, due to the shapes of the images themselves. (Haugeland 1985: 229)

An important advantage of the mental model theory is that it allows an indefinite number of hierarchical knowledge structures to be built upon a primitive base. This in itself does not solve the problem of commonsense knowledge representation, but it greatly reduces its magnitude.

The third difficulty concerns indexical expressions. Much of our reasoning involves objects and situations in the real world. This world includes oneself; it is what is experienced 'from here.' Part of what it is to understand that given entities are part of this world is to know their situation relative to one's own situation (Strawson 1959; Evans 1982). But knowing this involves the use of indexicals, whose content is notoriously inexpressible by means of linguistic concepts (Perry 1979). When, for example, I know that I am the person who has been tracking dirt on the floor, there is no way to specify verbally what it is that I know. A description will not serve, since for any description it would be possible for me to understand it and yet not know that I am the one described. Thus it appears that a crucial aspect of any nonartificial domain of discourse fails to be captured in a formal conceptual system (Cussins 1990).

If one reasons using mental models constructed from sensorimotor representations, there appears to be no need for a formal description of indexicals, since models are constructed from one's own point of view and include somatosensory information, and thus intrinsically represent one's own 'here' and 'now.' When, in particular, I reason about myself, I am represented not by a name or description but by the various sensory and motor structures that constitute self for me in my lived experience. How it might be physically possible for models to include such representations will be examined in the next section.

To summarize: studies of human reasoning indicate that the traditional computational model, in which symbol strings are manipulated according to formal syntax and the logical rules of inference, is inadequate to explain both the sorts of logical 'errors' human beings make in their reasoning, and the abilities in the areas of social and indexical knowledge that they do enjoy. The mental model approach can account for these phenomena more adequately. This is not to say that a complete theory exists, or even that there is a consensus among mental model theorists on the nature of such structures; nor does it mean that still other alternatives are ruled out. The studies constitute some evidence, however, that mental model theory is moving in the right direction.

4.   Evidence from brain organization

Even at this early stage of development, the sensorimotor theory predicts certain general forms of brain organization. Scientific work of the last decade supports these predictions. In this section we look at three of these areas. First, my version of the theory views language as a tool for communication rather than as the primary determinant of cognition. If that is so, then we would expect a dissociation between linguistic and cognitive deficits. Evidence suggests that while language deficits such as Broca's aphasia are usually associated with motor deficits, general nonverbal cognitive abilities tend to be spared. This evidence supports the position that language may be a cognitive subspecialty more closely related to motor and sequencing aspects of verbal expression than to reasoning ability. It should be noted that deficit associations are less reliable than dissociations as evidence of localization of function (Shallice 1988: 35). Nevertheless, the consistent association between linguistic and motor deficits in large numbers of patients is supportive of the claims of the theory, even if it does not constitute decisive evidence. Second, the theory holds that sensorimotor representations are held in working memory for use in reasoning. Regions in the premotor cortex involved in action planning appear to be organized in the requisite way. Finally, an essential claim is that concepts at all levels of abstraction can be represented by sensorimotor structures. Studies by A. R. Damasio support this view.

In addition to the above-mentioned studies of particular brain mechanisms, to be examined in this section, a currently popular hypotheses about overall brain structure is compatible with the sensorimotor theory. This is the Modularity Hypothesis; it holds that different cognitive tasks are accomplished by brain 'modules,' each determined by set of task-specific rules and cognitively isolated from other modules. Chomsky's (1980) theory of language competence is an example of such a theory, as is Marr's (1976) computational theory of vision. Marr's computational account of cognitive activity provides the basic argument for modularity: "Any large computation should be split up and implemented as a collection of small sub-parts that are as nearly independent of one another as the overall task allows" (1976: 485). Other support comes from work in the neurophysiology of vision (e.g. Zeki 1980) and in psychology (e.g. Fodor 1983; for fuller discussion of evidence for modularity see Shallice 1988).

The Modularity Hypothesis is relevant to the sensorimotor theory of cognition because it provides a theoretical basis for the independence of cognitive and language functions. At the same time, however, the evolutionary development of distinct functional systems from more basic sequencing abilities is allowed for, as is the use of sensorimotor imagery for conscious planning in all domains. It has been proposed (Corballis 1991) that a feature of human cognition common to many different domains is generativity: 'the ability to construct an unlimited number of different forms from a finite number of elementary parts' (1991: 65). In Corballis's view, the sort of generativity that characterizes human language is unique to hominids. It seems clear, however, that the ability of any creature to perform complex voluntary actions in response to novel circumstances requires generativity as defined above. If so, generativity could be one of the important features that ties the various highly evolved cognitive modules to their primitive origins in motor systems (see Leiner, Leiner and Dow 1993).

In looking at evidence for dissociability between linguistic and cognitive functions, we will first consider Broca's aphasia, one of the classic language deficits. True Broca's aphasia requires damage not only to Broca's area in the left frontal cortex, but also to surrounding areas which form part of a network associated with relational aspects of language, including grammatical structure. This network includes areas in the parietal cortex (concerned with somatasensory information) and the sensorimotor cortices (Damasio 1992: 532-534).[3] Patients with Broca's aphasia have difficulties in organizing sentences according to grammatical rules, and also in comprehension of sentences with complex relational structures as well as of isolated relational terms (Berndt and Caramazza 1980).

Broca's aphasia is also associated with motor deficits: lesions in Broca's area can cause "usually transient right-sided . . . paralysis. A residual clumsiness and sensory disturbance of the right hand may persist, especially involving the thumb and index finger. There may be an apraxia. . ." (Stuss and Benson 1986: 86). Apraxia is defined as the "impairment of ability to carry out purposeful movements by an individual who has normal primary motor skills . . . and normal comprehension of the act to be carried out" (Hecaen, quoted in Stuss and Benson 1986: 84). Grammatical difficulties similar to those associated with Broca's aphasia, including the comprehension of relative clauses, have been found in patients with Parkinson's disease, primarily a motor disorder (Natsopoulos et al.1991). This is further indication of the close relationship between motor and grammatical processing.

Greenfield (1991) marshalls extensive evidence for a common ontogenesis of language ability and object combination in an undifferentiated Broca's area. Her work is discussed further in the following section on evolution. Here we may note her evidence that agrammatic Broca's aphasics are deficient in the processing of hierarchical structures involved both in grammar and in nonlinguistic object combination (Greenfield 1991: 534-535). She also notes results of PET scanning studies (Fox et al. 1988) indicating that Broca's area is associated with the motor cortex in mouth, tongue and hand movements, and that it 'lit up' when subjects merely imagined hand movements, without carrying them out. (This is similar to the findings of Roland et. al. (1980) regarding the SMA, discussed below).

While Broca's aphasia is thus associated with disorders of language expression and related motor difficulties, it can be *dissociated* from nonverbal cognitive abilities. Kersetz (1988) reports studies of 75 global aphasics who performed well on a non-verbal test of intelligence, Raven's colored progressive matrices (RCPM). He concluded that the "relative preservation of nonverbal performance in the severely affected aphasics presented here argues for a dissociable process of language and high-level thought" (Kersetz 1988: 459). Broca's patients are usually aware of their language difficulties (Kandel and Schwartz 1985: 695), indicating preserved critical abilities.

The Modularity Hypothesis, according to which distinct tasks are controlled by cognitively-isolated, functionally-specified brain modules, is supported by such evidence of dissociation. That hypothesis alone, however, does not explain some finer distinctions among abilities surviving damage to specific areas. In an ingenious study, Canseco-Gonzalez and colleagues (1990) trained a patient with severe Broca's aphasia to learn abstract symbols representing verbs of two types: pure transitive verbs taking only one argument structure, such as 'fix' and 'locate;' and dative verbs taking two different argument structures, such as 'sell' and 'send.' Their hypothesis was that linguistic argument structure, which expresses action features such as agent and goal, is rooted in nonlinguistic visual experience, and they reasoned that symbols representing pictures of people performing actions would be easier to learn when the actions were commonly translated by pure transitive verbs, and harder to learn when common translations were the more complex dative verbs. The predictions were largely fulfilled, indicating that a classic Broca's aphasic was sensitive to argument structure presented in nonverbal form. The authors ask why, since grammar is always affected in Broca's aphasia, argument structure, a feature of 'text-grammar,' should be spared. They conclude that:

> information of relevance to argument structure is redundantly represented in anatomically distinct locations (including visual and language regions). In effect, we suggest that while argument structure representations serve an undeniable linguistic function, such representations may be the linguistic equivalents of nonlinguistic modes of organizing information, and thereby serve translation across cognitive domains. (Canseco-Gonzalez et al. 1990: 403)

This proposal is compatible with the view that certain functionally-distinct modules may have a common evolutionary origin, resulting in some isomorphism of structure among them.

It might seem that the association between aphasia and motor deficits, and dissociation between aphasia and cognition, undermines the sensorimotor theory. The position of that theory is that thinking is determined by sensorimotor structures; hence motor deficits ought to be associated with cognitive deficits. The sensorimotor theory, however, holds that cognition uses mechanisms of *action-planning,* which are associated with areas in the prefrontal cortex. The motor deficits associated with aphasia are not deficits of planning at this level, but of execution — with translating plans into detailed sequential motor programs. In contrast to Broca's aphasia, speech difficulties caused by damage to frontal areas such as the supplementary motor area, which are involved in attention and emotion as well as the initiation of voluntary movement, *are* associated with cognitive deficits. Patients exhibit akinesis (difficulty in initiating movement) and mutism, and on recovering "they describe a peculiar experience: the range and resonance of thought processes was reduced, and their will to speak preempted" (Damasio 1992: 537).

The other classical language deficit, Wernicke's aphasia, results from damage to the left posterior temporal area, located amidst multimodal sensory association areas. This deficit involves primarily comprehension of content words rather than grammatical structure. Wernicke's patients, unlike Broca's patients, are capable of fluent and grammatically correct but often meaningless verbal output. With respect to the above discussion of language disorders, in which I argued that motor expression is involved but nonverbal cognition spared, it might be objected that what is spared is precisely those cognitive abilities served by Wernicke's area, and hence that cognition may be linguistically determined after all. Because of the geographical separation of Broca's and Wernicke's areas, patients with deficits involving only those two areas are not likely to be available for testing this hypothesis. It is unlikely, however, that Wernicke's area alone could be responsible for the preserved higher cognitive abilities in Broca's patients, since these abilities involve much more than just the comprehension of single content words or phrases. They involve comprehension of complex relational structures (as in the work of Canseco-Gonzalez et al.) of the same sort as those expressed in the lost verbal abilities. Therefore, the claim that verbal structure does not appear to determine cognitive structure is still supported.

The above neuropsychological studies indicate that brain mechanisms subserving cognition, action-planning, and language are organized such that the language system is closely associated, both geographically and structurally, with certain motor processing systems, and that it does not independently determine the structure of higher cognitive abilities. This organization is compatible with an important role for language in the expression and comprehension of thoughts in verbal form. Patients with deficits in this area would be undeniably hampered in the ability to communicate complex thoughts, and even to remember them in cases where memories are mediated by verbal constructs. This role for language, however, is not the fundamental structuring role as seen by the linguistic theory of cognition; instead it is a facilitating role for communicative purposes.

My version of the sensorimotor theory holds that mental models make use of sensorimotor representations held in working memory, and that these representations involve mechanisms developed for action planning. To see how such a system might work we can look at the motor system, which is organized in the requisite way. It is believed to involve regions whose function is to develop abstract motor plans in light of sensory and somatosensory information, and to hold these plans in a memory buffer for various uses (Schmidt 1982). Psychological studies indicate that motor plans are formed in advance of the activation of motor sequences, and are used to activate and monitor them. Wright (1990) describes evidence such as anticipatory lip movements in speech that "suggests that a representation of the whole sequence — a motor program — exists before the sequence begins and is used to control the production of the sequence" (Wright 1990: 305).

Brain structures thought to subserve motor planning are located primarily in the frontal lobes. Neuroscientific work indicates a central role for the supplementary motor area (SMA), a region in the dorsal-medial part of the frontal cortex adjacent to the primary motor cortex. This area has many reciprocal connections with the posterior parietal area, a region involved in somatosensory perception and bodily orientation with respect to the external environment (Pandya and Yeterian 1985). It is believed that the SMA is involved in constructing plans for complex sequences of movements. These plans are abstract in the sense that they do not specify details of the movement, which are selected and activated by the primary motor cortex in light of computations of specific movement parameters (Kandel and Schwartz 1985: 496). Activity in the SMA is associated with the formation of a conscious intention (Stuss and Benson 1986: 87-88; Kurata 1992). The SMA, moreover, has been found to be equally active whether the subject is actually carrying out the plans or merely imagining them (Roland et al. 1985). Roland and colleagues also showed that the SMA is active during a number of pure thinking activities, such as mentally subtracting 3 from 50, or reciting every other word of a well-known jingle. Thus the function of the SMA shows that the brain does, in fact, appear able to do what the mental model theory requires it to do: form, hold, and use an abstract (and possibly conscious) representation of a spatial domain incorporating motor activity of the subject, in both motor and pure cognitive activity.

Other regions of the frontal lobes have been found to be involved in the holding of a mental representation related to cognitive and motor activity. Goldman-Rakic (1987, 1988) studied areas on the dorsolateral part of the prefrontal cortex, beneath the SMA, in both humans and monkeys. She found that damage to these areas in all subjects led to deficits in performance on various delayed action tests, in which the subject has to hold a representation of a certain operation on-line, awaiting an external signal to perform the operation. Humans with such damage are also deficient at the Wisconsin Card-Sorting Task, in which cards displaying symbols in various shapes and colors are sorted and matched according to various criteria, which are changed without warning. The new criterion is unavailable to the prefrontal patient for use in the task, even though, significantly, the patient is often able to verbalize the instructions. Goldman-Rakic proposes that the prefrontal cortex governs behavior by means of "internalized or inner models of reality" and that:

> the concept [of the required card-sorting category] may be thought of as a second-order representation that cannot be accessed by the patient to guide response choice. The capacity for this type of representational system may be a unique property of human intelligence linked to the emergence of language but presumably built on a first-order representational capacity shared with other mammals. (Goldman-Rakic 1987: 378-379)

It is not yet known how the planning regions perform their operations. What seems clear, however, is that reasoning is involved; as Goldman (1990: 332) notes, "effective planning requires effective reasoning about the results of possible actions." The above work shows that the brain contains in its action planning mechanisms the sorts of systems which could subserve the reasoning used in connection with mental models, in which results of possible interactions among diverse sorts of entities are represented.

Finally, in support of my argument against Jackendoff that sensorimotor structures are capable of representing amodal conceptual distinctions, I turn to the work of A. R. Damasio (1989), who has recently proposed a theory of distributed cortical processing for certain cognitive functions. Citing neuroanatomical studies by Hubel and Livingston (1987) and others revealing the segregation of processing pathways, Damasio holds that in perception and memory reactivated fragments of sensory representations occur in physically separated sensory and motor cortices, and are unified by means of synchronized activation across the cortices:

> The integration of multiple aspects of reality, external as well as internal, in perceptual or recalled experiences, both within each modality and across modalities, depends on the time-locked co-activation of geographically separate sites of neural activity within sensory and motor cortices, rather than on a neural transfer and integration of different representations toward rostral integration sites. (Damasio 1989: 39)

Cognition, in Damasio's theory, makes use of representations realized in the reactivation of sensory and motor experience in coordinated sequences. We can represent, and hence think about: natural and artifactual entities; features and dimensions of those entities; and events consisting of interrelations of entities. Abstract entities are "criterion-governed conjunctions of features and dimensions present in the concrete entities outlined above" (Damasio 1989: 42). Particular entities and specific biographical events, as opposed to categorical or generic ones, are individuated by context — by the constellation of other events, entities and features in which they occur:

> This cognitive/neural architecture implies a high degree of sharing and embedding of representations. Both the representation of abstract entities and of events are derived from the representation of concrete entities and are thus individualized on the basis of combinatorial arrangement rather than remapping of constituents. The representation of concrete entities themselves share subrepresentations of component features so that individuality is again conferred by combinatorial formulas. (Damasio 1989: 44)

The binding codes which control the co-activation are stored in 'convergence zones,' which receive input from the sensory and motor cortices and send feedback projections to them. The input does not transfer representations to the convergence zones; rather, "the signals represent temporal coincidences (co-occurrence) or temporal sequences of activation in the feeding cortices" (Damasio 1989: 45). This account supports the claim that cognitive activity makes use of sensorimotor representations consisting of combinations of features, and that these representations themselves can express the sorts of conceptual distinctions that Jackendoff ascribes to the level of conceptual structure. Damasio describes the aspects of reality — concrete entities, abstract entities, and events — that can be represented by distributed sensorimotor representations:

Entities are definable by the number of components, the modality range of
those components (e.g., single or multiple modality), the mode of assembly,
the size of the class formed on the basis of physical structure similarity, their
operation and function, their frequency of occurrence, and their value to the
perceiver.

As is the case with entities, events can be both internal and external, [to
the subject's body] and both concrete and abstract. The concurrence of many
events which characterize regular life episodes generates 'contextual complexity,' which can be defined by the number of entities and by the relational
links they assume as they interplay in such complex sets of events. Naturally,
during the unfolding of events, other entities and events are recalled from
autobiographical records. The records co-activated in that process add further
to the contextual complexity of the experiences that occur within a given time
unit. It is thus contextual complexity which sets entities and events apart and
which confers greater or lesser uniqueness upon those entities and events. In
other words, contextual complexity sets the taxonomic level of events and
entities along a continuum that ranges from unique (most subordinate) to non-
unique (less subordinate and more supraordinate). (Damasio 1989: 42)

On this account one's representations can reflect, for example, a TYPE/
TOKEN distinction by means of the degree of autobiographical context combined with memories of specific entities or events, and one could represent
logical relations among abstract entities with appropriate sensorimotor fragments and a highly reduced context. Attentional focus in connection with
sensorimotor representations is also involved in aspect selection; it can determine which aspect of a representation is salient. During the Stroop color
naming test, for example, subjects name the colors of visually presented
words, which are color names either congruent or incongruent with the presented color. Naming the correct color when the word is an incongruent color
name makes great attentional demands on subjects (Pardo et al. 1990), indicating that attention can select among visually-presented aspects, and that a
further level of representation is unnecessary.

One might wonder if Damasio's convergence zones correspond to
Jackendoff's conceptual structure, since both have a crucial role in the preparation of sensorimotor representations for cognitive use. But these roles are
somewhat different. The convergence zones are simply coordinating areas,
responsible for organizing and sequencing of the representations. Like motor
sequencing areas which organize movements from the behavioral repertoire,
the convergence zones organize sensorimotor traces. They do not impose new
distinctions not potentially present in these traces as selectively combined and
activated, as does Jackendoff's conceptual structure. It is significant, however,

that both theories require a separate system to operate upon the sensorimotor traces so as to render them cognitively useful, and it might be that Jackendoff's theory would require very few modifications to be compatible with the sensorimotor theory.

To summarize: studies of brain mechanisms of movement, language and cognition provide evidence for the hypothesis that cognition makes use of sensorimotor representations formed from traces of the subject's experience, and that these representations are held in working memory buffers for use in various cognitive activities. Neuropsychological evidence suggests that language functions subserved by the frontal lobes form a cognitive subsystem linked with specific motor abilities, and that higher cognitive abilities may function independently of language.

5.   Ape cognition and evolution

If sensorimotor patterns rather than language patterns structure thought, then, because of bodily similarities, we would expect to find strong cognitive similarities between humans and other animals. If language is a subsystem for communication rather than a prime determinant of cognition, then we would also look for evidence that human language evolved from communication systems in our ancestors. Both of these expectations have been fulfilled.

Premack (1988) investigated the mode of thinking in minds without grammar. He proposed that the intelligence of monkeys, apes and humans be represented by concentric circles, with humans possessing unique abilities, apes a subset of human abilities, and monkeys a subset of those of apes. His work with prelinguistic human children and with chimpanzees before and after language training showed that the unique abilities of humans are prefigured by those of apes.

An important difference between prelinguistic children and apes without language training is that many abilities manifested spontaneously by children can be acquired by training in apes. This is shown, for example, in tests involving grouping of like items. After training, apes roughly equal children in match to sample tests involving normal, nonmutilated or distorted objects, and in both groups skills transfer to other normal objects. When mutilated or distorted objects are used, children's skills are transferred but apes' are not; with training, however, the apes readily learn to match the non-normal objects.

The human cognitive advantage shown by these tests, Premack argues, lies in perceptual skills, which develop along a continuum: those in pigeons, for example, are a subset of those in primates (Premack 1988: 50). Human children also excel in recognition of physical similarity. Normal human children pass through stages in which they spontaneously recognize identity, featural similarity, and category membership; apes and retarded children show similar delays in development of these abilities.

Language enables human children to pass from recognition of physical similarity, which occurs spontaneously, to recognition of conceptual similarity, which does not. It also gives apes an advantage on certain kinds of tests. After introduction of plastic objects serving as 'words' for same/different, apes can recognize analogies of the type A:A'::B:B'. Premack concludes that language amplifies pre-existing abilities:

> These words ['same/different'] evidently call the ape's attention to the distinction, increasing its awareness of the distinction and thus its ability to use it. . . Though used only to refer to physical similarity between objects, the words none the less enable the ape to make judgments about the relation between the relations. We can understand this effect if we assume that the animal can recognize the analogy between the sameness/difference of objects, on the one hand, and that of relations, on the other. That is, evidently the animal can recognize:
>
> (A/A' same B/B') SAME (CC/DD same EE/FF)
>
> An individual who could recognize this simple identity would be close to using analogies in the manner claimed for the human adult (e.g. mapping one model of the world onto another model) and would have the potential at least for the recursive use of analogies.
> . . . The thoroughgoing superiority of the prelanguage child on every measure used indicates that the cognitive advantage to the human is not one introduced by language. . . What are the evolutionary implications of these findings? The addition of language to the proto-human did not create a difference but amplified one that already existed. For proto-human intelligence already greatly exceeded that of the ape. (Premack 1988: 63-64)

There are several implications of this work for the sensorimotor/mental model theory. First, that theory claims that more primitive structures are used recursively to represent more conceptually sophisticated or abstract relations. Analogical reasoning is central to mental model use: one takes structures used in reasoning about a familiar domain, and applies them in a novel domain. Premack's studies show that apes can apply relations between physical objects analogically to relations themselves, and thus that they have the basic cognitive apparatus necessary for mental model use in the absence of language. Second, as predicted by the sensorimotor theory, cognitive abilities of human beings appear to be continuous with those of apes. While the possession of a module specialized for syntax may account for certain defining features of human cognition (see Chapter Seven), many others, such as perceptual discrimination and spontaneous recognition of physical similarity, depend on the degree of development of nonverbal abilities shared with apes. Finally, Premack's work supports the attentional selection of abstract features or aspects of sensorimotor representations, as is proposed in Damasio's theory, rather than the existence of a separate conceptual system as in Jackendoff's. Language can aid in focusing attention on these distinctions because they are already represented, but only implicitly. If the concepts are explicitly represented in conceptual structure, as in Jackendoff's model, or if they are not represented at all prior to language, as some proponents of the linguistic theory might maintain, the role of language in facilitating use of the concepts is unexplained.

If key conceptual distinctions are available prelinguistically, what prompted the evolution of language? Several theorists have proposed an origin for language in motor sequencing areas of the cortex which were specialized for tool-making. Philip Lieberman (1991) argues that human language evolved from these areas, even though in the brains of nonhuman primates the areas homologous to the areas specialized for human speech do not control vocalization. Vocalization in nonhumans is not under voluntary control, and is subserved by subcortical regions (Lieberman 1991: 52-53). Human speech may, he argues, have evolved from a gestural system, which is under voluntary control and which is regulated by cortical regions adjacent to those controlling throat, mouth and facial movements. He quotes Doreen Kimura who theorized about the link between handedness and speech:

> It seems not too farfetched to suppose that cerebral asymmetry of function developed in conjunction with the asymmetric activity of the two limbs during tool use, the left hemisphere, for reasons uncertain, becoming the hemisphere specialized for precise limb positioning. When a gestural system [for language] was employed, therefore it would presumably also be controlled primarily from the left hemisphere. If speech were indeed a later development, it would be reasonable to suppose that it would also come under the direction of the hemisphere already well developed for precise motor control. (Kimura 1979: 203; quoted in Lieberman 1991: 79)

Lieberman's position is that grammatical syntax is made possible by the evolution of structures for coordinating sequential motor operations, specifically speech motor control. The structures are analogous:

> The sequence of symbols that define a sentence determines the context in which one symbol is substituted for another. Similar rules describe speech motor control for even seemingly simple motor tasks, such as providing a sufficient supply of oxygen while we speak. (Lieberman 1991: 107-108)

Lieberman does not deny the existence of brain mechanisms specialized for syntax, given the selective advantage of communication they confer. His claim concerns their evolutionary origins. The salient point for present purposes is that if we accept the evidence of Premack's work — that conceptual distinctions antedate linguistic ability — together with Lieberman's proposals concerning the evolution of language, then we have strong support for the view that language is an ability that serves a crucial but nevertheless cognitively specialized function in humans — communication; or, more generally, social interaction — and that the basic structures of cognition are independent of grammatical structures.

Lieberman's proposal has recently received empirical support in the work of Patricia Greenfield (1991), mentioned in the previous section. Greenfield cites evidence of a common neural substrate (Broca's area) for language and object combination during the first two years of life in humans. Evidence is both behavioral and neurophysiological/neuroanatomical. Behavioral studies show structural similarities in sound and object combination in infants up to the age of two, after which structures in language and object combination diverge. Neuroscientific work shows the development of brain circuitry such that an originally undifferentiated Broca's area becomes differentiated through a manual object combination circuit and a grammar circuit, with parallel connections to the anterior prefrontal cortex and the motor cortex (Greenfield 1991: 538-544). She also notes evidence from present-day primates consistent with the hypothesis that tool-use and language evolved together, and that there exists a neural substrate for these abilities homologous with that found in humans (Greenfield 1991: 547).

To summarize: if the sensorimotor theory is true, human cognitive abilities are developments from the simpler but structurally similar abilities in nonhuman primates, and language enhances these abilities but does not determine their nature. Premack's work with chimpanzees verifies this claim. In addition, there is evidence from ethnology, psychology and neuroscience that human language evolved from motor sequencing structures in prehumans, a finding consistent with the view that language is a subspecialty for communication and not an autonomous representational medium for cognition.

6. Parsimony

There is a final point in favor of the sensorimotor theory, which can be briefly stated. The sensorimotor theory requires only one basic set of rules for cognition and one representational medium, instead of two (one for cognition and one for motor behavior). Reasoning via mental models can make use of the very rule structures that are used to govern actual movements, and representation of the rules for mental models could utilize the same representational mechanisms as those used in action planning. This identification would be particularly valuable given that much more is known about brain mechanisms for motor behavior than is known about general reasoning mechanisms (although motor theory is still in its early stages). Conscious reasoning often makes verbal appeal to logical rules of inference, but the brain mechanisms underlying such reasoning are completely unknown. Identifying them with the systems underlying motor planning, or with extensions of those systems, would be a giant step.

7. Objections

It is objected by many people that they are simply not *ever* conscious, when reasoning, of imagery related to sensorimotor models. I think that this complaint cannot be taken seriously for several reasons. First, we tend to pay little attention to *current* proprioceptive background sensations even when they are essential for ongoing orientation and action. Perception of external objects is normally accompanied by enough bodily awareness to enable us to locate these objects with respect to ourselves; this awareness is in principle available to conscious experience (it can be included in the focus of attention) yet is generally not expressly noted. We are accustomed to *using* our bodily awareness to orient ourselves and deal with external objects, while at the same time ignoring this awareness and conceptualizing only the objects. Hence it is not at all surprising that when thinking about conceptual matters we would similarly ignore and even fail to recognize any sensorimotor imagery used in such thinking. This is particularly true given the prevailing ideology concerning linguistic thought; theories have a notorious effect on what people believe they experience.

Second, most people do not conceptualize the sorts of sensorimotor representations I have in mind as *images*, because that term has traditionally been reserved for the visual modality. If I ask someone what he did when he imagined clasping his hands behind his back, he might say that he didn't *image,* or *picture* the action, but simply *thought about* it. If the way we think about things is fundamentally by means of action imagery, but at the same time we do not call such thinking 'imaging', then the qualitative feels of such images may appear as nothing more than the way it *feels to think.* The relation between such feelings and actual bodily activity need not be subjectively obvious, especially when the imagery used for reasoning is vague or schematic compared with the imagery used for planning and executing actual motor activity.

The term 'image' is heavily theory-laden, and thus is liable to misleading interpretations. Why, in that case, do I not find a more neutral term? The reason is that there is a precise overlap between the visual experiences traditionally referred to by the term 'images' and the experiences, *in the visual modality,* that I believe constitute understanding. I want to exploit this overlap as one means of identifying the type of conscious experience that is the subject of this book. My claim is that what is usually called an 'image' is not an objective entity functioning like a picture or other symbol, but instead is an *experience,* generated in response to external events. The experience may be purely visual, or it may include elements from various nonvisual modalities. When the experience is visual, then it is similar to the experience we have when looking at an external object. It may be that even having a visual image involves nonvisual imagery, in that the experience of looking at something includes a background experience of eye focus, head orientation, and the like; perhaps for that reason the experience is mistakenly thought to involve mentally '*looking at*' a mental 'object.' If we think of imaging as creating an experience of sensorimotor events, rather than as contemplating a mental object, then many ontological difficulties can be avoided.

A third factor obscuring sensorimotor imagery is interference. We cannot consciously attend *at the same time and to the same degree* both to the imagery guiding our actions and to that serving as the medium for reasoning. I can think about a math or logic problem while riding a bike or driving a car if those actions can be performed automatically; motor images in such cases need not be conscious. If, however, I must concentrate on what I am doing, I cannot simultaneously reason about something else. Thus if I stop and analyze my mental experience at random moments while simultaneously walking and thinking, those experiences will be correspondingly varied: sometimes my conscious imagery will concern the activity, and other times it will concern the thoughts.

On the other hand, people do report thinking in words. If language is a cognitive subsystem evolved for communication, then why does it appear to play a central role in thinking? While a thorough answer is beyond our present scope, a general response can be sketched. I propose that there are two ways in which language occurs internally such that it can appear to be more fundamental than it actually is. First, fragmentary linguistic representations can stand in for physical objects in mental models.[4] As we noted earlier, language can serve to focus attention upon perceptual distinctions; words can hence represent these distinctions in communication and in thought. The structures in which these words occur, however, would be analogical ones. Bisiach (1988) offers a similar account in his argument, based on his studies of left-sided spatial neglect, against an autonomous representational role for language. He suggests that there exists:

> a passive, sporadic entailment of linguistic structures by fundamentally non-verbal thought processes, a sort of epiphenomenal resonance of the latter in the instrument they have at their disposal for overt communication. . . . Linguistic icons have been laid down alongside the nonlinguistic icons of objects, situations and events to which they are related. As such, linguistic icons might act as keystones supporting the assemblage of independent representations, and specifying the nature of their relations, in a compound act of thought. . . . By 'linguistic icons,' I literally mean sensorimotor representations of natural language items. (Bisiach 1988: 479)

On this view, images of words or phrases might be components of mental models; but reasoning with them would entail nonverbal structures.

It might be objected that when one interprets language, one's mental model is intended to represent the meaning of the utterance and/or the intentions of the language user, and that a mixing of the resulting imagery with the actual words and phrases of the linguistic material being interpreted would result in an incoherent model.[5] I agree that in a model used to represent a realistic scenario, images of words would have no role. There are, however, other uses for models, such as in solving word problems. Huttenlocher, for example, describes a common strategy for solving three-term series problems by constructing imaginary arrays: "The Ss represent items as words (or abbreviations) rather than pictures, but they do not imagine having to write out these words. Instead, each word 'appears' as E [the experimenter] reads it, and S then treats it as a material object which can be picked up and moved" (Huttenlocher 1968: 297).

The other way language occurs internally is in the mental rehearsal of acts of communication, as was mentioned above. We frequently imagine presenting our ideas to some specific or generic other. We internally try out the sound of arguments or explanations before expressing them aloud or in writing. The position of the sensorimotor theory would be that this mental representation of verbal forms is the result of largely nonverbal cognitive processing, constituting the reasoning of which the verbal structures are the final expression. Imagined speech can be vivid in consciousness, however, and hence can give the illusion of playing a dominant role in cognition and of verifying the linguistic paradigm.

8.   Conclusion

My purpose in this chapter has been to provide a context for the main subject of this book: the experience of understanding. As was explained in Chapter One, my view is that understanding anything is knowing the possible actions one might perform in relation to that thing, and being aware of that understanding is consciously imagining (some of) those actions. This view is best understood within the framework of the sensorimotor theory of cognition, as described and defended in this chapter. That theory is that cognition is determined by the structures of bodily action and sensation, and that reasoning involves the manipulation of mental models constructed by mechanisms similar or identical to those by which action-planning is carried out. The theory applies to the comprehension of content presented in any form, from abstract systems to physical states of affairs directly perceived, and to the consciousness of this comprehension. Thus the theory offers hope of a unified treatment of consciousness and intentionality in thought and action.

I have discussed three areas in which evidence favors the sensorimotor theory over its major rival, the linguistic theory of cognition. I have also sketched ways in which two common objections to the theory may be answered. The combined weight of the considerations raised here, it seems to me, is sufficient to justify efforts to develop this still somewhat inchoate theory of cognition into a detailed model, one which can generate specific predictions and testing. With this background, we are now ready to look more closely at understanding.

Recall that my view is a foundationalist one. Understanding a thing is relating it to something already understood; this means that there must be something understood in terms of itself. In line with the sensorimotor approach, this foundational entity must be something with which an agent is intimately familiar in a nonsymbolic way: the best candidate is the agent's own activity. In the next chapter we explore this basic level of understanding.

Notes

1.   For a related analysis see Geach 1957.

2.   The term 'metaphor' is used here in a general, not specifically linguistic, sense.

3.   Damage to Broca's area alone causes only temporary disorders associated with speech production.

4.   Freud (1900) proposed that linguistic fragments in dreams, as distinct from the language in jokes, are not used creatively because higher cognitive processes do not occur in dreams. Dascal (1985) argues that dream language is not creative because dream-creation is unconscious, and that, in general the boundaries between the different 'systems' of the mind, the *unconscious,* the *preconscious* and the *conscious,* are correlated with the extent to which language plays a role in each of them. (Dascal 1985: 105)
      Dascal holds that communicative intentions require consciousness, and hence creative communicative activity occurs in jokes but not in dreams. Dream-language consists of recollected fragments. The distinction between the occurrence of linguistic fragments as 'passive' components of a mental representation, and the active, creative communicative use of language is closely related to the two forms of internal language I propose here.

5.   I owe this suggestion to Maxim Stamenov.

CHAPTER THREE

Understanding Actions

1. Introduction: Searle's challenge

This chapter introduces the foundation of all understanding: the nonconceptual understanding an agent has of her own basic, goal-directed actions. We begin with a discussion of Searle's (1980) Chinese Room argument, which provides an initial motivation for the search for a foundation of understanding. We then develop a precise statement of this foundation by way of a series of refinements in its characterization.

John Searle states, in his famous example, that he does not understand Chinese. In the example, he imagines imitating a computer that takes Chinese symbols as input, matches them to other Chinese symbols according to a rulebook, and delivers the latter symbols as output. According to some accounts of understanding (e.g. Schank and Abelson 1977), if the input constitutes questions about a story, and the output constitutes correct answers to the questions, then the computer understands the story. But, Searle says, even though he performs the manipulations correctly, he knows he does not understand the symbols.

A great deal has been written about Searle's example and the argument he takes it to support: that syntax (as used in computation) cannot yield semantics (as manifest in human understanding). But very little attention has been paid to what I consider the most important question raised by Searle's example: *what is it to understand something in the way that Searle wants to understand the symbols?* Explaining human intentionality requires explaining the difference between understanding something in a way that satisfies us, that gives us confidence that we understand it, and failing to understand something in that way. In the Chinese Room example, the things that are not so understood are symbols, but in real life everything we encounter — a symbol, a physical object, or even an event involving our own bodies — is capable of being understood, or of not being understood, in the way that Searle has highlighted.

Margaret Boden (1990) points out that while Searle-in-the-room lacks an understanding of Chinese, he does understand how to manipulate the symbols. This type of understanding might even be attributable to a nonhuman computer, whose "procedures do embody some minimal understanding . . . of what it is to compare two formal structures, for example" (1990: 99; see also Sloman 1985). We may assume that Searle is satisfied with his understanding of how to perform the required operations on the symbols; he expresses no puzzlement about these actions or about the meaning of the *English* symbols that instruct him to perform them. Thus the Chinese Room scenario itself provides an example of the kind of understanding that Searle is missing in the case of the Chinese symbols, but we do not have an account of what this kind of understanding is. This chapter is an attempt at the beginning of such an account.

Ultimately, we need an explanation of what it is to understand symbols in general, which involves understanding both what they are symbols of, and what it is for something to be a symbol. I will give a general idea of my long-range view of understanding, most of which is beyond the scope of this chapter. Symbols are originally understood by being interpreted in terms of something else that one already understands. If in conversing with you I ask you to explain a word I do not understand, I am asking for a different word or for help in forming a mental picture that I can use in order to think the thought you want me to think. For example, if one does not understand the verb 'to perseverate,' one wants a translation of it into other words that one does understand. But how are *those* words understood? Some words must be understood in terms of nonlinguistic items (this, I take it, is part of Searle's intuition), and these must be familiar and recognizable (understood) as well. For example, I can understand the word 'cat' by thinking about actual cats, and I do this by imagining or recalling, in however vague or schematic a way, some of my own experiences with cats. In normal language use, of course, I do not pause to dwell upon how I understand common words like 'cat.' The experience of understanding is commonly a sense of confidence that I *could* summon appropriate images if necessary (Ellis 1995: 108f). But if my attention is drawn to the meaning of the word, I confirm my understanding by means of such recollections. I understand a cat that I see in much the same way: by interpreting it as one of *those things* that I had *such and such* experiences with. One understands nonlinguistic entities in terms of one's experiences with them, and activating or attending to one's understanding of such entities (or to the words referring to them) is imagining or recalling these experiences. Now, how are *those* experiences understood — i.e. how do we understand what is going on when we have them? Often in terms of further experiences; but this chain must end somewhere. I believe that there is a *basic level — a foundation — of understanding*, in which what is understood is not interpreted in terms of something else. The things we understand at this level are our own basic goal-directed actions. Roughly speaking, simply being able to perform such an action is understanding that action, and this is where understanding begins.

The goal of this chapter is to provide a noncircular account of the understanding of basic actions: the account must explain the understanding of a basic action without presupposing the understanding of anything else at all. This account is intended to provide a basis for a later account of the understanding of symbols. Examining the sort of understanding that would satisfy Searle is a means to this goal because, as I hope to make clear, that sort of understanding is close to the foundation that I seek.

2.   Understanding our actions

In this section I attempt to characterize, in a noncircular way, a sufficient condition for the understanding of a basic action. One way we understand actions is by being able to perform them. My aim is to identify that feature of our ability to perform an action which constitutes our understanding of the action. To do this I shall go through a series of formulations, each of which is correct in its way but may include more than I need to identify this feature. By means of successive refinements of these formulations I arrive at one which seems precisely to capture one way in which we understand an action, a way that does not depend upon our understanding of anything else, and which does not invoke conditions that are not themselves essential to that understanding.

3. Provisional characterization (1)

Suppose someone is teaching me to dance the Charleston, and trying to follow
her instructions I say 'I don't understand how to do this.' But I might be
actually doing exactly what she told me to do, and she would say 'Yes you do
understand; you *are* doing it!' I do it right, but I don't realize that I am doing it
right until I am reassured by my teacher. Under what circumstances might I
still insist that I don't understand how to Charleston in *that* situation? I might
say: I don't know what to do next. But then suppose the teacher says: 'You
don't do anything different; what you have been doing *is* the Charleston.' It
seems that in that case I would say: 'Is that all there is to it? Well, so *that's*
what doing the Charleston is!' In this example, the thing to be understood is an
action, and understanding it is being able to perform the action.

    Here I am thinking of understanding as a kind of knowing, to which one
can apply the distinction between 'knowing how' and 'knowing that.' Understanding can be knowing in two different ways: knowing *how* to do something,
and knowing what something means — knowing *that*, e.g., the Charleston is a
particular kind of dance. We can speak of understanding the term 'Charleston'
in the sense of knowing what the term means — 'knowing that' — and for that
it might be sufficient just to be able to describe the dance. So it is possible to
understand the term 'Charleston' without being able to *do* the Charleston (you
can, for example, certainly understand that you yourself can *not do* the
Charleston). Understanding the term 'Charleston' in this way is knowing what
thing the term refers to. But here I am interested in this term because it refers to
a particular type of thing: an action. A term referring to an action can be
understood in a different, perhaps a simpler and more primitive way, than by
knowing *that* it refers to things of a certain type. It can be understood by having
the ability to perform the action that it refers to, perhaps in response to that
term used as a command. We can say that one can understand a term that refers
to an action in two different ways: by knowing things about the action, and by
being able to respond to the term, when it is used as a command, by performing
the action.

    In general, understanding a symbol requires understanding (a) that it is a
symbol for a particular thing, and (b) understanding the thing that it refers to. I
have now been talking about (b) in cases when what is referred to is an action,
and distinguishing between understanding that action in the 'knowing that'
sense — e.g. being able to describe it — and understanding that action in the

'knowing how' sense — e.g. being able to perform it. Being able to perform it is at least a part of *one* way we can understand symbols referring to an action. Because the understanding of symbols is more complex than that of actions, I want now to focus on that ability to understand an action *itself* by performing it, independent of doing so as a response to the term referring to the action. So now let us look more closely at the Charleston case as an example, not of understanding the *term* 'Charleston,' but of understanding the thing to which the term refers — that particular kind of dance. In the example, the learner has just acquired an understanding of that dance by learning how to do it.

Could a person in that situation believe that she did not understand? There I think one might lack a feeling of familiarity or confidence in performing the movements of the newly-learned action. She might say 'I'm not sure I've got it.' But if the teacher says: 'Just keep doing what you're doing; that's doing the Charleston,' and the learner feels able to keep on doing the same steps, I do not think the learner would say 'But I still don't *understand*.' If the learner is able intentionally to repeat what she was doing, she understands what it is to perform the action. There is nothing more, in this example, to the learner's understanding how to do the Charleston than her being able to do it, and the ability to do it is one way of understanding this particular kind of dance. If you can Charleston, and you know you can Charleston (independently of any term by which you may refer to *that thing* that you can do), then you understand what kind of dance the Charleston is, and you know you understand it.[1]

It seems, however, that one could do some action like the Charleston correctly by sheer accident. For example, suppose I trip and, trying to regain my balance, perform what happen to be the movements of the Charleston. (We may even suppose that Charleston music is by chance playing in the background, and that my movements, again by chance, are in time with the beat.) In performing these movements I show that I am able to do the Charleston, in the sense that I am physically capable of articulating the movements in the right way. Nevertheless, in this case it is not so obvious that I would be said to understand the Charleston, because I am not clearly aware of what movements I am making; all I am thinking about is trying not to fall. If asked, I would probably deny any understanding or even clear awareness of what I had just done. Thus we need to specify that understanding an action is being able to perform it intentionally, not just accidentally. This, then, is a provisional characterization of basic understanding:

(1)   One understands an action if one has the ability to *perform that action intentionally.*

If one is able intentionally to Charleston, to perform the basic steps with the appropriate swivels and kicks in the right rhythm, then one understands the Charleston.

4.   Provisional characterization (2)

It won't work, however, to say simply that understanding an action is being able to perform that action intentionality. There is the possibility that I might intentionally perform some random movements which in actuality add up to all the steps and movements of the Charleston. These movements may have no meaning for me in combination but nevertheless I might perform *each one of them* intentionally. This possibility leads to a problem with (1). In performing these movements I am not guaranteed of understanding the Charleston, because I may not think of the random movements, all of which I happen to perform intentionally, as making up a single action. In that case, it seems to me, I do not understand *the action* that constitutes doing the Charleston because I do not think of what I am doing as *a single unified action* at all.

But if I am defining understanding in terms of the *ability* to perform an action, then why is this not a case of understanding? Someone watching me move about at random might say 'I thought you said you didn't understand the Charleston but you were wrong because look, you can do it!' I have said that understanding an action is being able to perform it, and in this case I am *able* to perform it, because I am able to perform all the movements that make it up. My behavior, moreover, is intentional. But I still think that in this case we would not say that I understand how to do (the dance that is in fact) the Charleston, at least not merely in virtue of what I have just done. The problem seems to lie in the fact that there is nothing in the way I perform the movements that binds them together as a single action, except for the fact that, on this one occasion, I performed them together. But understanding an action seems minimally to require understanding the action as *a single thing*, whose component movements are bound together by being components of an action. So just being able to perform each one of the movements of an action is not the sense of 'being able to perform the action' that we need.

It might be thought that what we need here is 'knowing that' to supplement the 'knowing how' of performing the action, in order to have full understanding. It could seem, that is, that understanding an action as a single thing, if accomplished through the ability to perform the action, requires as well the *knowledge* that the movements one performs constitute a single action — in this case, a type of dance. Why should anyone think that the difference between movements done as individual actions and as part of a single action can be captured in the performance of those movements alone, especially when the difference is not apparent to an observer?

This objection is partly right. Since the identical movements can be performed as individual actions or as parts of a single action, the physical process of moving the limbs and performing the movements itself cannot distinguish between the two. But I do not think we need to say that to understand what one is doing as a single action, one must *know that* it is an action of a certain type; one might be completely ignorant of any standard identification of the action. What one does need, it seems to me, is some way of *thinking about* one's movements when one does them such that the movements are experienced as a unity because of this way of thinking. In other words, while movements performed as a single action may seem no different to an observer from movements performed as separate and unrelated, they would seem different to the performer. I will illustrate what I mean by examining two closely similar cases.

Suppose we try to unify the movements in a performance, just in terms of the movements alone, by specifying that the movements constituting an action that one understands be movements that one has learned and can repeat in a particular order, rather than just random movements that one happens to perform on one occasion. Let us try a variation on the earlier example, in which someone intentionally and in the right order, but randomly and unknowingly, performs the individual movements of the Charleston. Consider a person who is being taught some exercises by a physical therapist.[2] Suppose the therapist gives the patient four different exercises, A, B, C and D, and says 'Do these ten times a day.' The patient may always do them in the order in which they were taught, ABCD, but only because that is the easiest way to remember them. Now let us say that these four exercises, when performed in the right order, are identical with the movements of the Charleston. Does the patient understand the Charleston (independently of understanding the word 'Charleston,' as discussed above), just by virtue of consistently performing the exercises in the right order? I think not, because understanding the Charleston is being able to perform the various movements in that particular order, and to do so *because* in that order they form a *unity* which has its own identity: *that* action. While the patient intentionally performs the movements in that specific order, and hence performs the movements constituting the Charleston, she still does not perform them *as a unified action.* The patient, in other words, sees no difference at all between performing them in the Charleston order, and any other order, except for the fact that she happens to have been taught them in what is in fact the Charleston order. Therefore they are not performed *as one action*, and hence she does not understand the Charleston.

On the other hand, now suppose that the therapist tells the patient: 'Doing the exercises in the order I taught you will have a special strengthening effect on your *kicking* ability. If you do them in the order DCBA they won't do that, but they will have a strengthening effect on your *jumping* ability instead.' If, on being told this, the patient now thinks of the four individual exercises done in the order ABCD as *the kicking exercise* — a single action which achieves the goal of strengthening one's kicking ability — it is more plausible to say that she understands the Charleston in the sense I am currently exploring: she understands the action to which the term 'Charleston' refers, because she has the ability to perform it *as* a unified action (although of course she does not thereby understand that the kicking exercise is identical with the action referred to by the term 'Charleston,' of which she may never have heard).[3]

How could I justify the claim that she understands the Charleston in the above case? Suppose later she hears of the Charleston and asks a friend to teach it to her. The friend, familiar with the patient's exercise program, might well say: 'You already can do it; it's the same thing as the kicking exercise!' If at least one way that a person can understand an action is by being able to do that action, which I have been assuming since my discussion of Searle-in-the-Chinese-Room, then in this case the patient understands the Charleston. The reason it seems right to say that she understands it in this case, but not in the case where the individual movements were performed at random, is that in this case the movements are thought of as comprising a unified action, even though the action is thought of as an exercise and not as a dance.

But the Charleston *is* a dance! Can you understand an action that is a dance, even though you can perform it, when you do not know that what you are performing is a dance? Consider a different example. Suppose a congenitally deaf person is taught to hit numbered woodblocks that correspond to the notes of the scale; the blocks included a padded one that is silent when hit. The deaf person is taught to hit the blocks in the following sequence: 3212333022203550321233332321000.[4] This sequence corresponds to the melody of 'Mary Had A Little Lamb.' Now, even if the deaf person comes to understand her action of hitting the blocks in the given sequence, it does not seem that she could be said to understand the playing of the corresponding melody. But she is able to play that melody, and she understands what she is able to do.

This case highlights the limits of the primitive action understanding upon which other understanding rests. A given action may be a part of a larger context in which it plays a specific role and is identified in terms of that role. One does not understand the action in terms of that role unless one understands the context in which the role is played. That is the case with a melody, identified in a context that essentially involves hearing. So a congenitally deaf person might not understand her action of playing 'Mary Had A Little Lamb' even though she is able (in a limited sense) to play it. But she can understand her action in terms of her own experience. This example is useful because it illustrates the way primitive action understanding can constitute the intentional core of complex events — the way, to take an analogous example, humans can unknowingly threaten the environment by their intentional activity, and how they can come to understand what they are doing.

In the case of a dance, performing the physical movements correctly is *almost* sufficient for understanding a dance; hitting woodblocks correctly but not understanding sound is much less sufficient for understanding the playing of a melody. Note that in order to constitute a dance, movements must be performed in a particular way that goes beyond the order of their performance. They must be done in a rhythmic way.[5] The Charleston is a good example for my purposes because it is difficult to do the steps *except* in a rhythmic way, since otherwise one tends to lose one's balance. But they could be done unrhythmically. Since the Charleston is a dance, consisting of movements ABCD done rhythmically in that order, one does not understand the dance unless one is able to do the steps in exactly that way. But it is not necessary that one think of what one is doing as a dance in terms of a wider social context. Thinking of it that way requires having concepts that go beyond the action itself, such as the concept of a festive entertainment. All that is necessary is that one have some way or other of thinking of that action — which could be a way as vague as 'that thing I sometimes do with the swivels and kicks,' or even

a wordless image — as a single action. That action is the very same single
action as the action one performs when doing the Charleston. The exerciser
does, in effect, do the Charleston when doing her exercises. Being able to
perform the action in that way, then, is understanding the (action that is the)
Charleston.

If my intuitions about these examples are right, then the understanding of
an action is not just the ability intentionally to perform all of the component
movements of the action. But our formulation of (1) allowed that possibility;
therefore perhaps we should amend (1) as follows:

(2)   One understands an action if one has the ability to perform that
       action *as a unified action* intentionally.

(2) provides a sufficient condition for understanding an action. As we noted
above, one can understand it in other ways, such as by knowing facts about it.
This way of understanding it is, as we said, understanding in the 'knowing
how' way. One manifests this kind of understanding *of a term* if one responds
correctly to that term used a command — e.g. 'Charleston!' More specifically,
I have argued, one understands the action to which the term refers if one is able
intentionally to perform it as a unified action.

5.   Provisional characterization (3)

I think that (2) is inadequate for illuminating the understanding of an action.
While it is true, we have not yet gotten at why it is true — why being able to
perform an action in the way described is understanding the action. (2) reflects
the recognition that understanding the action is being able to perform those
movements *as the components of a unified action.* Now in this formulation,
crucial work is done by the term *'as,'* which raises the question of how can we
define *this* ability — the ability to do something *as* a unified action — without
adverting to the concept of understanding we are trying to explain? I argued
earlier that that ability lies in the way the agent thinks about the action. Surely,
the thinking that underlies the ability to perform A *as a unified action* should
be explained as doing movement M *with the understanding that* movement M
is a component of action A. In other words, while a classification of the
performance of a unified action as intentional has desirable implications about

the state of mind of the agent, this state of mind is already characterized in terms of states that imply understanding.

We can solve this problem if, instead of characterizing understanding in terms of intentional action, we do so in terms of the ability to *intend to perform* an action. Talking about intentions instead of intentional actions will avert the threatened circularity because it will force us to talk about the nature of the agent's mental state, by which the movements are thought of as components of a single action. We have to be able to describe this mental state in a way that does not presuppose understanding. An action is intentional because of some mental state of the agent — an intention (which may or may not be an intention to perform that action). It is in the intention, if anywhere, that we will find a state of mind whose description does not presuppose understanding.

But how can this threatened circularity be avoided simply by talking in terms of intention instead of in terms of intentional action? Surely everything I have said so far could have been phrased in terms of intention, but the circularity problem would still have been there. Thus instead of (1) I could have said:

(1*)   One understands an action if one has the ability to intend to perform that action.

It could then have been objected that one could intend to perform all the components of an action, independently but in what happens to be the right order, and in that sense one intends to perform the action, but one still does not understand the action. Anything, it seems, that you can do intentionally, you can intend to do.

This objection is correct; it shows why it is that we must specify that what is intended is the performance of a unified action rather than just the individual components of (what happens to be) an action. Specifying this, however, can not be done without presupposing understanding if we talk just of the ability to perform an intentional action; we must talk of the ability to *intend* to perform an action. That is because the mental state that constitutes thinking of an action as a single unified action plays an active role in intending; this role concerns the determination of the *content* of the intention. At the time of the performance of an intentional action, the content has already been determined by the relevant prior intention. It is possible to state the content of an intention to perform a simple action A as follows: to perform action A *as* a unified action, *by* performing all the movements making up action A. Having the ability to intend this is, I maintain, one way of understanding action A, because it involves having a mental state whose content specifies action A as a unified action. Characterizing understanding in terms of this ability can be noncircular because, as I shall argue, we can talk about how the content of the intention specifies a unified action without using the concept of understanding. My point here has been to emphasize that while this content is what we need to look at, we must look at it in connection with intention, rather than just in connection with intentional action. Our job now is to see how this unification *is* accomplished in an intention. Seeing this will also illuminate the restricted sense of 'ability to perform' an action which, as I argued above, we want to ascribe to some disabled people.

To see this, consider what we do when we form an intention to perform an action. In the case of many of our intentions, it is impossible to talk about how we form them without presupposing understanding, because these intentions have conceptual components which must already be understood in term of other concepts before they can figure in the intentions. For example, the ability to intend to go to the opera presupposes understanding what the opera is, and that in turn presupposes the understanding of other concepts such as singing, public entertainment, etc. In order to talk about intention without presupposing the understanding of such complex conceptual components, we need the case of an intention to perform an action of which all the components are simple bodily movements of the agent. Dancing the Charleston, of course, is one such case, but let us find an even simpler one that a mere baby could perform.

Let us take an intention to grasp one's foot. (One might, if one is a baby, intend to do this for the sheer joy of it; if an adult, one might intend it as part of a more comprehensive plan such as assuming a yoga position. Either way, grasping one's foot is a single action, capable of being intended independently of any further intention.) How do we go about intending to do this? There are different types of possible answers to this question. One relevant for our purposes is the suggestion that one intends to grasp one's foot by individually intending all the bodily movements by means of which one will grasp one's foot. It is clear for many reasons that this is *not* the way one normally forms an intention to do this kind of action. Many, or even all, of the individual bodily movements by which one will carry out the intention in the case of such a simple action are not consciously decidable in advance of the start of the performance. They are calculated by the brain's motor system on the basis of information about initial positions of bodily parts, ideal trajectories, expected resistances, and so forth. The information required for these calculations is not normally available to consciousness, but is delivered to the effector mechanisms after the intention has been formed. In a simple physical action, the agent decides on a goal — e.g. grasping the left foot with the right hand — and unconscious mechanisms determine the individual movements by which the goal will be accomplished. Grasping one's foot can be thought of as a basic action in Goldman's (1970) sense; performing a basic action, like raising one's arm, does not require conscious calculations of how to do it:

> This is not to deny that there are mechanisms — indeed a very complex and interesting array of mechanisms — that do cause my raising my arm. What is crucial, however, is that my ability to raise my arm at will does not depend on having any knowledge (or belief) of these mechanisms. (Goldman 1970: 66)

In more complex actions, the unconscious mechanisms are inadequate and the agent must consciously decide on the means as well as on the goal.

What do I do, now, when I intend to grasp my foot? One thing I do is to think about my grasping my foot. I do not have to (indeed, I may not be able to) think about the individual movements by which I will do this. But I do think about myself doing it. How do I do that? A straightforward way is by imagining myself doing it. I form a sensorimotor image of doing it, and I decide to do *that*, the action that I am imagining myself doing. This image need not include explicitly all the detailed movements by which I will actually accomplish the action; it is a more or less schematic image of the way it will feel (and possibly look) to me when I perform the action.[6]

These sensorimotor sensations I imagine myself having are familiar ones. I have had them before; that is how I am able to imagine them now. In the past these sensations may have occurred separately from each other or as parts of different actions; in my current image, they are unified in the (imagined) achievement of the goal of grasping my foot. The image I have of grasping my foot, therefore, is a *blending* of memories of the experiences of various movements into a representation of a single action.

In the action-image, representations of the various movements making up the action are organized by the goal, which serves as the glue, or the thread,

binding the components together. The represented movements are not experienced as independent, like the distinct exercises in the earlier example, but as
serving the function of bringing about the goal. Here is that *'as'* again, but this
time it is innocuous. When we have an action-image we do not choose to
experience the separate movements as part of an action. We do not, that is,
contemplate a representation of movements and states, and *interpret* these as a
goal together with movements leading to the goal; such an interpretation *would*
require prior understanding. Instead, the movements and states being means to
a goal is already part of the image.

The type of representation I have in mind, in which the goal and its means
are represented as such, can be described in terms of the control-models of
goal-directed behavior familiar in cybernetic theory.[7] Control-models postu-
late an information-processing state which includes a system which causes
behavior, a representation of the goal-state, and mechanisms for comparing
feedback with the representation. These mechanisms detect errors and determine whether or not the goal has been reached. Adams and Mele (1989) list the
requirements for goal-directedness in a system S as follows (1989: 513):

(i)   S has an internal state R capable of fixing G as S's goal-state and S is
        capable of detecting G's presence or absence;

(ii)   Information about S's ongoing behavior B is fed back into the system as
        information input and compared with R;

(iii)   S's modifications of output behavior B in response to comparison
        between S's present state and goal state causally depend upon the
        correction process of (ii).

The internal state R, the guiding representation, is one in which the movements
by which G will be achieved are represented as means to G — as united with G
in a single unified action, as I have described it. This must be so if R is to do its
work in guiding behavior according to information input. Information that S is
in a certain state, for example, will be recognized as indicating that G has been
reached only if the conditions that constitute G are represented in R *as G* — as
what the behavior aims at — and not just as *a state of S*. Likewise, information
about states reached prior to G will avoid signal an error only if these states are
represented in R *as means to G*. In R, the content is what it is entirely by virtue
of the work that it does for the S using it.

In order for R to guide behavior, R must represent G in such a way that the representation will match the informational input if the goal is actually reached by S. That means, in cases where S a conscious agent, that G will be represented in terms of how it will feel to S to reach G. In that way, S can use conscious experience to know when the goal has been achieved; that is to say, the sort of experience by which we can tell when we have grasped our foot. We can tell, moreover, that we have grasped it in the way we intended — e.g. grasping the instep firmly with the right hand. It is in this way that imagining oneself performing a simple action is imagining a *single event*, even if the action takes more than an instant and involves many distinct bodily movements.[8] The resulting image, which binds together the means and the end into a single whole, is nonetheless rich enough to guide you in performing the action, if you have the appropriate motivation.

I am even able to imagine, in this vivid way, performing a simple action that I have never before performed, as long as I can imagine performing it by means of movements familiar from past experience. For example, to my knowledge I have never before touched my left little toe with just my left little finger, but I can imagine doing this clearly, because that action can be accomplished by means of simple movements that I have performed before. The important point, however, is that I do not need to represent explicitly and in detail each of these movements. When I select a goal, representations of them *are automatically collected and assembled into an image of a unified action.* The resulting action-image has a familiar feel to it, even if it is a novel action; it feels, as I imagine it, like an action that I can perform, and there is a definite sense in which this feeling is correct.[9] It is in that way that having the action-image is understanding the action.

In light of this account of forming an intention, I propose the following definition of the understanding of a simple action:

(3)   One understands a basic action if one has the ability to intend to perform it in a way that involves having an image of performing it as a unified action.[10]

My claim is that intentional understanding is grounded in the ability to have these intentions to perform basic actions. The idea is that the familiar feel of the thought — or sensorimotor representation — of the intended action is our intuitive, commonsense standard for intentional understanding.

6.   Final characterization (4)

(3) is not yet exactly what we want. Suppose a paraplegic was able to Charleston before his paralyzing accident. Now he is not only unable to do it, but also, because he is aware of his disability, unable to intend to do it. Still, we would want to say that he understands the Charleston, not only as well but also in the *same way* as someone who is able to do it, as long as he clearly *remembers how* to do it. The same thing is true, of course, in a more obvious way, in the case of an expert Charleston dancer who is tied to a chair and cannot move; that person also clearly understands the Charleston in the 'knowing how' sense. Both of these people know that they are physically unable to perform the Charleston and hence, if rational, could not intend to perform it. But there is a sense in which they are able to Charleston, in a way that a clumsy oaf on the dance floor, with full mobility, is not able to Charleston. Or at least, we might want to say, they have some central part of the ability to Charleston. Because of this ability we feel fully justified in saying that they understand the Charleston as we would if they were physically able to perform it. Thus the capacity for understanding an action in the 'knowing-how' sense does not require the ability to intend to perform the action, and hence our characterization in (3) was too broad.

The solution seems clear. If the basis of our understanding is the representation or image of our performing an action, then there is no need to specify in our characterization that the representation is a means of *intending* the action that is represented. There seems to be a redundancy in (3); if we can imagine the performance of a unified action, then whether or not the image is part of an intention, have we not shown that we understand the action?

The answer to this question seems to hang on whether being part of an intention is necessary to unify the action-image in the requisite way. In an intention, the goal is the central part of the image, since the goal is what holds the individual movements together. The question is whether in one's image of an action, formed in the absence of any intention to perform the action, the goal functions in that unifying way.

We can say that the action-image is unified in the requisite way in the absence of an intention if we view it as a plan along the lines of Mele (1992): a plan is the representational element in an intention. To be part of an intention, a plan must be combined with a motivational element. (Mele leaves the form of such representations open. In the simple actions I am interested in, they are sensorimotor images). Mele describes plans as follows:

> In the limiting case, an agent's plan for acting is a simple representation of his performing a basic action of a certain type.
>
> In other cases, the agent's plan is a representation of his prospective A-ing and of the route to A-ing that he intends to take. (Mele 1992: 109)

Such a representation could not be a representation of intrinsically independent movements that happen to be performed together, like a representation the exercise patient might have of his ABCD exercises when he thinks of them as separate exercises whose sequence makes no difference to what he is doing. As we have seen in the discussion of control-models of action, action-guiding representations must represent means and goals as unified actions. On Mele's account of intention, the representation guides action when combined with motivation. It could not serve that function, when combined simply with motivation, unless the individual movements were represented the way, or a way, to achieve the goal. If they were represented simply as independent movements then there would be no basis for taking the representation as a guide for achieving that goal. One might use further reasoning to confirm that a particular representation could serve as a guide to action, but that is not Mele's model of the functioning of the representational element in intention.

I conclude, therefore, that (3) contains a redundancy. We need to specify that the relevant action-image is adequate to serve as a guide to action, since only then are we assured of sufficient richness for understanding, but it constitutes understanding even when it is not serving as a guide to action as a component of an intention. Hence my final characterization of the understanding of a simple action is as follows:

(4)   One understands a simple action if one is able to imagine performing the action, with an image rich enough to serve as a guide in actual performance.

This characterization says that if I can imagine myself doing the Charleston then I can understand what you mean when you describe doing the Charleston to me, even if I have no intention of doing it and may actually be physically incapable of doing it.

It is important to be clear on what has been established in the above succession of characterizations. (4) represents the ability that on the one hand is sufficient for intentional understanding, but whose specification does not presuppose intentional understanding. Note that (2) and (3) also characterize this type of understanding correctly: being able to perform an action as a unified action intentionally, and being able to intend to perform it, are both cases of understanding the action. (2) and (3) were unsatisfactory, not because they were not accurate, but because they did not explicitly capture what it is about those abilities that constitutes understanding. (1) characterized the understanding of an action given that the action is performed as a unified action, which was not specified in that formulation.

7.   Searle's understanding

Our original goal was to characterize the sort of understanding that Searle missed in the Chinese Room, as a way of getting at the foundation of understanding in general. Recall that the aim of this chapter was an account not of the understanding of symbols, but of the physical actions performed in manipulating those symbols; we judged that Searle understood these actions in a way acceptable to him. We thus wanted to characterize the sort of understanding of an action that makes one satisfied and confident that one understands it. How close have we come to achieving that goal?

Our final characterization, (4), appears to succeed. It does this by providing two things. First, it shows what it is about the ability to imagine an action — and hence to perform it intentionally — that constitutes understanding it. Imagining it in the requisite way is representing the constitutive components of the action as such, in a form that is capable of guiding the performance of the action. Because the essential components of the action form the content of the agent's mental state, the agent can be said to understand it.

Second, this sort of understanding can produce the feeling of satisfaction and confidence that one understands an action, because the understanding consists in a mental state of which the agent can be aware, and with which she is familiar. What one imagines, moreover, is oneself successfully doing the action. The image provides the assurance that all the essential components of the action are at one's command. When we have this sort of experience in connection with something, we feel confident that we understand it.

To be sure, Searle-in-the-room is not entertaining images of his actions with the symbols. He is simply performing those actions — intentionally, as unified actions — without, presumably, giving them much thought. Instead, he is worrying that he does not understand the symbols. We do not yet know everything that understanding the symbols would involve, but at least we now can say something about his understanding of the actions.

Our goal in this chapter has been to develop an account of action understanding that can serve as a foundation for all other understanding. That account has been completed; we have not, however, considered action understanding in its foundational role. That part of the inquiry begins in Chapter Four, where we examine the relation of our understanding of physical objects to that of basic actions.

Notes

1. One also needs to recognize that the Charleston is precisely the repeatable action one is performing, rather than the token of the action one has just performed, or the action when performed under certain external circumstance, etc. These facts would, we may assume, become clear during the learning of the action. They are not further facts about the Charleston, but rather specifications that the Charleston is a certain repeatable physical action — an action type.

2. This example was suggested by Michael Bratman.

3. It might be noted that the patient already has this ability, in one sense, after being taught the exercises individually, because she has the ability to combine them on her own initiative into a unified action. She need not wait for someone else to do it for her. We can, of course, invent (and thereby understand) novel actions. The original exercise example works if we imagine that the patient has not thought of doing this and, while she has the ability to invent the action, and inventing the action would give her the ability to perform it as a unified action, she does not yet have the latter ability because she has not yet invented the action.

4. This example was suggested by Ralph Ellis.

5. There may be other criteria for performing the Charleston besides foot movements and rhythm, such as special hand movements. I am ignoring these; my point can be made if I stipulate that the foot movements and rhythm are all that is essential for doing the dance correctly.

6. The term 'image' is a somewhat dangerous one for me to use, since many people automatically think of 'visual image' on hearing this term. The reader is urged to think of an image as an activated trace of an experience in any modality, proprioceptive and kinesthetic as well as sensory (Newton, 1982).

7. For a discussion of the use of such models in explaining intention see Adams and Mele (1989).

8.   A little introspection will provide the reader with plenty of personal examples of such unified action-images. Imagine yourself, for example, picking up your coffee mug and taking a drink. Perhaps the most famous example of the compression of an extended and complex event (though not a single action) into a single momentary representation is provided by Mozart, who claimed to be able to hear an entire symphony in his head *all at once*.

9.   If an action that I can imagine but have never performed requires many different successive movements, then it is less likely to *feel* familiar and like an action that I can perform, even though I may *believe* with justification that I can perform it because I know that all its components are familiar movements. Perhaps it does not feel familiar because the representation of the action includes distinct temporal stages, which cannot all be retained in the same image at once. That may be true of my representation of dancing the Charleston, if I am a novice.

10.   One can in one sense be said to have the *ability* to do indefinitely many things by virtue of having the ability to learn to do them, or in general having the ability to meet some prior conditions for being able to do them. In that sense I have the ability to fly a plane, even though I have never even been in a cockpit. That is not the sense of 'being able to do something' that I have in mind here. Here I mean the ability to do a thing forthwith, needing no further preparation. In the case of an intention to perform a simple action, having the ability to form one here means that when one thinks of a goal, the imagery of performing the necessary movements for achieving the goal is automatically activated, and does not need to be consciously constructed.

Chapter Four

Understanding Objects

1. Introduction: object use as foundational

The term 'understand' is most commonly used in connection with language. We understand, or fail to understand, the meaning of certain words or sentences. Sometimes the sentences to be understood constitute commands. In those cases, as was discussed in the previous chapter, understanding them can involve not only understanding that what is said is a command, but also understanding the action we are commanded to perform, or knowing how to carry out the command. Talk of the understanding of language has thus, in the case of commands, led us to talk of understanding the things to which language refers.

In the previous chapter I characterized a sufficient condition for understanding an action type: being able to imagine performing an action of that type, with an image rich enough to serve as a guide to performance of the action. In this chapter I shall do the same thing for a far larger class of referents. In the case of an object or collection of objects that one perceives, I first formulate a sufficient condition for understanding as (roughly speaking) being able to use an object, or to imagine using it, in the course of performing an action. I then argue that if the notion of 'use' is broadened to that of 'incorporation into an action-plan,' the understanding of a wider category of physical objects can be characterized.

In developing a characterization of one sufficient condition for understanding a perceived object, I shall of necessity ignore a number of other ways we can understand an object. It may seem arbitrary for me to focus on just this one way; why not examine understanding in some other manifestation? For example, one way of understanding a thing is being able to give a detailed verbal account of the function of a thing, or its historical origin, or its material and structure; this way might appear to be on a par with being able to use it. If I can describe an object in all of these ways, but am not, for some reason, able actually to use it or to imagine myself using it (if, for example, the object is a right-handed tool and I am left-handed), do I not understand it every bit as thoroughly as if I were able to use it but could not give the verbal description?

The short answer is: not necessarily. Giving a verbal account of a thing constitutes understanding that thing only to the extent that the verbal account is itself understood. Since it is possible to utter words that constitute descriptions and, if Searle is right, even correctly to answer questions about the objects described without understanding what one is saying, it is possible to do these things without understanding the objects described, and even without understanding that one is uttering descriptions of objects. On the other hand, it is not possible to use an object intentionally without understanding the object *as a thing that one is using*. Thinking of an object in terms of one's use of it is a way of understanding the object, even though there are many other things about the object of which one may know nothing. If I can identify what it is about knowing how to use a thing that constitutes having an understanding it, I will then be in a position to show that this way of understanding objects is foundational for all other ways.

2.   Object perception

Another objection can be raised to the idea that object use is foundational. It will be noted that there are two fundamental bases of human intentional behavior: action and perception. Perception rather than action may be the ultimate foundation of understanding, since perception may seem necessary to action in a way that action is not necessary to perception. There is growing evidence against empiricism, and in favor of nativism, in accounts of basic object perception. Empiricism, as espoused by Berkeley and Helmholtz, held that the ability to perceive objects develops in the young child as a result of experience in reaching for and handling objects. Elizabeth Spelke (1990) describes recent tests of infant perception, which make use of a tendency in infants to look longer at novel displays than at familiar ones. Object unity and boundaries are perceived by means of observed motion in visible areas of the object. Spelke summarizes the results of this work:

> In summary, humans have some early-developing abilities to perceive the unity, the boundaries, and the identity of objects in visual scenes. These abilities are present before the onset of visually directed reaching or independent locomotion. Capacities to apprehend objects appear to emerge without benefit of trial-and-error motor learning. (Spelke, 1990: 117)

If our ability to perceive objects is indeed prior to motor abilities, then one can question the extent to which action understanding is the foundation for all other understanding. Perception is necessary even for a basic action such as grasping one's foot, the example used in the preceding chapter. Perhaps the understanding of such an action presupposes the understanding of the perceived foot as an object, possessing certain features (location, shape) that enable it to be grasped. If so, I was not successful after all in formulating a minimal sufficient condition for understanding, a condition not dependent upon the understanding of anything else.

There are two ways to respond to this objection. One way is to agree that the understanding manifest in object perception is the foundation for the understanding of an action such as grasping one's foot, but to argue that the understanding in object perception itself requires prior action understanding. A case can be made that object perception of the relevant kind is not an event that happens to the infant, but is something the infant does: it *looks at* the object. Looking at something requires at minimum the coordination of head position and eye focus. Looking at an object is a repeatable, goal-directed action that has as its goal the centering of the object in the visual field. If motion perception is essential to object perception, then tracking of the moving surface is required; visual tracking is an action. Thus we could say that this action-type — that of focusing on and tracking moving patterns by means of head and eye motions — must be understood in the relevant way in order for object perception to occur at all.

While the above is correct as far as it goes, it is not the only response I want to make. The reason lies in the phenomenon I am trying to explain. My interest is in the sort of understanding that we as human adults seek when puzzled by an entity encountered in the normal course of events. We want knowledge of an object's place — location and role — in our environment. Our environment is the domain of externally-existing physical entities and states of affairs of which we are the physical center, and within which we act.

Thus the relevant sort of understanding of objects presupposes the physical world. It presupposes that actions take place in space, among and by means of solid objects (parts of our own bodies as well as other objects). The infant's action of tracking movement is understandable in its own terms, but these terms are not ones that make reference to the spatial world in which our action takes place. While the act of looking at an object can be said to be understood by the infant, the object itself in such an act is not, or not obviously, distinguishable from the action by the infant. The object, in effect, is a result of the action taken as a whole — the perception of patterns of motion — and is not a thing in its own right toward which the action is directed.

I want a characterization of our understanding of something that we already know to be a spatially located object. Thus I may begin with objects as perceived, and need not unpack the perceptual act itself as the ultimate foundation. It may well be that what it is to be an object is understood, at least partly, in terms of the action of looking at an object. But here I am interested in what it is to understand, or to fail to understand, something which is perceived *as* an object in the external world.[1]

3. Object understanding as conceptual

In turning directly from the understanding of actions to that of external objects, I am leaping across a gap that will have to be filled eventually. The understanding of objects can be said to involve concepts; that is not so of the understanding of actions. In the terms used in recent discussion, the mental states in which objects are represented are states with *conceptual content*; that of those representing actions is *nonconceptual*. These terms were introduced by Cussins (1990): "Conceptual content presents the world to a subject as divided up into objects, properties, and situations: the components of truth conditions" (1990: 382). A theory of understanding must explain how this division is understood, and a foundationalist theory must explain how this understanding develops from nonconceptual understanding.

There are difficulties with these explanations that will require extensive argument and consideration of objections. The issue is in a certain way tangential to the discussion of the way object understanding is rooted in action understanding; for that reason it is postponed until Chapter Five.

4. Meaningfulness vs. correct meaning

The question of how we understand physical objects is not straight-forward, as the related questions of how we understand action types or words and sentences are thought to be. In the case of language, the commonsense view is that there is a single meaning, or a limited set of alternative meanings, that belong to a word or sentence. Understanding is knowing the correct meaning(s), or knowing which of the alternatives is meant in a particular context. In the case of action types, if real or imagined performance is taken as a way of understanding, the range of movements constituting performance of an action of that type is strictly constrained. For example, I understand what raising one's right arm is if I can do it, and I may do it in a variety of ways, but the arm I raise must be the *right* arm, and it must go *up*. In the case of an object, however, it is not obvious that there is any right way of understanding it. Unlike a word or sentence, an object that is not a symbol is not held to have *a meaning*. And unlike the action or imagined action that manifests the understanding of an action type, understanding an object is compatible with any way of acting in response to perceiving the object. There is nothing 'wrong' with using rocks as both missiles and paperweights, or using a jump-rope to fasten the trunk of one's car. To be sure, the jump-rope was manufactured for use in a game, but it *is* a rope with wooden handles, available for any use, whatever its creator's intentions. An object exists in its own right, independent of any interpretation or relation to one's actions. So what could it be to *understand* an object?

It is true that objects are not thought to have meaning in the way sentences have meaning. Nor are they, like action types, things that we perform correctly or incorrectly. Nevertheless, there are ordinary criteria for thinking about objects: we speak of knowing, or not knowing, *what a thing is* . While, as the jump-rope example shows, there may be no single right answer to the question of what a thing is, there are still wrong answers. It may not be wrong to call a jump-rope a trunk-fastener, but it is wrong to call it a sea-gull. Believing that a jump-rope that one perceives is a sea-gull is misunderstanding what it is that one perceives. Because one can misunderstand objects in this way, it must be possible to understand them correctly. Understanding an object correctly is knowing, roughly or exactly, what it really is.

The sort of understanding discussed in this chapter is not this sort. We are not yet ready to examine what it is to understand an object correctly — to know what it 'really is.' We are looking for foundations. In order to be able to understand an object correctly, one must first be capable of understanding it in *some way or other,* correctly or incorrectly. We sometimes speak of having '*an* understanding' of a thing, independently of whether or not that understanding is the correct understanding. In the same spirit, we speak of an objects being 'meaningful' to a person, again independently of that person's knowing the correct meaning. I am interested here in what it is for an object to be meaningful to someone — for the person to have an understanding of the object. After that is determined, we can talk about correctness. Nevertheless, it is true that the constraints upon having an understanding of an object may still be looser than the constraints upon understanding an action. This issue will be discussed later.

5.   Meaningful objects

In an article written in 1975, Bransford and McCarrell address the issue of what happens when we comprehend, or "what we know when an entity is meaningful for us." They argue that "objects become meaningful as a function of perceived interrelations with other objects (including ourselves)" (1975: 383).

Consider Figure 1 (from Bransford and McCarrell 1975: 379):

Figure 1: *A meaningless object*

This picture of an artificial object was intended to be meaningless; an observer does not know 'what it is.' In this case there can be no right answer to the question of what it is. Its designer intended that it not be any particular thing, and there is nothing but the designer's intention to determine its nature.

As Bransford and McCarrell make clear, however, knowing that it is 'nothing in particular' does not prevent one from trying to make sense of it, or find meaning in it, as one does with clouds or Rorschach ink-blots. If the object is viewed in relation to other objects, meaning can be *conferred*. Relations to other meaningful objects can identify a function, as in the following illustration:

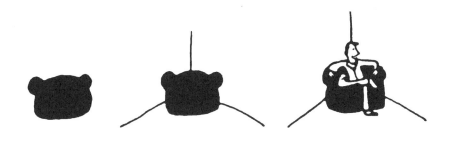

Figure 2: *Object can be interpreted as a chair.* (Bransford and McCarrell 1975: 379)

Or, perceived relations can identify an origin for the object:

Figure 3: *Object can be interpreted as a footprint.* (Bransford and McCarrell 1975: 380)

As Bransford and McCarrell conclude, "information about entities [sufficient to allow an organism to grasp their meaning] involves knowledge about their relations to other things that we know" (1975: 379-380). We do not understand objects considered in isolation from any context; rather, understanding them is knowing how they are (or could be) related to other things *that we know*. If we can relate them to these other things, then they take on a meaning for us.

The italicized qualification is significant. The following illustration depicts the original object in the context of relations to other objects, but our understanding is not much improved. We now understand its position in a 2-dimensional space also occupied by other objects, but nothing more about it.

Figure 4: *Object acquires a spatial context.*

If we do not know anything more about the other objects than about the one we are considering, it remains virtually meaningless.

It is significant, however, that with the addition of other objects, we understand *something* more about the object: its spatial position relative to the other objects. While we know nothing more about them than we do about the original object, we are familiar with spatial relations in general. Therefore, seeing the collection of objects shows us something that we know, and we can now understand something about the original object in terms of that knowledge. Since knowledge of a thing's relative position in 3-dimensional space is by itself minimally informative about that thing, however, our understanding is not much improved — particularly in contrast with the earlier illustration, in which the added objects are ones that are already meaningful in their own right.

If novel objects acquire meaning through their relations to other things which are already meaningful, then we may ask how those things acquired *their* meaning. Since every familiar object was novel to us at one time, then if any objects are meaningful there must be some way by which an object can acquire meaning, other than through relations to other meaningful objects. The question of a foundation for the understanding of objects thus arises, analogously to the way it did in the previous chapter.

In that chapter, we saw that basic action types can be understood in their own terms; they do not need to be related to anything else that is already understood. It might now seem legitimate to ask whether the same thing is true of objects. Is there a type of object that is meaningful to us in itself, independent of any relations to other meaningful objects, and such that other objects may become meaningful in relation to it? It is hard to see what sort of object that could be, since (unlike the actions we perform) every object, considered as an independently existing entity, is independent from us as well as from other things; how, then, could it be intrinsically meaningful *to us*? If, however, our account of the understanding of basic action is correct, then we do not need to search for a unique type of *object* that could play this role. Basic actions can play the role of things that we already understand, and we can understand novel physical objects in terms of those actions.

Accordingly, in what follows I develop a characterization of a sufficient condition for the understanding of a perceived physical object in relation to action types. The goal is the same as that in the previous chapter: a characterization of having an understanding of an object that does not depend upon the understanding of any other object. It will, however, depend upon the understanding of action types. This is desirable, since my goal is a foundational theory of understanding. The understanding of action types constitutes the foundation. As I shall show, the understanding of perceived physical objects constitutes the next level, resting upon that foundation.

6.   Characterizing object understanding

Two considerations guide the attempt to characterize minimal conditions for object understanding. The first concerns what other understanding, if any, we may presuppose. We are looking for sufficient conditions for having an understanding of a perceived object that do not presuppose an understanding of any other *object*. We may assume, however, the understanding of basic action, since that has already been characterized; hence we may allow understanding of the object to depend upon (apparent) relations of that object to basic action. I will refer to the sort of sufficient condition I want — one that does not presuppose any other understanding except for the understanding of a basic action to which the object appears to be related — as a *minimal sufficient condition* for having an understanding of an object.

The second consideration concerns the need for some criterion or sign of object understanding. Identifying minimal conditions for anything is often facilitated by imagining cases in which that thing is completely absent, and cautiously adding conditions until what is sought is, just barely, no longer absent. This method depends upon some reliable method of detecting the presence, or absence, of the object of inquiry.

In the case of the understanding of basic action, the criterion is the feeling of confidence that one is able to perform the action, a feeling that is provided when one can imagine the performance. In arriving at that characterization, part of my task was to argue that the ability to perform an action *should be identified* with the understanding of the action. Performance ability and understanding, in the sense of understanding that Searle applies to language, are not normally identified. In that discussion I was examining the foundation of understanding as it is ordinarily experienced, and I had to establish that performance ability can serve as that foundation. In the case of object understanding, the situation is in one way less demanding. I am not arguing that some state which is not normally thought of as understanding should be thought of that way. Rather, I am looking for a way to characterize what *is* normally thought of as having an understanding of an object — that is, having the sense that the object is meaningful. Thus in the present discussion we may use a criterion which is already commonly associated with understanding.

I am assuming, with Searle, that we can know, at least some of the time, when we understand something and when we do not. How do we know this? When we come to understand something after failing to understand it, there is a sudden feeling of satisfaction or confidence — the 'Aha!' feeling — that we are well acquainted with, and that we strive to attain or bring about when seeking understanding. The 'Aha!' feeling signals understanding, of course, only when understanding is first attained. When we are in the presence of familiar things there is no such feeling, but simply the absence of puzzlement. Thus in his discussion of the Chinese Room example, Searle does not mention his understanding of the English commands; we may assume that is because that understanding is a continuous, and hence unnoted, background state. In our search for minimal sufficient conditions for understanding objects, therefore, it will be useful to consider examples in which understanding arrives suddenly, such that a subject might experience the 'Aha!' feeling.

7.   First approximation

Let us begin by imagining trying to perform an action that involves a perceived entity. Suppose you are trying to carry a heavy, unwieldy object, such as a computer. You explore its convexities and concavities, trying to get a firm grip on it. Your hand finds its way under a protruding edge on the top of the machine, and suddenly you find that you can lift the computer easily. That edge is the handle.

When you discover that you are able to carry the computer by using the edge, there is a feeling of satisfaction — the 'Aha!' feeling. The satisfaction is due partly just to the success at accomplishing the goal of carrying the computer. But it is deeper than it would have been had the computer sported an obvious handle which you had recognized as a handle all along. Because you were having difficulty with the task, in effect a subtask emerged: figuring out which part of the computer could serve as a handle. When you found that you could use the edge for that purpose, you solved an extra puzzle. Figuring out how to lift the computer by using the edge was achieving an *understanding* of the edge: something that had previously been meaningless now acquired a meaning for you.

Of course, trying to lift the computer was not the only way you could have arrived at that understanding. The purpose of the edge might have been explained to before you had ever touched the machine; you would then have understood it just as well as if you had discovered its use on your own. That understanding, however, would have been dependent upon your understanding of the language used in the explanation. In the case we are considering, no understanding is presupposed except the understanding of the action you are trying to perform. All that is necessary for coming to understand the edge as a handle is the attempt to perform a action — lifting the computer — and the discovery that the edge can be used in performing the action. You did not need to know that the heavy object you wanted to carry was a computer, nor that its designer had intended the edge to be used as the handle. All you needed was to discover that that object — the edge — *could be used to achieve your goal.* It then became meaningful to you as a handle.

I might thus formulate a sufficient condition for having an understanding of an object as follows:

(1)   S has an understanding of an object O if S is able to use O in the intentional performance of an action.

This formulation allows that an object may be understood in terms of its relation to an action of the agent, even if nothing else about the object is known. It thus allows the understanding of an object to be not only nonverbal, but also nonconceptual: understanding is not just manifested by, but *consists in*, the ability to use the object. This point needs elaboration.

If understanding were just *manifested by* the ability to use it, then the ability could be a sign of some other mental state, the act of subsuming the perceived object under a pre-existing concept (e.g. the concept of a handle). Such a conceptual act, rather than the subsequent use of the object, would constitute the actual understanding. It is, of course, true that if before using or trying to use an object one already understands it as a handle, then there *is* a pre-existing conceptual state which is manifested in the ability to use the object (as a handle). Here my point is that while subsumption under a prior concept is a sufficient condition for understanding, it is not a necessary one, nor is it the minimally sufficient condition I am seeking. It presupposes the understanding of the concept of a handle, which in turn presupposes the understanding of other concepts. In saying that using a thing is itself a way of understanding it, we presuppose no understanding except that of the relevant action. The object need fall under no concept other than the immediate, action-relative one: thing used in the performance of this action.

The feeling of satisfaction to which I have alluded — the 'Aha!' feeling — is also not to be taken as itself the understanding an object. This feeling (called the 'click of comprehension' by Bransford and McCarrell, after a remark by Brown (1958)) is a qualitative state which frequently *accompanies* the sudden achievement of understanding, and which can as a sign to us that we have understood a thing. My purpose in talking about the 'Aha!' feeling has been to identify a sign of understanding that can be used in discussing the nature of understanding. When I claim that we understand a thing in some particular circumstances, it is convenient to be able to point to some common, tangible manifestation of that understanding. The 'Aha!' feeling would, I am presupposing, be taken as a sign of understanding in a commonsense context, even if one holds that understanding can exist without that feeling, or that the feeling could be misleading. (It is a sign, of course, only of having *an* understanding, not a sign that one's understanding is *correct*.) It is the satisfying feeling of things 'falling into place,' of 'getting the picture' — common descriptions of how we feel when we come to understand something. In my example of discovering that the computer can be lifted by using the edge as a handle, it helps to note that the 'Aha!' feeling would normally accompany the discovery. Pointing out that feeling adds convincing coloration to the case as an example of understanding.

In other words, the above formulation serves to locate a minimal sufficient condition for object understanding between two rival candidates: a conceptual mental state, not minimally sufficient for understanding, that results *in* the ability to use an object; and a qualitative state, not itself a state of understanding, that results *from* the ability to use an object. No matter what other mental states may exist, using an object in the course of performing an intentional action is having an understanding that object.

8.   Second approximation

Our first attempt to characterize the understanding of an object needs work. One difficulty is that while the characterization specifies that the *action* in which the object is used be intentional, the use of the object may nevertheless be completely outside of the agent's awareness. In that case we would not want to say that the agent understands the object, since we are interested in the sort of understanding of which one can be aware. For example, suppose I am hurriedly crossing a stream by walking on rocks. If I am confident of my footing and my attention is focused elsewhere, I will use individual rocks as stepping-stones without being aware of doing so. While I *could* become aware of a given rock that I am using in that way, we would not want to say that I understand it as a stepping-stone simply in virtue of the fact that my foot has happened to light upon it. Just as in the case of the understanding of an action we saw that for an action to be understood it must be intentional, and for an

action to be intentional the agent must be aware of performing it, so in the case
of the understanding of an object, we want to say that the agent must be aware
of using the object.

We could revise (1) in the following way:

(1')   S has an understanding of an object O if S is able intentionally to use
        O in the intentional performance of an action.

However, the above revision is flawed: it contains either a redundancy or an
irrelevance. If S intentionally uses O in the performance of an action, then it is
not necessary to specify that the performance of the action in which O is used
be intentional. There is an ambiguity in the phrase use of O in the performance
of an action. If O is used intentionally, then either it is used intentionally *for the*
purpose of performing action A, or it is used, during the course of performing
action A, for some subordinate or more narrowly defined purpose. If the
former, then action A is intentional by virtue of being the purpose of the use of
O, and the formulation is redundant. If the latter, then whether or not action A
is intentional, the use of O is part of a distinct intentional action, so the mention
of action A is irrelevant. For example, suppose I am crossing the Connecticut
River by stepping on rocks in the water. I may be fully aware that I am using
them for the purpose of crossing the Connecticut River, and in that case my
crossing the Connecticut River is necessarily intentional, and specifying that it
is intentional is redundant. On the other hand, I may be unaware that I am
crossing the Connecticut River, believing that I am in the middle of a flooded
field; in that case my crossing the river is not intentional. Nevertheless, I use
the rocks intentionally as stepping stones, because I am using them in the
action of, say, keeping my feet dry while walking on wet terrain. In that case,
the fact that my action of trying to keep my feet dry while walking on wet
terrain is the action that provides the context in which I understand the rocks,
and the fact that I am crossing the Connecticut River is irrelevant.

Since we want to say that an object can be understood as a means for
performing a certain action, to avoid irrelevant elements in our characterization the action in terms of which we specify the use of the object must be the
same one as that for which the object is intentionally used. Thus instead of (1')
our formulation should be:

(2)   S has an understanding of object O if S is able intentionally to use
        object O as a means of performing action A.

9. Third approximation

In the previous chapter, four formulations were considered before a satisfactory one was reached. We can benefit from that work in this chapter, by going directly from the above formulation to one that corresponds to our final characterization of understanding a basic action.

Let us briefly recall the reasoning that led to the final formulation in Chapter Three. It was noted that understanding an action by performing it intentionally requires that the action be performed as a unified action. For a noncircular account of performing an action as unified, the mental state that constitutes thinking of the action as unified should be specified in terms of the intention to perform the action, rather than in terms of the action as intentionally performed. It was then noted that the aspect of an intention that constitutes the understanding of the action is the mental representation of the action that serves as a guide during performance. We concluded that imagining performing the action, with the aid of such a representation, is sufficient for understanding the action. The final formulation was, therefore, as follows:

> S understands a basic action-type A if S is able to imagine performing a token of A with an image rich enough to serve as a guide in actual performance.

Accordingly, if understanding an object is being able intentionally to use that object as a means for performing an action, we may be able to move directly to the following formulation of a sufficient condition for object understanding:

> (3) S has an understanding of object O if S is able to imagine using O as a means for performing a token of an action-type A, with an image rich enough to serve as a guide in actual performance.

One minor change is necessary. I have argued that objects are meaningful, or understood, in relation to other things that are already understood, and that actions can serve as such meaningful things. The above formulation does not specify that the action-type A, to which O is imagined as a means, is already understood. As it stands, (3) allows that all that is understood is the segment of A that involves the use of O. It is true that on the above formulation, the performance of A is intentional, since that performance is the purpose for which O is intentionally used. Nevertheless, the entire performance of A is not included in what is imagined, but only that segment involving O, and so far we have characterized understanding solely in terms of what is imagined. Thus (3) should be amended as follows:

(4)   S has an understanding of object O if S is able to imagine using O as a means to performing a token of an action-type A that is already understood, with an image rich enough to serve as a guide in actual performance.

10. Imagining objects: the problem of illusion

While (4) is adequate for many cases of object understanding, there is a difficulty that we have not yet acknowledged in speaking of imagining the use of objects. A parallel difficulty did not exist in the case of imagining the performance of a basic action. Suppose I perceive an object and imagine using it to perform an action. What I imagine may be physically impossible. For example, I may see the edge on the top of the computer and think that it could be used as a handle — I might imagine using it to lift the computer — but in fact it may be too shallow or wrongly placed, and could not serve that purpose. In that case what I imagine is physically impossible. What I imagine may even be logically impossible. Suppose I perceive what looks like a rope lying on the ground, and imagine that I can use it to tie my car trunk closed. But I do not actually perceive a rope; a pattern of light on the grass has caused me to believe I see a rope. In that case I am perceiving nothing that could conceivably be used to tie my car trunk closed. Since there is no rope there at all, what I am imagining — that what I see could be used to tie my trunk shut — is a logical impossibility. Since I have imagined using an object to perform an action, I have apparently satisfied the criterion for understanding the object. But if what I imagine is misleading in either of the above ways, then my apparent understanding may be illusory.

The two cases described above pose problems with quite different solutions. Let us first consider the second case, where the 'rope' I imagine using is only illusory. This case has actually been covered in my introductory discussion of the understanding involved in perception (Chapter Three). There I pointed out that while object perception involves an interpretation of sensations similar in some ways to the interpretation of objects that is involved in understanding, since this interpretation is normally unconscious it does not fall within our topic. In the case of the illusory rope, light patterns have been interpreted as a rope prior to the act of interpreting in which we are interested: the interpretation of the 'rope' as something that can be used to secure the trunk.

There is no rope, but the subject believes that there is. Given that belief, there is the possibility either of understanding what the subject believes she perceives, or of failing to understand it. 'The rope' might be meaningless to the subject, who seems to see a only a long, flexible object which she cannot identify; alternatively, the subject may experience a sense of recognition, seeing the 'rope' as something with which she can secure her trunk. This recognition may involve imagining herself using the 'rope' to tie up the trunk. The fact that the rope is illusory is irrelevant for our purposes. While no object is actually understood as a result of what the subject imagines, she is now in the state of mind that yields the 'Aha!' feeling; she is, we might say, in an understanding state of mind.

Normally, what one perceives is really there; occasionally, one experiences an illusion instead. The issue is irrelevant here because we are interested in the difference between the internal mental state that constitutes failing to understand, sometimes accompanied by feelings of puzzlement or confusion, and the mental state that constitutes understanding, sometimes signaled by the 'Aha!' feeling. Those states, and the difference between them, are not affected by whether or not what is to be understood is actual or illusory. Thus the second case is not a real difficulty for our account.

Nevertheless, the possibility of an illusory object makes the above formulation unsatisfactory, since in referring to 'an object O' it implies without quite stating that the object is a real one. Since the possibility of illusion does not affect our account, and since we are interested only in a sufficient condition for understanding, we may narrow the formulation by specifying that the understood object be perceived (and thus not merely apparently perceived). That limits the characterization to nonillusory objects, which is acceptable since we are interested in normal conditions. Thus:

(5)   S has an understanding of a perceived object O if S is able to imagine using O as a means of performing a token of action-type A, that is already understood, with an image sufficiently rich to serve as a guide in actual performance.

The first case appears to be more of a problem. Here there is a real object, not an illusion, but what I am imagining is not a physically possible use of the object. It is the fact that the object is not illusory that causes the problem, since if the object is illusory there are no facts about it that contradict what I imagine.

This case, however, is actually ruled out by our formulation. Recall the account given in Chapter Three of the image, or representation, by which an action is imagined. It was there argued that an action-representation of some type is part of an intention, normally accompanied by a motivational state, and that this representation can occur 'outside' of an intention in the absence of motivation. While thus being able to serve purely imagistic purposes, the representation is nevertheless one which can guide performance in the event that the represented action is sufficiently motivated to be carried out. A representation of an action which could not guide performance is therefore not one that meets our conditions. That is the case when a subject imagines using an object in a way which is in fact not possible given the nature of that object. In that situation, we should say that the subject may only *seem* to have, but does not *actually* have, an understanding of the object.

It may be objected that it is artificial to distinguish the two cases in the way I have, since the latter case, like the former one, involves an illusion: that there is an object of such a nature that it can be used in the way imagined. Thus why not say that in both cases there is an illusion, and that in the latter case, but not in the former, some features of an object are actually perceived? If it is answered that in the latter case the image could not guide an actual perfor- mance, it will be pointed out that the same thing is true of the case in which the object is entirely illusory, but that there an understanding was still acknowl- edged to exist.

The solution lies in recognizing that there are indeed gray areas in which it is not clear whether we should say that there is an illusory object of which one has a real (albeit incorrect) understanding, or else that there is a real object of which one has an illusory understanding. Since, however, our interest is in sufficient rather than necessary conditions for understanding, we need not decide these cases. We may simply stipulate that we are characterizing the understanding of an object which is truly and accurately perceived, and such that a subject can imagine using it with an image that is in fact rich enough to guide actual use. In cases where the object is misperceived, or not perceived at all, we may say that to the extent that the object is illusory, there may exist an understanding to the extent that if the object imagined were actual, then the image could guide actual use. If the image is not of that nature, perhaps because it contains insufficient detail to guide the use of any object, then the understanding of the illusory object is itself illusory.

Illusory understanding can, however, trigger the 'Aha!' feeling, which we are using as a sign of understanding. Even a very dim or sketchy mental representation of the use of an object can be persuasive to the subject, and it is the that persuasiveness that marks the ultimate object of our search. So I do not want to suggest that what I am calling illusory understanding is not germane to our problem. Rather, I shall attempt to set aside the issue of illusion by observing that having an illusion of understanding an object requires that one have already a real understanding of other objects. That is because, as was the case with the understanding of actions, the mental representations by which the subject imagines using the object are derived from memory traces of the actual use of other objects. In the case of action, I can imagine performing an action with an image sufficiently rich to guide actual performance because I am able to draw upon memory representations of actual performances, even if the past performances were not identical with the currently imagined action, which is mentally constructed from fragments of those memories. Similarly in the case of objects, I am able to imagine using an object that I currently perceive only if I can draw upon memories of actual uses of similar objects in the past.

The illusion of understanding occurs when I imagine using an object with an image that, while drawn from memories of the use of other objects, is too loosely or schematically constructed to guide actual use. There is no real understanding because the image is not actually a sufficiently rich image of using the object. There is the illusion of understanding, however, because the image does draw upon actual memory experiences of the use of objects, in a way that leads me to think that the image represents the use of this perceived object. I say that illusory understanding of an object is dependent upon the actual understanding of other objects because the image that is the basis of the illusion is drawn from representations of the actual use, and hence under-standing, of other objects. Thus while the illusion can produce the 'Aha!' experience, our use of it as a sign of understanding is not compromised, because it *truly is* such a sign only in cases where the image is sufficiently rich to guide action.

The above move may appear circular. It is not circular, however, because I am using the 'Aha!' feeling as a sign of understanding only for the purpose of making my examples more recognizable. I am not using it as part of an argument that we understand objects if we can use or imagine using them. As was pointed our earlier, I need not argue for that claim, since it is a part of our commonsense notion of object understanding that having a use is one way that an object can have meaning, or be meaningful to the user. The 'Aha!' feeling is useful for my purposes because it serves as a vivid marker to lend recognizability to examples, when the right circumstances are carefully defined.

11. Kinds of objects

Now that a minimal sufficient condition for object understanding has been formulated, we must ask about the range of things to which the formulation applies. My examples so far have involved human-scaled, detached physical objects or their parts, such as rocks or a protruding edge on a computer. It seems clear that anything that can be physically acted upon in the pursuit of some goal is the sort of object that can be understood in the way characterized in (5).

If, however, we characterize object *use* as a minimal form of understanding, we are in danger of overlooking what it is about object use that qualifies it as understanding. The problem is different from related problems we encountered in formulating an account of action understanding. There our formulations were, until the final one, persistently too broad. Here, however, the formulation is too narrow: we are considering too specialized a sense of 'object use.' The problem becomes apparent when we think about the range of objects whose meaningfulness we wish to characterize. If we confine our characterization to detachable objects with which we physically interact, we will not have an account of how we understand other types of objects, such as elements of the landscape or our own bodies. But characterizing object understanding as object *use* seems to force us to omit these. At least in a common sense of 'use,' I do not use the tree I walk around to get across my lawn. And while in one sense I use my body to walk, in another sense I do not, since my body itself is what does the walking, rather than, e.g., the cane I may use to help it.

In focusing on the use of objects, I have risked losing touch with the foundation which is the basis of my account. What constitutes the understanding of an object used in performing an action is its *incorporation into the action*, which is already understood. The fact that the object is used as one *manipulates a detachable object* is irrelevant. If, in crossing my lawn, I swerve to avoid a tree, I am not 'using' the tree, but I still understand it in terms of the action: as an object to be skirted if I am to reach my goal.

Actions take place in environments. Some elements of the environment, such as distant mountains, can be ignored in planning and executing the action; others, such as obstacles one must climb over, cannot. The representation of the action, which serves the functions of guidance and control as described in the previous chapter, must include representations of these relevant environmental elements and their role in the action. For example, my representation of walking to the garage from my back door must include a representation of aiming first at the path through the hedge; otherwise I will bump into the hedge and not reach the garage.

If imagining using an object as a means to performing an action is having an understanding of the object, imagining avoiding an object as such a means is also having an understanding of it. The object, whatever its precise role, is understood in relation to the action. Understanding of objects that are perceived just as part of the environment may be thought of as merely implicit, rather than explicit. This broadening allows us to see that the ground we walk on, the walls of our rooms, the landmarks that guide us, are all meaningful in relation to our own actions, whatever their other meaning or lack of it might be. It also allows a way to characterize our understanding of our own bodies. As noted above, our bodies can play the roles both of agent and object in an action — e.g. my hand grabs my foot. As we shall see in Chapter Five, this duality in the role our bodies can play in action is reflected in the various ways the concept of 'self' is understood.

In light of this wider perspective on the relation of an object to an action, let us reformulate (5) as follows:

(6)   S has an understanding of a perceived object O if S is able to imagine incorporating O into the performance of a token of action-type A that is already understood, with an image sufficiently rich to serve as a guide in actual performance.

In the above formulation, "incorporating . . . into the performance of" is substituted for "using . . . as a means of performing." Objects are incorporated into a performance of an action if they figure essentially in the representation that guides the intentional performance of the action, in the way that they do if they are used — physically manipulated — in the performance of the action.

(6) allows us to say that some elements of the environment, as well as other aspects of a performance of an action, may be marginally meaningful to the agent. Seeing the sky and the horizon, for example, plays an essential role in determining bodily orientation, but because of the ubiquity of these features of the landscape the meaning they derive from this role is simply that of being a framework for actions performed outdoors. The meanings of other things, such as a well-designed tool or a dangerous cliff, will be more complex and more emotionally charged. Anything that may be a part of the performance of an action, but of which the agent is unaware, is to that extent meaningless to the agent; hence degrees of awareness correspond roughly to degrees of meaningfulness. One purpose of insisting that meaningful objects be represented in an action-image is that only elements of which the agent is aware can be so represented.

12. Conclusion: objects and objectivity

In the present chapter and the preceding one, I have explored the foundation of intentional understanding in goal-directed action. I showed, first, that the ability intentionally to perform a basic action, manifested in the ability to imagine performing it, is a way of understanding the action that presupposes no other understanding. Next, I showed how the ability to use a perceived physical object as a means to performing an action constitutes a way of understanding the object that is dependent upon the understanding of that action. Finally, I showed that an object that is intentionally incorporated into the performance of an (understood) action is itself understood in relation to that action.

In moving from the understanding of basic actions to the understanding of objects, we have crossed an important boundary. Under-standing basic actions does not require a concept of the objective, external world; that is how it can be a foundation for such a concept. But understanding objects, necessary for understanding other persons and language, does require such a concept.

Other writers, particularly Adrian Cussins, have recently theorized about this transition. Cussins (1990, 1992, 1993) introduces the notion of nonconceptual content in terms of Evans' account of embodied content:

> The Evansian begins like this: the subject sees the mug as graspable, as locatable, as being such as to resist manual-pressure, as being drinkable-from, as being push-and-then-fallable. . . . These descriptions that the theorist uses are not likely to be elegant or simple, for they are not available to the subject as descriptive conditions of the world. They are, rather, available to the subject in the kind of way in which I know, on the basis of my kinesthetic experience, how to raise my left hand to a point several inches above my right ear. I know very well how to do this. Moreover, I know that I know how to do it (I can, for example, make myself aware in imagination of each of the stages of the action-sequence). (Cussins 1992: 658)

Cussins contrasts nonconceptual content, which on the present theory corresponds to what is understood in a basic action, with objective content:

> A start on the objectivity of content is this: that the content's referent is given as public, as something which is, in principle at least, equally available to any subjective point of view. A sign of this objectivity is that the content can be incorrect: if the referent is given as a public object, then it is always possible that the subject is wrong about the object, even where the referent is the subject oneself. What we are after is a metaphysical distinction between subject and object, a distance which makes intelligible the *subject's being wrong (and therefore also being right) about the object;* which provides for the possibility of truth. (Cussins 1992: 660; italics added)

In order to explain the emergence of objective content, which allows the possibility of being wrong, from nonconceptual content, Cussins develops a theory about how a subject establishes 'cognitive trails,' or 'way-finding abilities' through 'feature domains' (Cussins 1992: 673f). While this theory is compatible with the present one, I think that the point of emergence of an understanding of objectivity from purely experiential understanding can be described more simply. If we take seriously the notion that the possibility of being *in error* defines objective contexts, and we note that error is possible only in a context of goal-directed activity, we can bridge the gap between subject and world entirely in terms of concepts derived from basic actions. The way we represent and carry out goal-directed actions is what makes the understanding of objectivity possible. This claim is analyzed and defended in the following chapter.

Note

1.   In Chapter Five I examine conditions for understanding objects as part of a world external
      to oneself. That discussion aims to identify, and to bridge, the gap between infant object
      perception and recognition of an independently existing external world.

CHAPTER FIVE

Error and the External World

1. Introduction: understanding the mind-world distinction

If intentional mental states can represent the external world, then we must be able to think and talk about the external world with understanding. What must be understood is not just the properties that distinguish different physical objects and states of affairs, but that they are part of a world that is external to our minds. The question is: how do we understand this idea of the external world as such?

Jackendoff (1991) raises this question, but his answer does not fully address it. In arguing that reality is 'observer-relative,' Jackendoff considers the commonsense objection that "I know the world is out there!" His answer is "That's what we are built to think! . . . Realism is a stance which we are built to adopt" (1991: 428). The difficulty with this answer is that while we can agree that we are built to take certain 'stances,' the notion of a stance is itself an intentional one! Taking a stance is understanding something in a certain way. I am asking how one achieves that understanding.

Evans (1982) argues for the ultimate indexicality of our conception of objective space. Thinking objectively about space is dependent upon a 'cognitive map:' a representation in which the spatial relations of several distinct things are simultaneously represented (1982: 151). Employing a cognitive map requires the ability to identify this map with egocentric space — a framework centered upon one's own body. The "ability to think about an objective spatial world at all:"

> presupposes the ability to represent the spatial world by means of a cognitive
> map. But nothing that the subject can do, or imagine, will entitle us to attribute
> such a representation to him if he cannot make sense of the idea that he might
> be at one of the points representable within his map. (Evans 1982: 163)

Understanding the idea of public, objective space requires understanding
egocentric space, whose content is given by our own experiences:

> Egocentric spatial terms are the terms in which the content of our spatial
> experiences would be formulated, and those in which our immediate behav-
> ioral plans would be expressed. This duality is no coincidence: an egocentric
> space can exist only for an animal in which a complex network of connections
> exists between perceptual input and behavioral output. (Evans 1982: 154)

While egocentric spatial terms refer to positions in public space, their sense is
derived from our actions and perceptions. This sense is nonconceptual; subjects do not identify points in egocentric space by descriptions, but demonstra-
tively, through responses made to it and actions taken toward it.

The dependence of our understanding of the external world on our own
actions and perceptions highlights the need to understand the way in which we
distinguish in general between things whose existence is dependent upon our
own actions and perceptions and things whose existence is independent of
them. Evans stresses the difference between egocentric and public space:
space defined by my perceptions and actions, and space defined independently
of these, relative to the perceptions and actions of anyone. But there is more to
the external world than its spatial definition. It is, primarily, ontologically
independent. The existence of external objects and states of affairs is independent of my intentions and perceptions. The indexicality of our ways of thinking
of the world coexists uneasily with this independence. On the one hand, we
think of the world as essentially related to ourselves, because we define its
center; on the other hand, we understand it as essentially other than ourselves,
because it does not depend upon us for its existence. The tension is most
evident in our concept of our own bodies, which are both essentially related to
our perceptions and actions, and a part of the objective world. It is these two
aspects of our experience of the world which must be united if the mind-world
gap is to be bridged by understanding. On the foundationalist approach, the
unification of these aspects — self and other — has occurred in experience
prior to the understanding of linguistic terms referring to external reality. The

essential features of this understanding are present in an experience which is wholly internal: the experience of deliberate, goal-directed action. The specific aspect of such action which constitutes the basis for understanding the onto-logical independence of the world is the experience of *error in action.*

2. Error as the basis of the mind-world distinction

Error is experienced when the results of an action are contrary to the ex-pectations which prompted and guided the action. Instead of talking about error we might speak, as Searle (1983: 89) does, of *failure* as what is experi-enced when an intentional action is not fulfilled. I prefer the term 'error,' however, because it includes the notion of correctibility. Error is the broader notion: it involves failure, but failure due to a mistake on the part of the agent. What is *mis*-taken can, in principle, be taken again. The notion of repeatability and improvement in action is, I will try to show, a component in our under-standing of the external world. The external world, I will argue, is experienced primordially as the ultimate ground of error in action; the ultimate basis for failure to achieve a goal, such that correction requires reconceiving rather than simply repeating an action. Actions are experienced as taken against a world which is not an adjustable component of the action but is external to the action. Even when an action-type has been successful in the past, and is repeated exactly, the goal may not be achieved; the failure, therefore, is due to some-thing *other than* the action; in that case, the only solution is a different action altogether. It is in this way that the otherness and externality of the world first manifests itself. This ultimate type of error is a *belief error*; a mistake in the calculation of the conditions and possibility of action. Correction requires revising, not just the action, but the beliefs upon which it was formulated. Thus action error can lead us to the necessity of formulating and correcting beliefs about the world, originally as a means of error correction. The connection between the mind and the world, on this account, is originally grasped entirely in terms of an inner experience: the experience of a mismatch between the goal of an action and the sensory experience which signals success. Thus my claim entails that without the experience of error, there would be no concept of the external world.

3. Action error

The sort of action at issue is conscious, intentional action, rather than involuntary motions such as tics. Because I want to show that our fundamental understanding of external reality is based on our familiarity with action error from our own experience, I want to characterize an event of which we are or can be conscious, occurring during intentional action. So we need to review the nature of intentional action.

An account of intentional action compatible with the discussion of basic action in Chapter Three is that of Myles Brand: "intentional action is action performed in following a plan" (1986: 213; see also Goldman, 1970, and Harman, 1986: 84). According to Brand, a plan is an abstract series of actiontypes (what I have elsewhere called an action pattern or schema). Plans can exist independently of persons, and they can also exist as mental representations, in which case a person *has* that plan, which can then be followed or not. Following a plan is more than just acting according to or in conformity with it:

> A subject follows a plan, I submit, just in case he has this plan, acts in accordance with it, and is moved to achieve the goal of the plan. Active attention or reflection is not necessary for plan following. We need only represent the plan to ourselves when following it; a plan is, as it were, a cognitive map through the maze of possible future action. (Brand 1986: 223)

Brand's account of intentional action differs from that of Harman (1986). On Harman's view, having a *positive intention* involves having a plan, but an action can be *intentional* without being *intended* if it is merely foreseen as part of an intended action but not aimed at (1986: 88ff). In what follows the actions I discuss are those *intended* in Harman's sense of that term. If I occasionally describe them as intentional, I understand them in Brand's sense as involving a plan, and not in Harman's sense as (possibly) merely foreseen but not intended. Something is intended if it is (a) an ultimate goal, or (b) selected as a means to reach that goal. If (b) it will also be a (sub)goal. As we shall see, if something is a goal then it guides subroutines.

Brand's account is compatible with recent work pointing to the existence of action schemata or programs in the motor cortex (see Chapter Two). According to this work, what is voluntary in an action is the selection of a goal; this event, unless followed by an inhibition, initiates a series of automatic actions or motor reflexes. These reflexes are not the same as ones operating at the level of the spinal chord, like the knee jerk in response to a blow to the patellar tendon mentioned by Brand (1986: 213): over such reflexes there is no possibility of gaining control. The higher-level reflexes drive actions like that in another example Brand uses: taking the soap from the tray in the shower, an action which advances his goal of going to the university and which could be articulated as part of his plan to do that, but which is included in a subroutine which need not be made explicit. The view that a (voluntary) action is initiated by selecting a goal which activates a plan is related to that of William James (as noted by Goldman, 1976 and 1990):

> We know what it is to get out of bed on a freezing morning in a room without a fire, and how the very vital principle within us protests against the ordeal. . . . Now how do we *ever* get up under such circumstances? . . . We suddenly find that we have got up. A fortunate lapse of consciousness occurs; we forget both the warmth and the cold; we fall into some reverie connected with the day's life, in the course of which the idea flashes across us 'Hollo! I must lie here no longer' — an idea which at that lucky instant awakens no contradictory or paralyzing suggestions, and consequently produces immediately its appropriate motor effects. (James 1890: 524)

Brand's emphasis is on plans as conscious cognitive representations, but he allows that plan following can occur without conscious attention, e.g. during athletic activity or any habitual action (1986: 223). Thus Brand's philosophical theory fits in well with empirical research on voluntary motor action. This compatibility is important for my approach to error, since I will want to appeal to such evidence when connecting the action context to other contexts.

How does error fit into the above account? An error can be initially characterized as a deviation from a plan or portion of a plan which is being followed. This deviation must be unintentional, since if it is intentional then it is by definition part of a plan. Error can result in failure to attain one's ultimate goal, but is not always identical with failure, since the goal may be attained in spite of the error. We can say, however, that in an individual action conceived of as part of a plan, (a subroutine), an error is identical with a failure: e.g. if, when aiming for the hot-water faucet to turn it off, one misses it and turns off the cold instead, resulting in a scalding that prevents one from attaining the goal of going to the university, one not only fails to go to the university, but fails to turn off the hot water, which failure is identical with the error which caused the scalding.

I suggest that our primary sense of error is derived from our experience of error in the performance of an action such that the error is identical with failure to perform the action. A paradigm example is the basic action of reaching for an object, and missing it; we can call such errors basic action errors. We can, of course, find even lower-order events which cause us to miss the object: e.g. incorrect timing of grasping motions. But to the extent that this timing is unconscious, and the grasping not an explicit subgoal in the overall action plan, it will not be manifest as an error. (It is important to note that there is flexibility in what is to count as basic action error. Athletes or musicians can train themselves to be aware of distinct motor events which are usually unconscious, and formulate explicit goals with respect to them; with such training failure to flex a muscle at a certain moment might be a conscious error.[1]) In terms of our account of action, this kind of error can occur when one is following an action plan containing no consciously discernible subroutines — e.g. when one's plan is simply to 'turn off the hot water' with no particular method ('move arm to right, flex fingers' etc.) being part of the cognitive representation of the plan.

Being aware of an action error *as an error* requires feedback which informs you that what you have just done is erroneous. That is why the sort of error at issue must coincide with failure to realize a goal. The goal is represented in the action plan (or schema, or motor program) driving the action. Motor feedback provides continuous information about one's performance, allowing one to make adjustments (which are generally unconscious). When the performance is complete, feedback from the final stage can be compared with the goal, and a mismatch signals an error.

In the case of the goals of complex actions, failure can result from events beyond the agent's control and hence, we might want to say, in the absence of error on the part of the agent. That is also possible with basic actions: e.g. an object can unexpectedly move or fly away just as I am about to seize it. Feedback informs me of failure (my fingers close on unresisting air) but what error am I guilty of?

My error was in representing a certain goal as attainable by means of a certain action. I am not necessarily to be blamed: perhaps I had been assured that the bird was stuffed. Nevertheless, I erred in attempting to achieve by this type of action what could be achieved only by a different type of action. This example suggests that our account of the primary sense of error should include the stipulation that the error be in principle correctable. In the future I can either improve my skills or give up trying to catch birds with one hand. (If I am doomed by some form of brain damage to spend my life hopelessly repeating the action without learning from experience, then we must say that the action is not an intentional one in our current sense, since the selection of the goal is not voluntary.)

The above example suggests that within our limited context of single-goal basic actions, two types of error can occur. Error can be caused by the failure of a component specified by the action plan, or it can occur because the plan was the wrong one for achieving a desired higher-level goal. In the first type the error occurs in the carrying out of a plan; in the second type it occurs in the selection of the plan. We can characterize these two types as production and planning errors. (This distinction is to some degree a relative one, except at the extremes of the action hierarchy: an error is a production or a planning error depending on how the action is characterized. This relativity is not a difficulty for us since in the later parts of this chapter we will be concerned primarily with these extremes: basic actions and ultimate planning and goals.)

A similar account is offered by Donald Norman (1981; see also Reason 1984). Norman refers to the sort of error I have been discussing as a 'slip:' "A slip is a form of human error defined to be the performance of an action that was not what was intended" (1981: 1). Norman's theory of action is similar to the one under discussion. On his view "action sequences are controlled by sensorimotor knowledge structures, or *schemas.*" Schemas are selected and activated by "a mechanism that requires that appropriate conditions be satisfied for the operation of a schema" (1981: 3). Many schemas may be active at a given time without being *triggered*; a schema is triggered "by current processing activity whenever the situation matches its conditions sufficiently well" (1981: 4). Norman's account of the hierarchical structure of action schemas is similar to Brand's account of plans and subroutines:

> [A schema is] an organized body of knowledge, including procedural knowledge that can direct the flow of control of motor activity. Each schema is assumed to cover only a limited range of knowledge or actions. As a result, any given action sequence must be specified by a rather large ensemble of schemas, organized in a hierarchical control structure. One schema may need to invoke other schemas, passing to them particular values that the variables of the schemas must assume for the particular actions to be performed. Information passes both down from the higher-order schemas to the lower ones and also back up from lower-order schemas to higher ones.
>
> . . . The highest-level schema is called the *parent* schema, with the subschemas [Brand's subroutines] that are initiated by the parent schema for the control of component parts of the action sequence being called *child* schemas. (Norman 1981: 4)

Norman classifies slips into three types (1981: 8):

(a)   Slips that result from errors in the formation of the intention.

These are what I have termed 'planning errors.' This type includes what Norman calls 'mode errors,' in which the situation is erroneously classified. My example of trying to grasp a live bird by means of actions appropriate to the grasping of a stuffed bird is an example of a mode error.

(b)   Slips that result from faulty activation of schemas

In these cases components from the wrong schema are activated, or schemas may be deactivated prematurely. Forgetting what one was doing is an example of the latter.

(c)   Slips that result from faulty triggering of active schemas.

In these cases child schemas are triggered out of order or not at all. (b) and (c) are what I have termed 'production errors.' That is, the schema is appropriate to the goal, but is incorrectly carried out. The case of turning off the cold water instead of the hot water could be a mode error or a faulty activation error; the correct classification would depend on further data which we need not invent. The important point to note for our purposes is Norman's position that for the detection of error of any type, a feedback mechanism is necessary:

> In order for discrepant behavior to be detected, two things are necessary: a feedback mechanism with some monitoring function that compares what is expected with what has occurred; [and] a discrepancy between expectations and occurrences. (Norman 1981: 11)

As noted above, the level of error upon which our basic concept of error rests is that wherein error is equivalent to failure to achieve a goal, since it is only in that case that we can immediately compare the action performed to what was intended. Norman also makes the point that detection of errors must take place at the level of the error:

> Each level of specification of the intention must be decomposed into more basic levels in order for an action to take place . . . until some primitive level of act specification is reached. Feedback and monitoring is required at each level. (Norman 1981: 13)

Some monitoring and correction of errors in basic actions undoubtedly takes place unconsciously, but some of it we clearly are or can be aware of.

So far our account of action error consists of five criteria:

(a)   the following of a plan or motor procedure, which aims at
(b)   a selected and represented goal;
(c)   feedback during the procedure;
(d)   a deviation from the goal, signaled by
(e)   a recognizable mismatch between the representation of the goal and the indicated end-state of the procedure (indicated by feedback).

It might seem that (c) and (e), a feedback mechanism and the recognizability of mismatch between goal and actual results, are essential not to the existence of errors, but only to their discovery. But that is a mistake. Error requires *deviation* from a goal, and you can't deviate from a goal without having *aimed* at the goal — that is, without having a plan or procedure which is *guided by* that goal. For an action to be guided by a goal, two things are required. First, there must exist a representation of the goal, in the form of what it would be like for you to achieve it — that is, the representation must be sensitive to the sort of sensorimotor feedback which would signal that the goal had been achieved. Second, continuous feedback during the procedure must exist to allow the agent to monitor progress, in order to effect a convergence of the successive stages of the procedure on to the desired end-state.

Without such continuous feedback and a representation of the desired goal in terms of appropriate end-state feedback, the procedure (or plan or activated schema) could not be guided by the goal and hence could not be a procedure *for* achieving that goal, but only a series of movements which had a certain probability of reaching that end-state. A procedure *for* achieving X is an intentional procedure, which means that its nature is, in part, determined by its purpose.[2]

But can't one make an action error without the possibility of being informed of it by feedback: can't you try to achieve a goal without there being a way of knowing whether or not you have succeeded? For example, couldn't someone who has been totally deaf from birth try to speak some words while alone and without help, and rightly believe that either an error had been made or that the attempt had been successful, without having a way of knowing which had occurred? But the difficulty lies in the notion of *trying* to achieve a goal without following a procedure which aims at that goal. In the absence of any basis for believing that one's movements are bringing one closer to a goal, one cannot be said to be trying to achieve that goal. Performing movements at random while *hoping* that they will result in X is not *trying* to achieve X.[3]

To aim at a goal, then, a procedure must be guided by a representation of that goal, and it cannot be so guided if there is no feedback to signal (correctable) deviations from that goal or stages leading to it. In the simplest cases (basic actions) the only feedback one is conscious of is that which reveals a match or mismatch between the representation of the goal and the end-state of the procedure. In order for a match to be detected, the representation of the goal must take the form of some possible feedback information, for otherwise the representations would not share the common features necessary for matching.

The above account contains what might seem a major defect: error exists only relative to the way a goal is represented by the agent. Isn't it part of our concept of performing an action that there is an objective fact of the matter as to whether or not it was performed, such that the agent might falsely believe an error had been made, or not made? If my goal is to turn off the hot water faucet, isn't it possible that I do not in fact turn it off, and hence commit an error, even though for some reason I misrepresent the feedback from the desired state and believe that I have turned it off?

It is here that the difference between production and planning error becomes important (and especially so for the purposes of this chapter, since the same sort of objection and response will show up in the epistemological context.) The objection is based on the fact that error as we have been discussing it is solely production error; but as we have seen, it is possible to be free of that and still commit a planning error. In reply, I shall first defend the current focus on production error; then I shall grant the point of the objection, and expand on it, as regards planning error.

Of course you can misrepresent what it will be like for you to bring about a certain (objectively described) state of affairs. But recall that we are here characterizing our basic understanding of action errors, and this understanding must be formed in the *experience* of making an error. The only way to have such an experience is by means of comparing the expected results of one's actions with their actual results, where the latter are immediately felt by the agent. This can occur only with production error, where in the case of a basic action the end-state does not match the representation of the goal. We must note that while an agent's having the experience of making an error means that the error exists relative to the agent's intentions and not to some external state of affairs, the existence of an error is still an objective fact: either there is a mismatch between intentions and results, as represented in terms of feedback, or there is not. Since we have taken the position that action schemas or plans are physically realized as patterns in the motor cortex, we can note that a mismatch can *automatically* trigger a reaction of disappointment or dissatisfaction, while a match can trigger feelings of pleasure. A matching is positive feedback, mismatching is negative feedback. Whether feedback is positive or negative does not depend on a decision of the agent, such that it would be easy to mistake one for the other. It is part of the 'reflexive' (in Evarts' (1979) sense) nature of the motor procedure that feedback can be processed appropriately without conscious attention by the agent (although not always without the possibility of such attention). At the minimum, learning takes place, which requires distinguishing between success and failure. So the existence of action error on this level is a real, objective fact, all the conditions of which can be completely grasped by the one who commits the error.

But for higher organisms, the experience of error has significance beyond the noting of a mismatch between an intended and an actual end-state of some motor procedure. We have discussed the errors which are equivalent to failure to achieve a goal. While they are *detectable* only at that basic level, our commonest type of response to them cannot be explained only at that level. We need to understand why errors matter; why making an error is undesirable. The proposed counterexample presented a case of error which is (at least temporarily) beyond the agent's experience. We can describe it is a type (a) error after Norman's classification (a planning error): activating a schema for bringing about a state-of-affairs in which I receive feedback of type X is not the correct way to achieve goal Y. The parent schema contains an error; however, the child schema which results in feed-back of type A is error-free. We can now characterize production errors as ones whose possible detection is a function of the mechanism for performing the action; planning errors are ones whose detection lacks such a mechanism. Because of the possibility of planning error, even if I know that a particular action I have just completed has been performed 'correctly,' I can still wonder if I have made a mistake: is what I have just done what I really wanted to do? E.g., imagine that I have a long-range goal of assassinating the King, and my plan is to do this by shooting him when he appears on the balcony. As I take aim I represent the achievement of my

goal as (the sight of) the man on the balcony falling over dead just after I press
the trigger. I press the trigger and see the man fall over dead; thus I have a sense
of success. But I may still ask: was the man who keeled over really the King?

If the man I shot was not the King, normally I will discover it in due
course. But the discovery need not occur in the process of performing any
particular subroutine in the higher-level action of killing him. (I may discover
it by accident, years later.) The distinction crucial for our purposes is that with
production errors a mechanism for their detection is a part of the mechanism
for performing the action in which they occur. If a planning error has occurred
this means that the subroutines are in error, but they lack a mechanism for
detecting this sort of error. If an error occurs that could not have been detected
by the mechanisms for performing an action, and the error is the result of a
planning error, then the ultimate source of the problem points us to the external
world.

4.   Action planning and external reality

Planning an action involves two components. There is the set of background
beliefs representing possible actions, including implicit beliefs about the compatibility of the actions, and there is the formation of an intention, which
involves selection of a goal and a plan for achieving it from the background
beliefs. Therefore planning errors can be of two types: errors of selection, and
errors of belief.

Norman describes what I call errors of selection as "slips during the
formation of the intention," and mentions two specific types: "errors in classi-
fying the situation and errors that result from ambiguous or incompletely
specified intentions" (1981: 5). He offers the following as an example of the
former: "My office phone rang. I picked up the receiver and bellowed 'Come
in' at it." In this sort of case 'the resulting action may be one that was intended
and appropriate for the analysis of the situation but inappropriate for the actual
situation' (1981: 6). An example of the latter is "the replacing of the lid to the
sugar container on the coffee cup." Here:

> an appropriate intention has been formulated, but the description of the
> desired act is insufficient . . . leading to ambiguity in the selection of in-
> formation from memory. (Norman 1982: 7)

Looking again at our earlier example, I may fail to kill the King even though I successfully shoot the man on the balcony because, while I had known that the man on the balcony was not the King, and I was only rehearsing for the next day when the King would appear, I unthinkingly carried out my shooting plan instead of my rehearsing plan.

Finally we come to belief errors. An action may be erroneous because the beliefs on which it was based are false. For example, in my desire to assassinate the King I may fail simply because my information about the man on the balcony that day was incorrect. In this case the intention and the action plan were formed and carried out correctly. When an action error is caused by a belief error then one cannot, as one can with other forms of planning errors or production errors, correct the error by reforming the intention or reperforming the action. One must correct the belief.

If I set out to revise my beliefs because I suspect that they have been responsible for my action error, I have formed a new intention, and with it a new action plan. It is not a plan for motor action, although some of the subgoals of the plan may involve that. But revising my beliefs has now become a goal like the goals that motivate motor action, because this revision is now itself a subgoal in the longer-range plan which was interrupted by an error. Thus revising my beliefs requires an action plan. In following the plan, I apply criteria for belief revision. On these criteria, my beliefs must correspond with reality. Acknowledging that my beliefs were false constitutes understanding that there is an *external reality* that is *independent of those beliefs*.

But why 'reality' rather than just an ideally coherent set of beliefs? Because what the notion of a higher-order coherence must explain is the *continual occurrence of error*. In the action context, there is an upper limit to the errors that can occur, determined by the overall goal, that for the sake of which every subgoal exists. Every type of error that can occur with respect to that intrinsic goal is explained in terms of some aspect of the planning or production of actions to achieve that goal. The possibility for belief error, on the other hand, is open-ended. Only if we posit as a 'goal' something fixed, which we nevertheless can never attain, can this be explained.

Positing an ideally coherent set of beliefs does not explain why belief errors keep on occurring because there is no intrinsic reason, *apart from the continual occurrence of error,* why such a set cannot be attained. The only thing that prevents us from having perfectly coherent beliefs is the continual acquisition of new beliefs stemming from the occurrence of error, including the failure of our beliefs to predict new experiences. There is no way we can conceive of an upper limit to this process: there is nothing about a system of beliefs considered in isolation which would characterize it as maximally coherent, no internal criterion of completeness (even though many rationalists have believed that there might be). I have no idea of what it would be like to know that I had made all possible mistakes, in the way that I know what it would be like to achieve other sorts of goals. Thus if we want an explanation of belief error which is comprehensible in the way that action error is comprehensible, then we must posit a fixed upper limit against which any belief system can turn out to be erroneous: that is the function of external reality.

I am suggesting that a defining characteristic of our concept of external reality is that in terms of which our beliefs can be false. 'Real,' in this view, primarily means 'not mistaken, not mere appearance, not dependent upon our perception.' Because there is such a thing as external reality, the fact that our beliefs can let us down is explained. External reality, in contrast to our beliefs, is eternally fixed. It is difficult to characterize the concept in a more positive way.

5. Action, belief, and metaphor

Let us take a general look at how the above claims about error are related to the foundationalist view of understanding. Lakoff (1980, 1987) and Johnson (1980, 1987) hold, as we have seen, that "structures of our experience work their way up into abstract meanings and patterns of influence" (Johnson 1987: xix). The structures of our experience take the form of 'image schemata;' an image schema is:

> a dynamic pattern that functions somewhat like the abstract structure of an image, and thereby connects up a vast range of different experiences that manifest this same recurring structure.' (Johnson 1987: 2)

In Lakoff's words, we structure our experience by means of 'idealized cognitive models:'

> Cognitive models are directly embodied with respect to their content, or else they are systematically linked to directly embodied models. Cognitive models structure thought and are used in forming categories and in reasoning. Concepts characterized by cognitive models are understood via the embodiment of the models. (Lakoff 1987: 13)

The idea is that we begin with the experiences of bodily motion and motor interactions with objects in our environment. These experiences form image patterns (schemata) in terms of which we understand new experiences in new, wider domains: we structure the new domains with the schemata derived from our bodily experience. In that sense we 'understand' these domains in terms of bodily actions. The motor images described by Jeannerod (1994), or the 'response images' of Goldman (1976), developed to control concrete physical actions, are used in the performance of non-basic, perhaps more abstract, higher-level cognitive activities.

6.   The bifurcation of cognitive understanding

There are two ways these patterns can be used. The first is *nonreflectively* as organizers of the higher-level activities. For example, just as when I decide to take a sip from my coffee cup I set in motion a series of ('reflexive') actions which I correct by monitoring feedback until the represented goal is attained, so in deciding to drive to the university, or to move to France, I begin to monitor and correct a nested set of subactions in the same way. The second way the patterns can be used is *reflectively*. Then I take the patterns as objects, specifically as models, and divide up a new field of inquiry into various aspects by mapping it onto the model and treating the relationships among the aspects of the new field as though they were identical with the relationships among elements in the model.

The second, reflective use is what Johnson and Lakoff have in mind. They hold that when we form *concepts* with respect to a given domain, we use the structures of these image schemata:

> . . . I want to suggest that the image schemata constrain inferences (and thus reasoning) in certain basic and important ways. They can do this because they have definite internal structure that can be figuratively extended to structure our understanding of formal relations among concepts and propositions. . . . Because schemata are so central to meaning structure, they influence the ways in which we can make sense of things and reason about them. (Johnson 1987: 38)

In order to be used this way, image schemata or motor patterns must be available to be thought about, and not merely function to activate motor sequences. It is no contradiction that most of time we may be consciously unaware that we are making such use of image schemata. The point is that this is a higher order use of image schemata, and thus, unlike the use of them as motor sequence activators, would be unavailable to the simpler animals.

In contrast, I have in effect been arguing that we use action patterns in both ways. In the context of the present discussion, we use them nonreflectively in belief formation and belief revision. That is, these activities are goal-oriented and goal-directed in the same way as motor actions are, and our natural methods of forming and revising beliefs do not depend upon a *conscious decision* to employ an action model. This means that lower animals which could not be said to reflect could nevertheless be said to have beliefs which facilitate their action planning in the way that humans do. I have also argued that when we develop epistemological theories (whether sophisticated or commonsensical) we use the patterns reflectively. We map the belief context on to the action context, and treat elements in the belief context as though they possess the same interrelations as the elements of the action context. We do the latter in response to the occurrence of action error, when we have ruled out a cause of this error in action performance and plan selection. Because of this reflective use of action patterns, we come up with a view of belief error as the failure of correspondence of a belief to reality. Thus it is reasonable to say that this second use of action patterns (or the action/error model) is metaphorical, while the first — the development of a belief system as a facilitator of action planning — is not metaphorical but is simply a higher-level type of action.

But while the above distinction between the two roles of image schemata is useful, in the long run it may disguise the unity of a principle underlying all behavior: one involving nested or serial iterations of basic motor and perceptual events.

Notes

1.   It is noteworthy that the 'motor image' theory of action has made its way into the training of athletes, who are taught to image themselves successfully performing the desired feat and thereby to create a 'neuromuscular template' which controls future performances.

2.   The requirement that a goal guide an action by means of the matching of motor feedback from phases of the action with a representation of the goal is what may underly Harman's claim that intentions are self-referential. If I intend X I intend that my intention shall cause me to do X (Harman 1986, Ch. 8.) Harman's account of intentions is discussed at greater length below.

3.   There do seem to be cases in which one can try to do X in the absence of any definite procedure which includes feedback, as long as there is a way of telling whether or not one has achieved X. For example, I can try to wiggle my ears by simply moving facial muscles at random while watching my ears in the mirror. But in this case I am not really trying to wiggle my ears so much as trying to *learn to* wiggle them by a method which does involve monitering feedback: making random motions while noting the frequency of certain results. This is the method of learning bodily control by biofeedback; here the continuous feedback *is* the seeing whether the ears wiggle or not. The ultimate goal is not a single event of ear-wiggling, but the development of a procedure (plan or schema) for wiggling them at will.

CHAPTER SIX

Understanding Persons

1. From actions and objects to language

In the preceding chapters I explored a foundational level of intentional understanding in the performance of goal-directed physical actions involving physical objects. This is a necessary first step in the development of an account of the intentional understanding of language.

Understanding language is complex. Before one can understand the meaning of a particular word, one must understand what a word (and, in general, what language) is, and that requires understanding the concept of a symbol. Understanding the meaning of a particular word requires, moreover, having at least some understanding of the objects or states of affairs themselves to which the word refers. This complexity is the reason for the gap now confronting us between intentional language understanding and the foundation of intentional understanding in general.

It might seem that the gap is a narrow one, since language is, after all, a tool. It is used in various social actions, all of which involve producing an effect on other people. As a tool, language is a type of object. Since we have defined the understanding of an object in terms of its incorporation into an action, perhaps language understanding could be defined simply in terms of our prior definition of object understanding, along with a reference to the sort of action — communication — into which it is incorporated.

That will not do, however, because while understanding a tool as such can be defined in terms of what we have already established, understanding a given type of tool must be defined in terms of the understanding of the task to which the tool is applied. I do not, for example, understand a shovel unless I understand digging. Thus we will need an account of how we understand communication, and that is no simple matter since it entails understanding the concept of a *person*.

2. Persons, understanding and communication

While linguistic communication is a way of transmitting information, it is more than that. I transmit information to the engine of my car when I turn on the ignition. I do not, however, communicate with the engine, because I do not believe that the engine *understands* the information, with the sort of intentional understanding we attribute to persons. The engine responds appropriately because the physical form of information itself directly causes the response.

One can imagine similar circumstances in the case of linguistic communication. For example, if I see someone about to run off a cliff I might shout 'Stop!' and the shouted word might startle him so much that he stops. In that case, however, it is not his understanding of the *meaning* of what he heard that caused him to stop, and for that reason we would not classify this as an example of normal linguistic communication. As I argued earlier, linguistic understanding requires that two things be understood: the meaning(s) of the linguistic items, and that the items are symbols. Since a symbol is such only because of the role it plays in an act of communication, understanding that a given stimulus object is a symbol means understanding that it is a component in an act of communication. Understanding this, in turn, requires understanding the communicative act itself, and that requires understanding its other components. Since two essential components of a communicative act are the transmitter and the receiver of the information, in order to understand one's activity of communication one must understand the other party to that activity: a being that itself understands. That is what I mean by a *person*. One must also understand oneself as a receiver, and understander, of the information.

It is thus clear that understanding one's action of communication requires a level of self-understanding different from that required for the performance of other actions, such as grasping an object. In the latter case, I must understand myself as a moving object, interacting with other objects in the world. This level of understanding need not be completely reflexive: I do not need to understand myself *as* one who understands, in order to understand my action. That is because the agent's understanding is not a *component* of the action of grasping an object (although the components of the action are understood by the agent, if the action is intentional). In the case of communication, however, understanding *is* such a component. The action of communicating is not complete unless the communication has been understood by the recipient of the information. This understanding, in turn, requires that the communication be understood as a communication — that is, as information intentionally sent by a person. Thus a successful act of communication requires the understanding, on the part of both parties to the transaction, that both are persons.

This chapter is an examination of that understanding. I will show how our understanding of what a person is can be explained in terms of the foundation — the understanding of our own actions and of the physical objects incorporated into them — and hence how our understanding of what a person is can be similarly nonconceptual. Since, as I will argue, the former understanding is not a simple extension of the foundation — other people are not mere objects upon which we act — but rather employs it recursively, the explanation is complicated. Therefore I shall begin with a summary of basic intentional understanding as explored in the previous two chapters.

3.   Understanding as knowing how

At the beginning of Chapter Three, we saw that an action can be understood in two ways. One can know *that* it is an action of a certain kind — e.g. that the Charleston is a dance popular in the 20's — and one can know *how* to perform the action. 'Knowing that' is conceptual or propositional understanding; it requires prior understanding of the concepts included in what is known. 'Knowing how' requires no prior conceptual understanding. Knowing how to do a thing is just being able to do it intentionally. Clearly 'knowing how,' in presupposing no other understanding, is closer to the foundation. Eventually I shall examine the precise way that 'knowing that' is built upon 'knowing how;' here I shall simply use the term 'understanding' in the 'knowing how' sense, since that is the sense used in the discussion thus far.

Understanding a basic action-type has been defined as follows:

> S understands a basic action-type A if S is able to imagine per-
> forming an action of that type, with an image rich enough to serve
> as a guide in actual performance.

Note that there are two components to the definition. One concerns the *nature* of understanding — having an ability to act — and the other concerns the mechanism by which this ability is *manifested* — imagining acting. Intentionally performing the action is also a manifestation of understanding, but imagining (i.e. consciously representing) is part of an intentional performance: the performance is initiated and guided by means of a representation of the goal and the steps to achieving it. Thus while the nature of this type of understanding is captured in an action, the action need not be carried out but may exist only as a representation in the agent's mind.

The definition of object understanding proceeded along the same lines:

> S has an understanding of a perceived object O if S is able to imagine incorporating O into the performance of a token of an action-type A that is already understood, with an image rich enough to serve as a guide in actual performance.

The definition of object understanding has the same two components as that of action understanding; unlike the former, however, it presupposes that something else is already understood. Thus in effect the account of object understanding constitutes our first example of building upon action understanding as a foundation. It is also the most straightforward example. There is more than one way to use one's understanding in a given context in order to make sense of something else. Let us look at the different ways this can be done.

4.   Literal and metaphorical understanding

Object understanding as characterized above represents one way to build upon a foundation: *incorporation*, in which something is understood as bearing a direct relation to other things that are already understood. The novel object or state of affairs is included in the pre-existing system of related components. Using an object in performing an action is the most obvious example; another would be recognizing that an unexpected object looming on the horizon is a tractor plowing the far end of a field on which one is standing. In both cases the context in which the object is understood includes one's body and current spatial location; the object is understood, in part, in terms of its relation to oneself and one's actual circumstances.

As we have seen, however, this sort of understanding can be manifested in mental imagery alone. For example, I can see an object and imagine how I *might* use it without actually doing so, and hence form an understanding of it. For example, I understand the chair in the corner of my room as something I could sit on if I were to walk over to it now. Once this possibility is recognized, it is a short step to recognizing that what one imagines can be counterfactual to varying degrees. The paralyzed ex-dancer in Chapter Three understands the Charleston as something he *could* do *if* he were not paralyzed. I understand the snow covering my yard as something that I could shovel away *if* I were strong enough and had a place to put it.

In the above examples, the understanding is achieved by imagining a direct physical relationship between the object or state of affairs to be understood and actions of types that I have actually performed, in the context of certain (counterfactual) circumstances. The imagined relationship includes the object or state of affairs *itself*, as I perceive it. The counterfactual circumstances alter my imagined abilities to act, but they do not involve substantive differences in the thing that I understand by this means, or in the action-type into which I imagine incorporating it. I propose to term this sort of understanding 'literal understanding,' because in what is imagined the object and the action incorporating it are represented as the actual perceived object and actual tokens of the relevant action-type. I imagine *really* shoveling *that* snow that I see.

The other way later understanding builds upon the foundation of action understanding is through *metaphorical extension* of what is already understood. Metaphorical understanding is possible only because action understanding is manifested in a complex mental representation. This manifestation allows one to apply an understanding of an action-type to a novel set of objects which one could not actually incorporate into a token of that action-type, even if one were able to perform the action. The novel objects and the ways one might act upon them are interrelated in ways to some degree isomorphic with those constituting the components of the original action, but they could not be actually incorporated into an action of that type. In effect, when encountering novel objects or states of affairs one sometimes understands them by imagining them *standing in* for the components of a familiar action.

To take a simple example, suppose one is trying to use chopsticks for the first time. One's instructor says: 'Pretend the upper chopstick is a pencil.' One then understands where to place one's fingers and what sort of pressure to use, on that chopstick at least. Or, imagine that you are trying to understand the behavior of a difficult co-worker. 'Just think of him as an overgrown three-year-old,' a friend suggests, and you find that that method enables you to work with him.

In the first of these examples, one uses a mental representation of a well-understood action — writing with a pencil — as a guide to an action with a different object. One does not write with the chopstick, but one pretends to. There is more to understanding how to use a pair of chopsticks than this, but one can understand how to hold the upper chopstick as: the way one holds a pencil.

The second example is more complicated. Dealing with a three-year-old child is not a basic action-type. There is, however, a certain general style which we know how to employ when interacting with a three-year-old. With a real child, there are details to the behavior that could not be used with the co-worker: an extreme clarity and simplicity of speech, for example, or an exaggerated brightness of expression. But representations of certain general features of the style can be used in the situation with the co-worker; for example, stressing the consequences for his own comfort and convenience of recommended actions. Being able to treat him in part as one treats a child is one way of understanding how to deal with him.

I shall term the two ways of extending action understanding to novel material 'literal understanding' and 'metaphorical understanding.' These terms are derived from linguistic contexts, but are used here in a nonlinguistic sense. In literal understanding an object is understood entirely in its own terms; it is taken at 'face value.' In the example used in Chapter Four, the protruding edge on the computer is treated not as *like* some other thing that functions as a handle, but as a handle itself. In metaphorical understanding, on the other hand, one in effect pretends that the object to be understood is of the type commonly incorporated into a certain action-type, while remaining aware that the object could not actually be so incorporated.

5.   The mechanism of metaphorical understanding

Literal understanding is straightforward, since one can just imagine doing certain things to the very physical objects that one thereby understands. Metaphorical understanding is not straightforward, since while one also imagines doing things to physical objects, the objects in one's imagination are not, and are not intended to be, the objects that one thereby understands. The question thus arises of how, in metaphorical understanding, the thing that is imagined is related to the thing that is understood.

The examples we have considered provide a clue: one imagines incorporating the novel object into a familiar action, but one's representation omits features of the action that are inappropriate to that object. Since the chopstick is known not to be a writing instrument, one imagines *holding* a pencil but omits a representation of actually writing (and perhaps of the visual appearance of a pencil). In the example of the childish co-worker, one imagines certain features of one's behavior with children, but omits others. The two cases are different in the following way. In the chopstick example, one *stage* of the familiar action of writing with a pencil — grasping the pencil — is imagined in full detail, while later stages are omitted. In the colleague example, certain *aspects* of a general style of behavior are imagined, while other aspects are omitted. One type of thing I do when trying to persuade a young child to do something is to stress the immediate benefits to the child of doing what I suggest; another is to use a 'childish' tone of voice. When treating my colleague as a child, I select the former aspect but not the latter.

I will have more to say about metaphorical understanding as such in Chapter Seven. In those discussions, it will be useful to be able to draw upon simple examples of such understanding dating from early in a child's development, in the we did in Chapters Three and Four for action and object understanding. Analyzing the way a child comes to understand the concept of another person will provide us with such an example. If understanding an object by incorporating it into an action is our earliest example of the literal understanding built upon action understanding, understanding another person is our earliest example of metaphorical understanding.

6. The infant's 'theory of mind'

In recent years cognitive psychologists have tried to explain how humans and other animals are able to predict one another's behavior. This problem is different from that of predicting the behavior of inanimate objects, which requires some minimal understanding of laws of physics. The behavior of humans and probably many other animals is intentional, meaning that it is a

result of mental, not just physical states. If a ball is hit by another ball it will
roll in direction predictable by its weight, position, the force of the impact, etc.
If a human being is hit by a ball, her reaction will depend not only on these
physical factors but on her mental, or intentional, states as well. Thus interacting with others of one's kind requires understanding these intentional states of
mind. Since very young infants are successful at such interactions, the understanding cannot require very difficult reasoning. What is it, and how is it
acquired?

A dominant view has been that, at least in the case of humans, infants
develop a 'theory' of intentional states. This view has recently been defended
by Alison Gopnik:

> Empirical findings show that the idea of intentionality is a theoretical con-
> struct, one we invent in our early lives to explain a wide variety of evidence
> about ourselves and others. This theoretical construct is equally applicable to
> ourselves and others and depends equally on our experience of ourselves and
> others. (Gopnik 1993: 2)

An assumption at the root of the 'theory theory,' as it is sometimes called, is
that humans are equipped with the ability to form theories about mechanisms
operating in various environmental domains by generalizing to the best
explanations of observed events in those domains. These generalizations lead
to 'naive' or 'folk' doctrines, such as naive physics or folk psychology, by
which we predict and 'explain' observed events. Thus in the domain of human
behavior we explain many events as being caused by 'intentional' states such
as 'beliefs' and 'desires,' while we explain the behavior of inanimate objects in
terms of nonintentional 'forces.' The 'intentional stance' (Dennett 1987) is a
useful construct yielding many successful predictions, not only of human
behavior but also sometimes of the behavior of nonhuman animals or even
computers, but it is nevertheless a construct, or a theory, and a very imperfect
one. As such, it is subject to replacement by a more adequate scientific theory.

The 'theory theory' has come under attack from several directions (e.g.
Gordon 1986, Goldman 1993). In this chapter I shall join the critics. My views
have much in common with those of Gordon and Goldman. Like Gordon, I
shall argue that we understand other people by simulating their states; like
Goldman, I shall argue that the concept of intentionality is not 'invented;' not,
at least, *ab initio* . The basis of my argument is that the understanding an infant
has of its own intentional actions is the most likely root of its understanding of
the intentionality of other persons. What this means is that the concept of

intentionality is not entirely invented, nor is it innate, on certain understandings of those terms. The concept develops naturally and organically out of the child's understanding of its immediate experience.

As an introduction, let us look at some recent work on the development of the child's theory of mind. Researchers in cognitive psychology have studied the condition known as autism, as a way of identifying the elements of normal understanding of others. Autism is a cognitive disorder affecting social interaction and communication. Victims appear, to varying degrees, unable to grasp that others have intentional states; they seem, in short, not to understand that others are 'persons,' but treat them in much the same way that they treat inanimate objects. If they do indeed fail to understand the concept of a 'person,' as I characterized it above, then the disorder can be a major clue to the nature of the normal understanding of persons.

Simon Baron-Cohen (1991, 1993) has studied joint-attention behavior in both normal and autistic children, on the hypothesis that a capacity for joint-attention is a precursor for a theory of mind. It will be useful to look at his analysis, both for the insights it offers and for what it leaves still unexplained regarding the understanding of persons. Baron-Cohen writes:

> From observational studies, it appears that joint-attention behaviors occur far less frequently in autistic children than in non-autistic control groups. . . These behaviors include 'referential looking' (as occurs when I look at what you are looking at, and attempt to get you to look at something by using the direction of my eye gaze), and gestures such as giving, showing and pointing. In normal children, referential looking is present in the majority of eight-month-olds . . , and gestures such as giving, showing and pointing emerge between nine to 12 months old . . . Joint-attention deficits are likely to be the earliest social deficits in autism yet identified. (Baron-Cohen 1991: 239; references omitted)

Baron-Cohen studies 'proto-declarative pointing' — pointing "in order to comment or remark on the world to another person" (1991: 240) — as a paradigm example of joint-attention behavior. Proto-declarative pointing entails understanding *attention* in another person, and this in turn requires

> understanding that vision (or audition) can be directed selectively, and that its direction depends on the person finding the object or event of *interest*. (Baron-Cohen 1991: 244)

How does the infant represent *interest*? Baron-Cohen believes that this ability may require metarepresentation. Unlike primary representations, which store literal information about the world, metarepresentations "refer to other representations" (1991: 234): thoughts, dreams, pretend objects, etc. Being able to represent others' thoughts may be necessary in order to recognize their personhood sufficiently to communicate with them.

A metarepresentation is a data-structure which takes information from the observed behavior of another person and constructs a representation of a relationship among three components: an agent, a state of the world, and a 'decoupled' representation of that state. The result could take the form:

> mother PRETENDS [of] the banana [that] 'it is a telephone.' (Leslie and Roth 1993: 87)

This type of structure could be used to represent another person's attitude of interest in a particular state of the world.

While a mechanism for handling metarepresentations may be an essential component in treating others as persons, postulating such a mechanism is not the same thing as explaining how one *understands* that another person is a person. One need not be conscious of one's metarepresentations (Leslie and Roth 1993: 89). Such information-processing mechanisms are doubtless at work in all our cognitive activity. Our interest is in how we understand the entities with which these mechanisms allow us to interact. 'Understanding' here refers to a state of which we can be conscious; it normally, in adults at least, *accompanies* the activity of a metarepresentational mechanism when one interacts with another person.

Imagine, for example, that you are interacting with an object you take to be a computer — you are, let us say, participating in a Turing-test competition. You believe that the entity on the other end of your 'conversation' is a computer program, but suddenly its response makes you think it is a human being after all. Something changes in the way you think of the entity. Before you thought of it 'as a machine;' now you think of it 'as a person,' and you can tell the difference. What *is* that difference? Explaining that your metarepresentational mechanism has kicked in does not account for the experiential aspects of it.

Meltzoff and Gopnik (1993) suggest an answer. They are proponents of the 'theory theory,' according to which a representational model of the mind develops between the ages of three and six, and "supplants an earlier 'nonrepresentational' understanding of the mind" (1993: 335). In their view, only with the acquisition of the representational model is the concept of intentionality acquired; as noted above, Gopnik holds that it is a 'theoretical construct.'

Nevertheless, Meltzoff and Gopnik argue that the earlier, nonrepresentational understanding that an infant has of other persons is a precursor of the later representational understanding. As I shall argue, I differ with them primarily with regard to the origin of the understanding of intentionality.

Meltzoff and Gopnik argue that an infant perceives other persons as similar to itself:

> Infants are launched on their career of interpersonal relations with the primary perceptual judgment: *'Here is something like me.'* . . .
> We propose that infants' primordial 'like me' experiences are based on their *understanding of bodily movement patterns and postures*. Infants monitor their own bodily movements by the internal sense of proprioception, and can detect cross-modal equivalents between those movements-as-felt and the movements they see performed by others. (Meltzoff and Gopnik 1993: 336; my italics)

The ability to detect similarity between self and other is expressed in imitation:

> We suggest that for the youngest infants, persons are: 'entities that can be imitated and also who imitate me,' entities that pass the 'like me' test. Such a rule would be effective in sorting the world into people versus things, and could be operative in the opening weeks of life — because the data show that infants imitate at birth. (Meltzoff and Gopnik 1993: 337)

The authors hold that the full concept of intentionality is a later stage in the development of a theory of mind which has its origins in the ability to imitate. My quarrel is not with the claim that the *concept* develops after the age of three. My interest is in a preconceptual, experiential understanding of intentionality; I shall argue that this essential aspect of the acquisition of the concept exists much earlier. The extent to which the issue is substantive rather than terminological will be discussed further on.

7. Understanding the actions of others

An infant, as we have seen, can be said to understand its own intentional bodily actions. We are now considering a claim that infants can judge the perceived bodily movements of others to be 'like' their own actions, as evinced by the fact that as early as 42 minutes after birth, an infant can imitate facial expressions (Meltzoff and Gopnik 1993: 342). Making this judgment may be equivalent to recognizing another as a person.

To settle this matter we will need an account of what is meant by 'person.' Judging another to be 'like' oneself is relevant only to the extent that one understands *oneself* to be a person, or a being with intentional mental states, and that has not been discussed. As we saw above, understanding one's intentional actions does not entail understanding oneself as a being that understands — has intentional mental states — and thus understanding that another's actions are like one's own actions does not appear to entail understanding the other to be a person in the intentional sense.

Thus understanding another to be like oneself may not be a sufficient condition for understanding the other's personhood. It may, however, be a necessary condition. Since we must start somewhere, let us begin by exploring how another entity is understood as a person in the sense of a being like oneself. Then we will look at how one might understand *oneself* as a person.

An account of the understanding of another person might take the following general form:

> S understands another entity as a person if S is able to imitate the perceived bodily movements of the other entity.

Recall that our account of the understanding of a person should depend upon no other understanding except that closer to the foundation: one's own actions and the objects incorporated into one's actions. In the above formulation, a person is understood by means of S's own action of imitation. For this to qualify as understanding in the requisite foundational sense, then one's own action of imitation must itself be understood.

The following question now arises: is the action of imitating the other entity (which happens to be a person) understood in a way that is distinct from the resulting understanding of the entity as a person? Is imitating, in other words, just another action, understood on the same level and in the same way as any other basic action? Or is imitating a special kind of action, one that can be performed only in response to a special kind of entity: one-that-can-be-imitated? This question is important. If the former is the case, then it would seem that understanding another person is straightforwardly like understanding any other entity with which one may use or otherwise incorporate into one's action. If the latter is the case, then the account seems circular: one can imitate only those things that are understood to be persons, while that understanding is possible only in terms of the act of imitating. We have a dilemma. It might be thought that by adopting the former account we lose nothing and gain simplicity, but the difficulty is that we also lose the special character of person-understanding. If imitating is a sort of action that can be performed with just any entity, then since it is after all possible to imitate the movements of inanimate objects, we have not yet captured what is unique in that concept.

One might, it is true, appeal to the results of acts of imitation: a person responds in certain ways to being imitated (mother smiles again, more broadly, when baby smiles back at her) while an inanimate object fails to respond at all. This move would locate the concept of a person in the act of imitating together with the response: a person is an entity that responds in a certain way when imitated.

While the above account might describe part of a fully-developed concept of a person, the main difficulty here is that of getting imitative behavior off the ground. A newborn infant who imitates someone sticking out her tongue must have some ability to recognize the perceived gesture as imitatable. This ability would seem to require the infant's prior awareness of a similarity between the other person and herself. The difficulty is that a newborn infant is not aware of possible appearances of her face, while the facial appearance is all that she is aware of in the other (she is not, that is, aware of the other's proprioceptive sensations in making the gesture — but it is only those that are (presumably) similar to what she is aware of in her own case). If so, whatever gives her the idea in the first place that she can imitate another by sticking out her tongue? How, in other words, does the 'like me' judgment arise?

Two possibilities have been suggested. One is that there is an innate mechanism that triggers facial imitation in newborns in the manner of a simple reflex. However, experimental data showing that the imitative response can be delayed, and also that infants appear to work on perfecting the response, suggest that the response is not a simple reflex but an intentional action aimed at matching the target presented by the other (Meltzoff and Gopnik 1993: 341-2). Meltzoff and Gopnik thus prefer an alternative account (proposed by Meltzoff and Moore 1992): that there exists a:

> primitive *supramodal body scheme* that allows the infant to unify acts-as-seen and acts-as-felt into a common framework. . . . We suggest that the supra-modal body scheme revealed by early imitation provides the foundation of the development of the notion of persons and self-other equivalencies in infants. . . . (Meltzoff and Gopnik 1993: 342-3)

On this view, what is innate is not an imitative response reflex (although there may be an innate tendency or desire to imitate), but a framework within which various perceptions can be matched and treated as equivalent. The 'reflex,' one might say, is the identification of what is seen as a 'bodily action' in terms of this framework. To be sure, the *tendency* to respond by imitating the action is innate, but the tokens of behavior are still intentional, not reflexive (like many life-sustaining behaviors such as eating). Positing the supramodal body scheme solves our problem of how an infant can know enough about itself and the other to *imitate* the other — the problem of what imitation could possibly mean to an infant. The answer is that in imitating another's gesture the infant is simply trying to perform the gesture that it has represented in the way it represents its own (actual or possible) actions. In other words, *trying to perform* the gesture is not the original imitative impulse. That originates in the *representation* of the *other's* gesture in the infant's *own* body scheme.

What does it mean to say that behavior at such an early stage is intentional? It means that it is guided by a representation of a goal, and that progress toward the goal can be monitored by comparing a current state with the represented goal. As the authors note, infants often begin imitating with only an approximation of the adult's gesture, and "appear to home in on the detailed match, gradually correcting their responses over successive efforts" (1993: 342). This matching process requires the infant's awareness of proprioceptive feedback from her efforts, as well as an awareness of the desired goal as represented in the 'body scheme.' The infant's awareness would necessarily be minimal, in that its content is only certain immediate sensations. Nevertheless, the way the infant uses those sensations to achieve a goal marks the behavior as intentional. As we saw in Chapter Three, an action is intentional if the agent can intend to perform it. In this case, the infant clearly intends to imitate the facial gesture, since she (by hypothesis) attempts to bring her behavior into conformity with the facial gesture as represented in the supramodal body scheme. Her behavior conforms to the control-model of goal-directed behavior proposed by Adams and Mele (1989), discussed in that chapter. She aims at producing proprioceptive sensations which signal that the goal — a match with the perceived gesture — has been achieved. Thus, these imitative actions are intentional.

On the view we are considering, imitating the gestures of another is a response to an identification of the other as 'like me,' an identification constituted by the mapping of the perceived behavior of the other onto the infant's supramodal body scheme. Let us see if this account can provide a sufficient condition for the understanding of a person (in the sense of 'an entity like me'). Our rough initial attempt was as follows:

> S understands another entity as a person if S is able to imitate the perceived bodily movements of the other entity.

We can now see that while this characterization is not inaccurate, it is not the minimal sufficient condition we seek. The ability to imitate is the ability to perform an intentional action with the result that one's behavior matches (to one's own satisfaction, at least) the behavior of another. If, as argued above, imitating is successfully performing an intentional action, then we run into the same type of case as that posed by the paralyzed dancer in Chapter Two. Someone, infant or not, might be prevented by extraneous constraints from successfully carrying out an imitative act, but nevertheless be capable of intending to imitate; and it is this ability that marks the understanding of an entity as another 'like oneself.'

We can treat this case in the same way as we did the other: what counts for understanding is the ability to *intend* the action, rather than the ability to carry it out. And, once again, the relevant aspect of *that* ability is the ability to *imagine* carrying it out. Now, the above analysis of how the infant imitates a perceived gesture provides us with what we need. The infant has a representation of her own performance of the gesture in the supramodal body scheme itself, with which she attempts to bring her motions into conformity. That bodily representation, activated by the sight of the gestures of the other entity, serves the infant as her guide to performing the imitative act.

The action that the infant attempts to perform is at once her own action, and the action of the other. That is because the perceived and the intended action are represented within a common framework. Since there is just a single action-representation, understanding her own (attempted) action *is at the same time* understanding the action of the other. Thus, we might reword the above characterization as follows:

> S understands another entity as a person if S is able to imagine performing the actions of the other entity.

This is not yet what we want, because while it correctly describes the way an infant understands another person (according to the account of Meltzoff and Gopnik) it also captures something that older humans can do in the case of other entities that they do not understand as persons. I can imagine performing the actions of something I know to be an insect, or a robot, because I have learned to use my imagination in a way an infant cannot. We cannot appeal to the fact that infants (presumably) imitate only other persons, since we do not even know that that is true.

The solution lies in acknowledging that I can appeal to prior understanding in explaining the understanding of an entity as a person, since I am acknowledging that there is a foundation for the latter. Thus we can use our formulation of a sufficient condition for action-understanding in a characterization of person-understanding:

> S understands another entity as a person if S can understand the actions of the other entity as she understands her own: by imagining performing them, with an image rich enough to serve as a guide in actual performance.

But one might ask why this formulation is an improvement on the previous one. If S can imagine performing the actions of a robot that is known to be a robot, then does the above formulation not characterize S's state as well as the previous one?

The answer is that in this formulation, it is specified that the actions of the other entity are understood *in the way that S understands her own actions.* I understand my own action because my representation, or image, of performing the action is rich enough to guide actual performance. That means that the components of the action are represented as playing their proper roles: the means are represented as means, the goal as goal. The experience of entertaining that representation is the experience of understanding that action — which means, of being able to perform the action. The infant who imitates another by representing the other's perceived actions in her supramodal body scheme is representing the other's action as performed, that is, as performable, by the infant herself, in the same way that she performs her own actions. That is the same thing as saying that the infant perceives the other as acting in the way the infant herself acts — that is, intentionally.

The infant might well imagine this in the case of a robot, but an adult normally would not, knowing the nature of a robot. I might imagine making the movements a robot makes, but I would not imagine the robot making them *in the way I would make them*: with the same bodily sensations and experiences.

If I were to imagine them in that way, I would be imagining the robot as a person, not as a robot. It might be easy to fool an infant into doing this, but less easy to fool an adult. (An adult or older child can, of course, *pretend* to herself that the robot is a person by imagining its actions in that way.)

We should note that if an infant is fooled into thinking that a robot is a person, with the result that she represents its actions in her supramodal body scheme, then she does not really understand the actions of the robot; she misunderstands them. But as discussed in Chapter One, we are not concerned here with correct or accurate understanding as distinct from misunderstanding. We are concerned with what it is to have *an* understanding of something — that is, for a thing to be meaningful, and to be meaningful *as* such-and-such. I have been describing what it is for an infant to have an understanding of another's actions, and I have argued that when an infant has the same kind of understanding of another's actions that she has of her own actions, then she has an understanding of the other *as a person*. This account allows that her understanding of the other may in fact be mistaken, if the other is not really a person.

8.   Understanding persons

I have argued that an infant understands another as a person if she can understand the actions of the other in the same way that she understands her own actions. But as we have also seen, she does not need to understand herself as a person in order to understand her own actions; understanding one's own actions is foundational, requiring no other understanding. Understanding personhood thus appears to have sprung from nowhere.

It appears that way because what we understand when we understand that another entity is a person is *nothing other than* understanding its actions in the way that we understand our own. That is all there is to understanding personhood. Since the special characteristic of persons that separates them from things like robots is intentionality, we may say that when we understand another's actions as we do our own, we attribute intentionality to the other. But we can say that without also saying that we attribute intentionality to our own actions when we understand them. We do not, that is, understand our own intentional actions by applying a prior understanding of intentionality to an action we are performing or imagining. Rather, it is the intentionality of our own actions — their being guided by a represented plan — that allows us to understand them in the first place. Thus intentionality is *constituted by* our ability to understand our own actions. When we understand the actions of another in the same way, we are thus automatically (preconceptually) attributing intentionality to those actions, and hence, to the other. It is in this sense that imagining performing the actions of another is taking the *intentional stance* toward that other.

9.   The intentional stance and metaphorical understanding

We can now see how the understanding of personhood is built by metaphorical extension upon the understanding of our own actions. Metaphorical understanding in general is understanding an object by representing it in a certain way. As stated above, when understanding something metaphorically one in effect pretends that the object to be understood is of the sort commonly incorporated into a certain action-type, while one remains aware that the object could not actually be so incorporated. In the case of an infant's understanding of another entity as a person, the infant pretends, in effect, that the other entity is 'incorporated into an action-type' *in the role of the infant herself* — the familiar agent of actions of that type. The infant, however, remains aware that the other is really an *other*, not one and the same being as the infant herself. How does this work? Recall that we are presupposing a more basic level of perceptual understanding of an external object. Thus the infant perceives the other as an external object, and hence as other than herself, but at the same time perceives it as if it were she herself, the agent of her imagined actions.

Her ability to do this may well be 'built in,' depending upon an innate mechanism for constructing a supramodal body scheme and an innate tendency to represent the perceived actions of others within that scheme. (It may be these features that are missing when a child is autistic.) But while these necessary features of imitation may be innate, a given individual action of imitating another by making use of these innate features would be an intentional, not a reflex, action. As such, it would involve the infant's awareness of performing the action. The awareness of performing this imitative action is the experience of understanding the other as a person.

Understanding another as a person fits our account of metaphorical understanding because it involves a kind of pretense: that the other is oneself. The fact that the mechanism allowing this pretense is built in may lead some to conclude that the action, being so basic, could not be one of intentional understanding, but only if it is forgotten that understanding must have a foundation. No prior understanding is presupposed in the understanding an infant has of its own actions, an understanding made possible entirely by built-in mechanisms. When the infant, in imitating the other, understands the other's actions as she understands her own, understanding of personhood *begins*; no prior 'person concept' is required. All that is then required for the initial understanding of personhood to serve as a foundation for later understanding is that the early imitative actions be available to consciousness, so that they can later be represented or imagined in novel contexts, and we have seen that consciousness of the actions follows from the fact that they are intentional.

Originally, an infant 'takes the intentional stance' toward another entity when the infant represents the actions of the other entity in her supramodal body scheme, which allows her to imitate the other. The older subject can take the intentional stance toward another just by representing the other's actions in the subject's supramodal body scheme without overtly imitating the other. In representing the actions in that way, the subject is pretending to be the other. The understanding is metaphorical rather than literal because the subject remains aware that she is not literally the other, since the other is *other* — an entity separate from the subject in space and other physical circumstances. These circumstances are left out of the representation in the supramodal body scheme; only the other's actions are represented as identical with the subject's actions. The subject continues, meanwhile, to represent the other physical circumstances of the other person as they actually are. This is the same process as we saw in the example of the chopsticks: the learner represents holding the chopstick as identical with her remembered holding of a pencil, while continuing to represent the nonpencil-like features of the chopstick as they actually are. We might say that in metaphorical understanding the subject pastes a bit of her previous experience onto her representation of the novel object. The result is a kind of collage, in which the subject's own past experience blends with the novel object in a *meaningful composite whole* . In understanding something in this way, one makes it one's own.

10. Imitation and communication

Recall the views of Baron-Cohen, discussed above. He argued that joint-attention behaviors such as referential looking and pointing, often absent in autistic children, are early precursors of a 'theory of mind.' Such joint-attention behaviors are also early instances of communication, which presupposes the understanding of persons. Now that we have seen a way that understanding persons can arise, let us look at how that understanding enables the infant to understand communication.

Baron-Cohen argued that early joint-attention behaviors require that the infant understand the other's *attention to* and *interest in* objects of perception. These are intentional mental states. Now that we have an account of an infant's understanding of basic intentional actions in another through imitation, we can see that imitative behavior can also illuminate these mental states. All that is required is that the infant be able to represent the other's attentional behavior using the same framework within which she represents such behavior in herself. When she herself pays attention to an object, she is interested in it, and we may assume that her interest is a phenomenon of which she is aware. If the other's attentional behavior is represented within her own supramodal body scheme, then the interest that accompanies such behavior in herself will, as I put it above, be 'pasted on' to her representation of the other's behavior. Thus she herself feels 'the other's' interest.

The earliest imitative behavior, in which infants imitate others' facial gestures, cannot be called 'communication,' since (we may assume) the infant's imitative gesture is not intended by the infant to be 'understood' by the other person. Before that is possible, the infant must learn that others will respond to her gestures. Then, as she represents their responses in her supramodal body scheme, she will (more or less automatically) represent appropriate mental states along with the behavioral responses — in the way that, we are told (citation), we feel subjectively happier when we form the muscular movements of smiling. Thus in acting to bring about a specific behavioral response in another, the infant will at the same time be acting to bring about the appropriate mental state, which she will represent as accompanying the behavioral response.

For example, consider referential looking, in which a subject tries to get another to look at something by using the direction of the her own eye gaze. Her attempt is intentional in that she employs a representation of what she is trying to bring about: the other's looking at the same object that the subject herself is looking at. If the representation makes use of the supramodal body scheme, then the subject's own action of looking is already represented in that scheme, along with whatever subjective feelings of interest she experiences as connected with her action. The represented action of the other will then share in the feelings of interest: in trying to get the other's action to match the represented action, she is simultaneously and automatically trying to get the other's feeling to match her own feeling, since the other's state is represented in the same framework as her own.

We may now say that communication begins when an infant attempts to cause imitative action in another, such that the desired response of the other is represented in the infant's own supramodal body scheme. In trying to get the other to do what she does, she is trying to get the other to feel what she feels. 'Communication' is a misleading term, since it implies the transfer of information *from* one *to* another, while what is really going on is an effort to effect a *unity or a matching between* oneself and another. The sense of this matching, or the experience of trying to bring it about, is the experiential content of the concept of communication. Communication is possible only between persons because only persons can share the same representational framework of embodiment within which the matching takes place. Communication is understanding personhood because sharing one's body scheme with another for representational purposes is understanding oneself and the other as persons.

11. Conclusion

In this chapter I have shown how it is that the understanding of one's own actions and of the objects incorporated into one's actions become components in one's understanding of persons. These more fundamental levels of understanding are used in connection with a perceived other to create a metaphorical understanding of that other: aspects of that other are imagined as 'standing in' for aspects of oneself, as the subject of understood actions. Communication is understood as an attempt to cause the other to act and feel in the way one represents oneself as acting and feeling. As I have analyzed our understanding of personhood, the possibility of communication is as fundamental to it as the possibility of acting is fundamental to our understanding of our selves: we understand ourselves as agents, and we understand others as extensions of our agency made possible by communication.

We now have uncovered the elements that make up the understanding of natural language — that is, the knowledge of how to use it. In the next chapter we look at how these elements are combined in actual language use.

CHAPTER SEVEN

Understanding Language

1. Introduction: language as a tool

Semantics is the usual context for discussions of understanding; one is said to understand a language if one knows what its words and sentences *mean*. The property of having a meaning (of being 'about' something) is said to make linguistic and other symbols *intentional*. Because of this intentionality, our understanding of symbols seems uniquely different from our understanding of nonsymbolic entities; we must know not only how to use them, but also what they mean. On the foundationalist theory, however, all aspects of language understanding rest on the same sensorimotor base as any other type of understanding. If to understand something is to know how to incorporate it into an action plan, then language is like any other tool: one understands by knowing how to use it to accomplish a goal. Semantic understanding, on this view, would be assimilable to other kinds of action and object understanding. As Gendlin says, "Linguistic analysis only looks like an analysis of language. What is actually analyzed is something very different: namely, our 'knowing how to use' words in situations" (Gendlin 1973: 284).

A similar view has recently been propounded by Laurence Nemirow (1995). Understanding in general, he argues, is "knowing how to follow a rule." *Knowing how* to follow linguistic rules is distinct from simply knowing the rules — *knowing that* a language is bound by certain rules, or having a linguistic theory for a particular natural language. In Searle's Chinese Room, the English speaker has a written set of rules which he follows, but having these rules available is not the same thing as having the ability to follow them in the requisite sense. For that, the rules must be internalized so that they 'fuse' with the rest of one's representational system:

> In the beginning, the student [of a language] knows the relevant linguistic rules, but cannot act in accordance with those rules without expressly invoking them — a relatively slow and painstaking process. By the time she reaches the second stage, she has so mastered the rules that she knows how to follow them immediately — without considering their formulation. She then 'understands' the language, in the full sense of the term, precisely because she is no longer rule-bound. She has integrated language and concept. (Nemirow 1995: 41)

Language understanding on this view is acquired similarly to the way one acquires other tool-using skills such as bicycle riding. At the beginning one is consciously aware of the 'rules' — the sorts of things one must do with the tool in various situations — and then the rules become internalized, fusing with the rest of one's abilities. At the end of the first stage the learner *knows that* use of the tool is controlled by certain rules; at the end of the second, the learner *knows how* to use the tool, and hence understands it.

But language requires a more complex analysis than do tools that are not symbols. While with most other tools, understanding consists entirely of mastering the appropriate physical manipulations, the semantic aspect of language seems to be something distinct from the syntactic rules that govern its use. Compare a hammer with the sentence 'Clinton won the 1992 election.' For both, there are occasions when their use is appropriate, and understanding them entails being able to use them correctly on those occasions. In the case of the sentence, however, there seems to be another dimension of understanding: the sentence *expresses a proposition,* which is a thing distinct from any actual or possible use of the sentence, can be true or false, and can be independently understood. There is no equivalent dimension in the case of a nonsymbolic tool. Therefore, semantic understanding seems to require a separate analysis. This requirement has been a huge stumbling-block for a theory of language understanding. Efforts to assimilate semantics to syntax by means of a computer model have failed. While much has been written on the relations between sentences *themselves* and the propositions they express, there is no model yet that provides a unified account of both syntactic and semantic *understanding* on the part of a language user.

I believe that the present theory can provide such a unified account. The key lies in recognizing that language is a tool whose use involves more than one type of goal-directed activity. Language use, even on single occasions, is multifaceted. One uses it to elicit desired behavior in other people, when one is the speaker; one uses it by creating an appropriate mental state in response to instances of the language, when one is the hearer. It is by creating this mental state that we understand the proposition expressed by a sentence. These uses are normally blended when we communicate with others, but they can be distinguished in their relations to different kinds of *nonlinguistic* activities that a language user knows how to perform. On this view, language is nothing but a tool, qualitatively no different from any other except in the complexity of its use. Learning a language is acquiring a set of skills. Some involve overt, public linguistic behavior directed toward hearers; others involve responding mentally and behaviorally to the linguistic behavior of speakers. All of these skills are developments from nonlinguistic abilities.

More specifically, the claim is as follows: language is an implement that induces responses in human beings; these responses include both overt behavior and covert mental states. Understanding a language thus requires both knowing how to use it oneself to induce the desired overt and covert responses in another person, and how to respond appropriately, overtly and covertly, to another person's linguistic behavior. It is because of this complex nature of language understanding that the analogy with nonsymbolic tools is misleading. If that analogy held, then understanding a hammer would have two aspects: knowing how to wield a hammer — to, say, pound a nail — and also knowing how to be hammered — to play the role of the nail. It is precisely this duality that distinguishes symbol understanding from that of other tools. There is, of course, a sense in which one could be said to understand how to be hammered, in that one's body automatically responds appropriately to being hammered: it bruises, etc. But that is a *nonintentional* response, even lower than the level of primitive intentionality of basic action discussed in Chapter Three. On the foundationalist theory of language understanding, the intentionality associated with language is a development out of abilities that are simpler, but equally intentional.

In more formal terms, the present theory of language understanding can be expressed as follows:

(1)   If S understands a language (L), then S can be a producer (P) and a consumer (C) of L.

(2)   S can be a P of L if S knows how to use L to produce a desired response upon a C.

(3)   S can be a C of L if S knows how to respond to L, as used by P, by generating the response desired by P.

In other words, understanding a language is knowing how to perform two distinct types of linguistic actions. If, in line with our general premise, language understanding can be analyzed in terms of basic action understanding, then we must first examine the two types of actions and see how each is derived from, and understood in terms of, basic actions; and second, we must explain how these two types of linguistic actions are related to each other in complete language understanding. We will see that the distinction between the two types of linguistic action is a development from the basic duality in the way an infant understands another person, discussed in the previous chapter. The other person is an *other* (an external object), and yet unlike other objects is understood in the way that the infant understands her *self*.

The remainder of this chapter aims to carry out the above program. We first look at what it is to be a producer and to be a consumer of language, and how each of those activities is understood according to our general account of understanding. We then examine how these roles are combined in full language understanding. Some aspects of the theory follow in a straightforward way from what has already been argued concerning the understanding of actions, objects, and persons. Others, in particular certain claims about the role of mental imagery in language 'consumption,' are less straightforward and more problematic; greater attention will accordingly be devoted to these.

2.   Language production as tool use

Tools, or implements, are objects used in actions to produce desired results. We can classify tool understanding as a type of object understanding, in terms of the analysis in Chapter Four. It was argued there that an object is understood if one can imagine incorporating it into an (understood) action. That definition was a broadening of an earlier candidate: understanding an object is being able to imagine using it as a means for performing an action.

We saw that the earlier candidate was too narrow, excluding objects like items in the landscape that one takes account of in one's action but which are not, strictly speaking, means to a goal. We can, however, use that earlier formulation to characterize the understanding of tools:

> S understands a perceived object O *as a tool* if S is able to imagine using O as a means of performing a token of action-type A, that is already understood, with an image sufficiently rich to serve as a guide in actual performance.

Understanding an object in this way is, of course, dependent upon a prior understanding of action-type A, which includes understanding the goal of that action. The goal of a linguistic action involves another person, not just an external object or a state of oneself; it is for this reason that language is unique as a tool. Before we examine the goal of language use, however, we can see that while language is unlike most other tools in not being a perceived physical object, it is no different from any other tool in being incorporated into an action as a means to the goal of the action.

Language use is often treated by philosophers of language as though it is an end in itself; as though one's primary goal in speaking is to express a thought in language, or to refer to some object or state of affairs. This impression is derived from the common focus upon explaining the relation between linguistic symbols and their referents. But of course one does not normally verbalize without some extralinguistic reason for doing so, or else people would verbalize continuously, without regard for circumstances. To be sure, speaking and understanding others' speech are distinct activities. We might say a language user stands continuously ready, if not to speak, then at least to understand whatever is uttered in her hearing. But even so, the user either tries to ignore, or else tries to follow, what is said — succeeding better or worse at either goal — depending upon other circumstances.

Language, unlike most tools, is abstract, consisting in rules that guide concrete instances of behavior. In that way, instances of a particular natural language are more like action-types than like objects. Thus in defining language as a tool, we must use a broadened characterization: it is not only perceived physical objects that can be tools, but anything, including another action, that is used as a means of performing a given action-type.

If we broaden the characterization of 'tool' in this way, however, then the understanding of the action-type *without* the means becomes an issue. In the previous chapter, we saw that a physical object is understood as a means to performing an action if the action is understood independently of that object. But a given action-type can be a means to performing a token of a more inclusive action type, when the more inclusive action-type is not understood independently of that means. For example, in understanding the action-type of climbing to the top of the stairs from the bottom, I must understand the intermediate stages of climbing the middle steps; on the other hand, climbing the middle steps is a means to climbing to the top. The question is: can an essential part of an action-type also be a means to performing that action-type?

The issue is important because if it is not settled, the account may seem in danger of circularity. It need not be circular, however. In the stair-climbing case we do not need to explain the understanding of stair-climbing as a means independent of the understanding of the action of climbing to the top of the stairs, since we can explain the understanding of stair-climbing as a general action-type as a means to the goal of getting to the top, a goal that does not necessarily involve climbing the steps (one could, for example, use a rope). Likewise, in the language case, if a particular linguistic token is understood as a means to performing a token of a given action-type, and that type must be already understood, then that linguistic token cannot be an essential part of that action-type. There is no difficulty, however, in characterizing any action with a nonlinguistic goal independently of any linguistic acts that it includes as means. If the goal is nonlinguistic, then it can be represented and understood nonlinguistically. For example, suppose my goal is the very general one of conforming to social conventions at a formal reception. This goal is achievable by a large disjunction of intermediate acts, many of which are nonlinguistic, such as smiling and shaking hands at appropriate moments. Or suppose my goal is the more specific one of getting this person to give me a ride home from the reception. Again, I can represent the achievement of that goal independently of any linguistic means of attaining it. It is only our representations of *basic* actions that blend means and ends into seamless wholes. As soon as an action is sufficiently complex to require conscious decisions about means, then the goal must be representable independent of any given means. And if, as argued above, every linguistic act is a means to a nonlinguistic goal, then it is a part of a more comprehensive action-type that can be understood independently of the linguistic acts that may make it possible.

But while the more comprehensive goal must be understandable nonlinguistically, if even one possible means involves the use of language *per se* (and not just, for example, the production of vocal sounds) then there must be prior understanding both of persons and of communication. This is because language use requires that the consumer as well as the producer understand it. Things that understand are persons, and producing understanding in another person is communication.

Any goal that is achievable by language use must thus involve the understanding of both persons and communication. As was argued in Chapter Six, understanding another as a person is achieved by means of metaphorical extension of one's understanding of one's own actions:

> S understands another entity as a person if S can understand the actions of the other entity as she understands her own: by imagining performing them, with an image rich enough to serve as a guide in actual performance.

Understanding another as a person is, in effect, *pretending* that the other is, in certain respects, oneself. (In general, viewing something as *like* another thing is pretending to oneself that it is, in certain respects, the other thing.) From here it is a short step to the understanding of communication, which begins with the built-in ability of an infant to represent the actions of other humans in its supramodal body scheme, and hence to imitate them. When the infant's goal is another's behavioral response to her gesture, and she represents this desired response in her own body scheme, she is at the same time representing what she desires the other to experience (since that experience is a part of her representation). We can thus say that she is communicating an experience to the other person. The states produced in the consumer are understood, by the producer of language, as experiential states: in terms of the way the producer feels when her behavior is of the kind she aims to produce in the other.

3. The neuroanatomy of language production

Language is a rule-governed system of action-types that appears to have evolved for the purpose of affecting the behavior of other persons by means of the production of mental states in them. There is evidence in neuroanatomy of the connection between language use and both tool-making and social interaction. In Chapter Two we examined the work of Lieberman and Greenfield on the relation between grammatical ability and tool-making, and the connection between Broca's area and motor abilities as revealed by deficit studies. If language is primarily a tool for communication, then such connections would be expected.

4.   Language consumption as model construction

 It is clear that conceived as a set of abstract rules that guide specific actions, language is unlike tools that are physical objects, and also that it is like other activities, such as dancing or cooking, that serve as means to more general goals. It is set apart from both by its semantic aspect, to which we turn in this section.

Just as the most common example of language production is speaking, the most common example of consumption is hearing, or being spoken to. The distinction is not cleanly captured in these two roles, however, since a speaker must understand how the hearer will understand what is said, and the hearer must understand the production of the heard speech. For purposes of the present discussion, however, my primary example of the language consumer will be the person who is addressed.

In being hammered, it is appropriate for a nail to remain passive; in being spoken to, however, the hearer is expected to do something. Sometimes the hearer's behavior is nearly automatic, such as an expression of an emotional state ('Don't speak to me!') or a move to advance a social goal unrelated to the semantic content of what is said ('Fine, thank you; how are you?'). Often, however, the appropriate response is not so automatic; then the hearer may engage in creative mental imagery.

5.   Language understanding and imagery

The theory that the decoding aspect of language understanding is a constructive or creative process has been urged by Johnson-Laird and others, as we saw in Chapter Two. Johnson-Laird argues that one actively works at understanding linguistic descriptions by constructing mental models to satisfy the constraints in the description. Johnson-Laird does not hold that these models must be images; he leaves open the question of how they are realized in the brain. Damasio, however, specifies the use of sensory images in cognitive activity. Images, in his view, are firings in sensory cortices generated by activated 'dispositional representations,' codes stored in 'convergence areas' in regions such as the hypothalamus, brain stem, and limbic system.

> Acquired knowledge is based on dispositional representations in higher-order cortices and throughout many gray-matter nuclei beneath the level of the cortex. Some of these dispositional representations contain records for the imageable knowledge that we can recall and which is used for movement, reason, planning, creativity; and some contain records of rules and strategies with which we operate on those images. . . .
>
> The appearance of an image in recall results from the reconstruction of a transient pattern (metaphorically, a map) in early sensory cortices, and the trigger for the reconstruction is the activation of dispositional representations elsewhere in the brain, as in the association cortex. (Damasio 1994: 105)

Damasio argues that "thought is made largely of images:"

> It is often said that thought is made of much more than just images, that it is also made of words and nonimage abstract symbols. Surely nobody will deny that thought includes words and arbitrary symbols. But what this statement misses is the fact that both words and arbitrary symbols are based on topographically organized representations and can become images. Most of the words we use in our inner speech, before speaking or writing a sentence, exist as auditory or visual images in our consciousness. If they did not become images, however fleetingly, they would not be anything we could know. . . . The point, then, is that images are probably the main content of our thoughts, *regardless of the sensory modality in which they are generated* and regardless of whether they are about a thing or a process involving things; or about words or other symbols, in a given language, which correspond to a thing or process. (Damasio 1994: 106-108; italics added)

The theory that thought is made largely of images is plausible only if images are understood to be multimodal; hence the italicization above. Because of the close association between the concepts of images and pictorial representations, which can be dangerously misleading, it is important to pay special attention to the issue at this point in the argument.

6.   Images are multimodal

On the basis of what is now known of the neural basis of imagery, there is no support for the view that an experienced mental image is a visual object, a sort of 'mental picture.' As we saw in Chapter Two, images are activated traces of sensory experiences; they can occur in any modality. When one images, one reactivates an experience, or parts of an experience, that one had previously; an image is a type of episodic memory. This is not to say that memory images are veridical. They do not necessarily correspond to a single past event; as Hume and other associationists noted, we can mix and match elements of past experience in boundless creativity, and often created images are mistaken for episodic memories of actual events. Because images are not only visual I can form an image of drinking milk that tastes like wine; I can form an image of a familiar pain in my foot, or of the sound of my mother's voice saying things she never said. And as we have seen, one forms motor images when planning actions.

An interesting suggestion about the use of imagery in an unusual modality is made by Ellis (1995). Ellis argues that one way students may learn to recognize common inference patterns in logic is through rhythm-pattern imagery.

> Once the students can recognize the patterns in a *visual* diagram, then they have to learn to recognize the same pattern in a *temporal rhythm* which they hear or imagine hearing when someone speaks an argument. . . . For instance, . . . we could say that 'this implies that; this; therefore that' is *modus ponens,* whereas 'this implies that; that; therefore this' is the fallacy of affirming the consequent. . . . We can hear these temporal rhythms just as we would hear a recognizable pattern in music. (Ellis 1995: 83-84)

Rhythm pattern imagery may also be a factor in counting. For example, one may forget to pay attention while counting objects, even though one continues to count. The final number can sometimes be retrieved, however, (if it is low enough) by means of a trace of the unique rhythm pattern of the counted number that lingers in working memory.

7.   The descriptionalist challenge

The view that images are purely visual has led to erroneous beliefs about cognition. Many have argued against an imagery theory of thought, and in favor of a descriptionalist theory, on the grounds that the pictorial nature of visual images limits in various ways their usefulness in representation (Pylyshyn 1978). For one thing, indeterminacy in some particular respect may be a feature of some representations, but while descriptions can be indeterminate, visual images are determinate. Thus if I think of a tiger I think of an animal with an indeterminate number of stripes, but in a picture or a visual image of a tiger the stripes are countable. For another thing, a description can contain information that a visual image cannot. An example is given by Dennett:

> Another familiar puzzle is Wittgenstein's duck-rabbit, the drawing that now looks like a duck, now looks like a rabbit. What can possibly be the difference between seeing it first one way and then the other? The image (on paper or on the retina) does not change, but there can be more than one description of that image. (Dennett 1969: 137)

The point is that while there is a difference between seeing the drawing as a duck and seeing it as a rabbit, that difference is captured only in the description. In his discussion of this example, however, Dennett overlooks another difference. A constraint upon one's experience of seeing the picture is that one cannot see the two aspects *simultaneously* ; as with the Necker cube, one must switch from one to the other. That constraint is not captured in the description: one can refer in a single description to a figure which depicts both a duck and a rabbit. Therefore, each mode of representation appears to have a constraint that the other lacks.

A view of imagery that goes beyond the visual can incorporate both constraints: the difference between the two aspects, and the inability to see both at once. To see this, one can simply note by introspection what it is that changes when one switches from seeing a duck to seeing a rabbit. A major difference between the two aspects is the orientation of the figure in each case: as a rabbit it looks (say) to one's left, and as a duck to one's right. Noting this difference entails a reference to the viewer's position and bodily orientation *vis a vis* that of the figure. This reference to the viewer's spatial location is more highly structured in the case of the Necker cube: on one interpretation the viewer is above and to the right, and on the other below and to the left.

The point is a very general one: an experience of seeing something is not just a visual experience. In seeing an object one is aware, not only of various nonvisual features of what is seen, such as any sound, smell, etc., but also of various aspects of one's own body, in particular one's spatial location and state of motion relative to the object. These bodily experiences are part of understanding what it is that is seen, as Evans explains.

If that is the case, then having an image of a seen object is likewise not just a visual experience. If one images an object as having a particular spatial location and orientation, then the spatial location and orientation of one's body relative to the imaged object is part of what one imagines experiencing. In experiencing, or imagining experiencing, one's spatial properties, one must activate nonvisual bodily representations. The basis of the view that imagery cannot distinguish between a duck and a rabbit in the example is the mistake of thinking of 'an image' as one thinks of 'a picture.' But an image is not a picture, it is an experience. If it is a visual image, then it is an experience of seeing, but seeing is not having a purely visual experience.

The same mistake lies at the root of the claim that a description, but not an image, can represent an indeterminate number of stripes on a tiger. While it is true that one could (probably) count the number of stripes in a clear picture of a tiger, or on a clearly seen tiger, it does not follow that one could count the stripes *'on an image'* of a tiger, since an image is an experience, not a picture. One can surely have an experience of a tiger as having an indeterminate number of stripes; one simply has a *visual impression* of stripes. Visual impressions are experiences that cause one to think something has certain visual properties, without enabling one clearly to identify the precise defining boundaries of those properties.

Thinking of an image as an experience rather than as a picture allows us to explain how an image can represent *select aspects* of an object, in very general terms. A visual experience involves the experience of attending to specific aspects of what is seen. Visual attention is thought to be accomplished in the brain by means of cortico-thalamic connections, which subject certain visual features to enhanced processing activity (Crick 1984; see also Crick and Koch 1990). This heightened activity increases the salience of particular aspects of the visual field, and the accompanying experience of *attending to* those aspects is a familiar one. Imagery can reproduce the heightened activity, and hence the experience of attention, as well as the more purely visual features of the experience (Farah 1989). There are, however, other problems with the representation by images of indeterminate states of affairs; these are discussed below.

Finally, we should note that images have an affective aspect. If I form an image of a shark appearing in the water while I am swimming, a sense of fear will be part of the experience I imagine having. The distinction between imaged emotions and 'real' ones is not so clear as that between images and other sorts of sensations. Emotions are activated similarly by novel experiences and remembered ones (LeDoux 1992).

In what follows, the term 'image' will be used without any prior assumptions as to modality. The term will be used to refer to the mental creation of a sensory experience, with the understanding that such an experience can include proprioceptive sensations, motor imagery and emotions, as well as visual, auditory, olfactory, and tactile sensations.

8.   Understanding and image creation

Suppose someone is describing her new house to you by saying such things as 'When you go in the front door, there are stairs going up on the right, with a closet to the left of them;' to make sense of the description you try to picture what she must be thinking of. You probably picture the door of the closet on the left side of the wall facing the front door, as it would appear to you if you stood at the front door. But if she then says 'Opposite the closet door is the door to the dining room, on your left' now you may switch to an image of the stairs coming out of the right wall, with the closet, also on the right wall, beyond them. As long as what she says is what you would say if describing a given scenario, you will accept an image of that scenario as representing what she is talking about.

Johnson-Laird and others have proposed that the understanding of discourse proceeds by the construction of mental models, analogical representational structures created by the language consumer in response to linguistic expressions (see discussion in Chapter Two). These structures represent domains, possibly abstract ones, in which the entities referred to are located and in which they interact. These models are constructed by procedures on the basis of the meanings of expressions; this 'procedural semantics' relates language, "not to the world, but to mental models" (Johnson-Laird, 1983: 248). As we have seen, mental model theorists do not specify that models must be mental images; there is a close relation between models and images, however:

> There is plainly a relation between images and mental models, and I shall assume that images correspond to *views* of models: as a result either of perception or imagination, they represent the perceptible features of the corresponding real-world objects. In imagining, say, a rotating object, the underlying mental model of the object is used to recover a representation of its surfaces, reflectances, and so forth — what the late David Marr (1982), in referring to the process of perception, called the '2 1/2-D sketch.' (Johnson-Laird 1983: 157)

Since our general topic is *conscious* understanding, we are particularly interested in the imageable aspect of mental models. The present theory holds that novel things are understood in terms of things already understood. If I am aware of understanding a description of a novel state of affairs, then I am consciously relating it to a state of affairs that is familiar. Thus the image I create will be composed of elements from my previous experience, related to each other in ways that I am familiar with. I have not seen a room exactly like the one you describe to me, but every element in your description *that I am able to understand* corresponds to something in my previous experience.

The above account may seem unobjectionable when applied to our understanding of determinate, physical states of affairs. There are serious objections, however, to the claim that everything can be understood by the construction of images. One is an obvious one: most of the time, we are not only unaware of using imagery, but fail to discover it upon introspection. Many people heatedly deny using imagery in the ways described.

Ralph Ellis has pointed out a feature of imagining that explains this unawareness: we can become aware that we understand something on the basis of the initiation of the imaging process followed by the *inhibition of irrelevant aspects of the image*. Ellis discusses the inhibition of imagery in connection with our ability to understand states of affairs by means of subjunctive conditionals: the understanding of what *would* happen if I were to perform various physical actions in the context of that state of affairs:

> When we say that we have 'understood' a situation, we therefore mean that we have succeeded in imagining the essential conditions which would allow us to feel confident of being able to predict what will or would happen, while inhibiting our imagination of the irrelevant aspects. This involves truncating efferent neurological responses so that only the ones corresponding to more general characteristics of objects are allowed to occur. And this is true whether the concept is a causal one or merely the concept of a unitary entity or relation. Even when we imagine a unitary entity, such as a physical object, we are imagining what would happen if we were to manipulate it in various ways. (Ellis 1995: 82)

A truncated act of imagining provides the sense that we understand something in giving us the confidence that we *could* imagine it in detail. Just as I can see a puddle and feel confident that I could jump across it, while having no intention of doing so, in the same way I can know that I could construct a detailed sensorimotor image while not actually doing so. The result is a feeling of understanding that is founded upon imagery construction without actually involving fully realized images; this result is compatible with the unawareness or outright denial of imagery by those unfamiliar with the sensorimotor theory of cognition.

Two further difficulties stand out: indeterminate states of affairs, and abstract entities.

9.   Imagery and indeterminacy

We have already discussed briefly the claim that an image cannot represent an indeterminate state of affairs. It was argued that if images are treated as experiences rather than as pictures, then a particular image, such as that of a striped tiger, can be indeterminate in some respects. In the case of understanding discourse, however, mental models may be unavoidably determinate in a way that conflicts with other requirements of the representation. In the example at the beginning of the previous section, the description of the room initially prompted one image, but that image had to be revised with the addition of more detail. This means that the initial parts of the description were indeterminate in certain details; nevertheless, a determinate (and incorrect) image was constructed to represent it. Does this complication render implausible the present account of the understanding of descriptions?

Not on the view of Johnson-Laird, who considers the reconstruction of images as one standard way of coping with indeterminacy. When you describe something to me, I will construct a likely image, standing ready to revise it if necessary. This process can be demanding and confusing, however, and there are alternatives. One is to construct alternative models; this method, however, can lead to a combinatorial explosion of possibilities, and would work only for small numbers of possibilities. Another is to introduce a 'proposition-like element of notation into an analogical model' by some sort of mental 'tagging' of elements in the analogical representation (Johnson-Laird, 1983: 164). While there is no single foolproof and efficient method of constructing models in response to indeterminate descriptions, this fact is not an argument against the mental model theory of language understanding, since such understanding can be difficult in exactly the ways predicted by the indeterminacy problem. We struggle to understand someone whose descriptions are imprecise, we interrupt and request specifics, we express our confusion. In light of the prevalence of *misunderstanding*, the intrinsic determinacy of particular mental models as compared to descriptions should be viewed as support for the theory, rather than as counterevidence.

10. Imagery and abstraction

Another common objection to the mental model theory concerns the representation of abstract entities and states of affairs. Suppose someone is explaining a mathematical function to you, and you are trying to understand it. What possible images could apply here?

While the view that images cannot represent abstractions is a common one, there is a long tradition of responses to it. They can be divided roughly into two types. One is that concrete images can be used to represent abstract entities by means of an abstraction process on the part of the subject, who limits the use of the concrete image in ways corresponding to the definition of the abstraction. For example, while in thinking of triangularity in general I can form an image only of a particular triangle, I can still use this image in calculations involving triangularity in general either by *ignoring* features applying only to this imaged particular, or by first initiating and then truncating the process of imaging a particular triangle, as described above.

The other type of response takes the bull by the horns, declaring that abstract entities can be represented directly by images that are primarily nonvisual. This approach has become more popular in recent years, beginning with the work of Lakoff (1987) and Johnson (1987), and finding support in the neurosciences. Lakoff and Johnson, as we saw in Chapter Two, argue that meaning on all levels is created by 'image schematic structures' derived from basic experiences of embodied action. These structures define basic actions and also higher-level conceptual structures, including abstract ones, that are meaningful for us. Lakoff explains the roles of these structures:

(1)   There are at least two kinds of structure in our preconceptual experi-
       ences:

       A. Basic-level structure: Basic-level categories are defined by the
           convergence of our gestalt perception, our capacity for bodily
           movement, and our ability to form rich mental images.

B. Kinesthetic image-schematic structure: Image schemas are relatively simple structures that constantly recur in our everyday experience: CONTAINERS, PATHS, LINKS, FORCES, BALANCE, and in various orientations and relations: UP-DOWN, PART-WHOLE, CENTER-PERIPHERY, etc.

These structures are directly meaningful, first, because they are directly and repeatedly experienced because of the nature of the body and its mode of functioning in our environment. . . .

(2) There are two ways in which abstract conceptual structure arises from basic-level and image-schematic structure:

A. By metaphorical projection from the domain of the physical to abstract domains.
B. By the projections from basic-level categories to super- ordinate and subordinate categories. (Lakoff 1987: 267-68)

Lakoff specifically applies this theory to the foundations of mathematics, citing Saunders MacLane on the origins of the various mathematical structures:

The real nature of these structures does not lie in their often artificial construction from set theory, but in their relation to mathematical ideas or to basic human activities . . . mathematics is not the study of intangible Platonic worlds, but of tangible formal systems which have arisen from real human activities. (MacLane 1981: 470)

The claim is that for any conceptual structure to be meaningful, one must grasp it in terms of structures that are already meaningful in one's own experience, and these will be sensorimotor structures. In particular, meaningful representations of abstract concepts are composed of kinesthetic images. We have already seen that such nonvisual images are available for action-planning and movement control (Jeannerod 1995); all that is required beyond that is the ability to use such images in abstract contexts as well. We have also noted recent work on the cerebellum, indicating that its mechanisms, evolved for motor control, are involved in abstract reasoning processes (Leiner, Leiner, and Dow, 1993). Thus in light of all this work, we can claim strong support for the view that the understanding of abstract structures is founded upon the understanding of embodied ones.

11. Imagery and mental models

With the broadened view of imagery defended above, we can now combine the mental model theory with an imagery theory of representation; we can, in other words, defend the claim that understanding language as a consumer can involve constructing mental models out of sensorimotor structures drawn from experience. When language is used to describe a state of affairs, the consumer understands the description in terms of her own sensorimotor activities in analogous situations. Even when the descriptions refer to completely novel and/or abstract entities and relations, these can be understood by being modeled as entities and relations familiar to the consumer. These will be, at root, embodied states, involving actions by the consumer incorporating perceived physical objects, stored and reactivated as image schemas.

On this view, understanding a description of an abstract theory involves processes essentially the same as those involved in understanding a description of a physical scenario, like the entrance to the friend's house in the example above. This is true because any state of affairs we can understand, however abstract, involves a domain consisting of entities and their interrelations, which can be represented by the image schemas developed for physical actions on physical objects. A domain is a space, to use Fauconnier's (1985) term. Whether the space contains trees, numbers, clashing ideologies, or Plato's Forms, we know how to represent it, and we understand the logical rules its inhabitants must obey.

If our way of understanding descriptions in language is really so simple and universal, one might suppose that introspection would reveal to every subject the common representational medium. In fact, however, the enormous disagreement about this medium makes sense in light of the creative and individual element in an act of understanding. In response to your description, I construct my mental model from my own experience, in a way that is meaningful to me. The details of the elements in any construction will be unique to the subject, who selects from an indefinite number of possible images in a variety of different modalities, all equally capable of representing what the speaker is talking about in ways adequate for the hearer's purposes. The more abstract the state of affairs described, the greater the number of kinds of images that will serve. An individual's description of her particular interpretation of an abstract description may thus fail to highlight the underlying structural similarities to that of another individual, unless the two already subscribe to the sensorimotor theory of understanding. Individuals differ, moreover, in the salience of their imagery on a given occasion or in general. In the case of kinesthetic imagery in particular, it is easy to overlook it, since such imagery is probably a constant part of one's background experience.

The individual, creative elements of a given mental model do not, it must be emphasized, render them incommunicable. They are always constrained by the structural demands of what is interpreted. Mental models, however they are subjectively experienced, can be represented in terms of stereotypical actions and relations, corresponding to the objective structures of the linguistic material under interpretation.[1] Thus communication between two individuals can never be complete. The greater the constraints, however, of the structural elements upon possible interpretive imagery, the more successful it will be.

To summarize: there are two general aspects to language understanding. The user understands both how to produce it and how to consume it. Understanding the former requires the understanding of two more fundamental components of language use: the user understands language as a tool, and also understands other persons as beings, like herself, who respond to stimuli with experiences as well as behavior. Language is understood as a tool specifically for inducing desired experiences and behavior in other people.

The consumer responds to the language of the producer by means of appropriate overt behavior and also by constructing a mental model in response to the producer's description. The mental model is constructed from image schemas derived from the consumer's embodied experience. It is the familiarity of these image schemas to the consumer that constitutes an important part of the consumer's experience of understanding what the producer is talking about. In this way 'knowing that' the producer is talking about such and such is based upon 'knowing how' to respond to the producer.

12. Combining the two aspects of language understanding

The two aspects of language understanding seem on the surface to be opposites. The producer's understanding is objective: language is a tool for producing an effect upon another being. The consumer's understanding is subjective: language arouses an experiential state. But in spite of this opposition, we want to be able to say that the producer understands language as consumed; the consumer understands it as produced. How are these blends of the subjective and the objective achieved?

The subjective and objective aspects of language understanding can be combined in the same way as the corresponding aspects of the understanding of persons. A person is an *other*, meaning an object external to the subject; at the same time a person is one *like oneself*, whose actions are represented, by an infant, in its supramodal body scheme. In our understanding of other persons the subjective and objective are blended: a person is an *other* that we understand *from the inside*, as we understand ourselves. On the basis of this blend, other subjective/objective composites are possible — specifically, language use. In using language as a tool upon another person, I simultaneously represent the effect that my use of the tool will have on the other; I represent it as consumed. That means that I represent the way in which I would understand my words, if they were said to me. That understanding forms part of my understanding of how to use language as a tool upon another person. In understanding language as a tool used upon me, I construct a mental model of the state of affairs the language represents, and I simultaneously represent the producer as another person who desires that I construct that mental model, or a similar one. In other words, as a producer I must represent the consumer, and as a consumer the producer, both objectively and subjectively.

This ability to represent another both subjectively and objectively is what Gordon (1986) calls 'simulation.' The simulation theory is intended to explain our folk psychology, or our understanding of the propositional attitudes of others — that they believe, fear, desire what it is that they describe. When, in a conversation with you, I attribute a belief to Smith, I am inviting you to engage with me in a game of pretending to be Smith:

> Stepping into Smith's shoes I might say: 'Dewey won the election.' Such assertions may then be used as premises of simulated practical inference. But wouldn't it be a great advantage to us practical simulators if we could *pool our resources*? We'll simulate Smith *together*, cooperatively, advising one another as to what premises or practical inputs to practical reasoning would work best for a simulation of Smith. . . . Of course, I couldn't come straight out with the utterance: 'Dewey won.' I need to flag the utterance as one that is being uttered *from within a Smith-simulation mode* and addressed to *your* Smith-simulation mode. I might do this by saying something like the following:

1. Let's do a Smith simulation. Ready? *Dewey won the election.*

The same task might be accomplished by saying,

2. *Smith believes that* Dewey won the election.

My suggestion is that (2) be read as saying the same thing as (1), though less explicitly. (Gordon 1986: 167)

In this description we see the two different aspects of language understanding at work together. Objective language behavior elicits subjective language behavior; the words induce the hearer to engage in a creative mental activity. The ability to simulate Smith in response to the words 'Smith believes . . .' constitutes the understanding of those words. The same process can explain the understanding of other types of linguistic content: what you probably 'have in mind' if you make certain claims, describe some state of affairs. It can also explain how I understand what I am doing when addressing another. I represent my action as having the goal of inducing certain behavior on the part of the (objective) other; I also represent the subjective state of the other when he responds to my words.

How are these multi-aspectual representations effected coherently? It is clear that when I represent both the state of affairs that you describe to me, and you as a goal-directed language producer, I am representing entities in two quite distinct contexts, and this distinction must itself be represented. If, for example, you are telling me about the actions of another person, I cannot represent that other person and you the present speaker as coexisting in the same domain. The mental 'spaces' idea, introduced by Fauconnier (1985) and developed further by Dinsmore (1987), suggests a promising solution. Mental spaces, which are 'domains used for consolidating certain kinds of information' (Dinsmore 1987: 2), represent specific contexts. Dinsmore explains the process of 'knowledge partitioning' and its relation to simulation:

The process of distributing knowledge over spaces according to context will be called *knowledge partitioning* . For instance, the knowledge that George believes *p* is represented by the assertion of *p* in a 'George believes that' space. Knowledge partitioning seems to belong to the processes by which mental models are constructed in Johnson-Laird's (1983) theory. The reciprocal process of using contexts to access knowledge, thereby realizing global consequences of simulative reasoning, will be called *context climbing*. For instance, if *q* has been derived in George's belief space relative to the real world, and is therefore represented there as true, then by context climbing the proposition that George believes that q is available as a true proposition in the real world. (Dinsmore 1987: 7)

The process of assigning new information acquired during discourse to the proper space does not require that each new item be explicitly tagged; the appropriate space can be implicit:

> The same kinds of inferencing involved in processing discourse about the real world would seem to be involved in processing discourses about other spaces, since the structures of the discourses seem to be similar. I will call the space with respect to which a discourse is understood the *focus* space for that discourse. The most obvious kind of example is provided in fictional discourses. However, another interesting example is found in a discourse that is initiated like this:
>
> > (1) Arthur believes it is the duty of everyone to fight what he thinks is an invasion of space frogs. Before this situation gets out of hand, every homeowner should defrog his own yard, taking care to _____
>
> After the initial shift in focus space, the discourse could continue indefinitely with the implicit understanding that we are talking about Arthur's belief space rather than about the real world. This space has become active and inference processes relevant to discourse understanding apply locally to this domain. (Dinsmore 1987: 13)

Dinsmore goes on to apply the model to the understanding of conditionals, counterfactuals, and to problems involving presuppositions, and he indicates that the model might support analogical and metaphorical reasoning. The sensorimotor theory of understanding, of course, holds that all reasoning that is not about one's own immediate goal-directed actions is metaphorical, and hence that in principle the mental spaces model will be adequate for all such reasoning, including that involving abstract domains. Representations of logical or mathematical domains are constructed by means of the same image schemata, to use the term of Lakoff and Johnson, as are used in representing physical domains. Thus consider an example similar to Dinsmore's case of Arthur's belief in space frogs: 'Goldbach believed that every even number is the sum of two primes. Any number ending in 0, 2, 4, 6, or 8 can be written as the sum of two numbers such that . . . ;' the statement would continue by defining prime numbers. Understanding such statements involves processes identical to those described by Dinsmore, except that the space devoted to what

Goldbach believes is constructed from sensorimotor image schemas representing numbers and relations between them, rather than physical scenarios such as frogs on lawns.

13. Neural correlates of knowledge partitioning

Single mental models can be realized in the brain through the activation of image schemas, and these, in turn, through the mechanisms proposed by Damasio: the "reconstruction of a transient pattern (metaphorically, a map) in early sensory cortices, [triggered by] the activation of dispositional representations elsewhere in the brain" (Damasio 1994: 105). But what sort of imagery could be associated with the representation of distinct contexts, or 'spaces?'

While details remain vague, enough is known about the action-planning functions of the frontal lobes to justify speculation that the answer will be found there. Complex action-planning would require just the sort of partitioning of knowledge that is proposed for language-understanding. Action-planning involves the consideration of alternative possible actions and outcomes. Representing these would require that the relevant knowledge be assigned to the appropriate contexts, by means of 'spaces' and rules for interrelating them. Reasoning about actions and outcomes would take place within these distinct spaces. The close similarity between action-planning and knowledge representation in this particular respect is, of course, what one would predict on the basis of the sensorimotor theory of understanding.

Notes

1.   I am grateful to Maxim Stamenov for this observation.

CHAPTER EIGHT

The Elements of Conscious Experience

1.   The phenomenality of conscious experience

When we are aware of understanding some aspect of the world that confronts us, we have an experience that is like the experience of performing a familiar, goal-directed action. Memory images of past actions involving physical objects some of which (persons) we understand by imitation, are blended with contemporary sensorimotor input: the result is our ubiquitous sense of being at home in the world. The goal of this book has been to elaborate and defend that claim.

Throughout the discussion I have made ready use of references to conscious experience. I have avoided defining consciousness, and instead relied on the reader's familiarity with certain types of experiences (such as the 'Aha!' experience) as a phenomenological base for many of my claims. The time has come to fulfill the promise made in Chapter 1: to offer some account of how such experiences can exist in the first place. Even if my descriptions of what understanding 'is like' are acceptable, we still need to ask the question: *why is understanding like anything at all?* Or, more generally, what is it for experience to be like something?

Phenomenal consciousness, as noted in the introduction, is most frequently discussed with respect to sensory experience, particularly the experience of color. In this book our focus has been on the experience of imagery: activated traces of past sensorimotor experience. Can conscious imagery be understood in terms of mechanisms similar to those at work in conscious perception?

The brain mechanisms of imagery and perception appear to be highly similar (Farah 1989). Imagery and perception are inseparable components of cognition; in effect, they are two sides of a single coin. First, imagery is necessary for the conscious perception of novel sensory stimuli, as is pointed out by Ralph Ellis:

> Seeing occurs only when we *attend to* (i.e. *look for*) the object on which we are to focus. And *looking for* involves asking the question about a concept or image, 'Is this concept or image instantiated by what is in my visual field right now?' (Ellis 1995: 3)

Recognizing what is seen requires mapping input onto memory traces of similar objects; hypotheses regarding neuroscientific details of the process have been proposed by Damasio (1994) and Edelman (1989). These proposals will be discussed later in this chapter.

The other side of the coin is the dependence of imagery upon novel input. This process is not so well documented as the former, but it is entailed by the distinction between images and hallucinations — and by the subject's ability to distinguish between imagery and perception. My awareness that I am entertaining images is made possible in part by a mismatch between the memory traces and my current sensory and proprioceptive input: I know I am only *imagining* swimming in the ocean, because I am aware that I am *actually* sitting at my desk. I know, moreover, that it is *I myself* who am imagining: conscious imagery, like conscious perception, appears to involve self-consciousness. Sensory deprivation experiments, in which previously normal subjects quickly begin to hallucinate, make clear how tenuous is this anchoring in reality.

Damasio summarizes the relation between memory representations and novel somatosensory input:

> Although the early sensory cortices and the topographically organized representations they form are necessary for images to occur in consciousness, they do not, however, appear to be sufficient. In other words, if our brains would simply generate fine topographically organized representations and do nothing else with those representations, I doubt we would ever be conscious of them as images. How would we ever know they are *our* images? Subjectivity, a key feature of consciousness, would be missing from such a design. Other conditions must be met.
>
> In essence those neural representations must be correlated with those which, moment by moment, constitute the neural basis for the self. (Damasio 1994: 99)

Because of this interdependence between internally generated input and external input, an account of conscious perception will also be an account of conscious imagery. This chapter offers such an account. The goal is to confront, not the specific content of individual phenomenal experiences, but what we might call the 'phenomenality' of those experiences: what it is for experience to have phenomenal qualities in the first place. The real problem is not what our experiences 'are like,' but why they 'are like' *anything at all.*

The 'phenomenality' of experience is such a mysterious property that it frequently slips aside unnoticed, even in the most straightforward attempts to explain consciousness. For example, Churchland (1985) conflates the properties of the *content* of qualitative experience with the property of *being* a qualitative experience in a criticism of Nagel:

> What interests me is [Nagel's] claim that reductions of various substances elsewhere in science *exclude the phenomenal features of the substance.*
> This is simply false. . . . The phenomenal features at issue are those such as the objective redness of an apple. . . . Redness, an objective property of apples, is identical with a certain wavelength triplet of electro-magnetic reflectance efficiencies.(Churchland 1985: 18)

But given an ambiguity in 'phenomenal features,' Nagel's claim is not false of existing reductionist theories, which do fail to explain the phenomenality of phenomenal properties.

When this phenomenality is not overlooked, it is sometimes viewed from the other extreme, by those whom Flanagan terms the 'New Mysterians,' as being quite beyond the reach of any logically or nomologically possible physical theory. For example, David Chalmers argues that "We know that a theory of consciousness requires the addition of something fundamental to our ontology, as everything in physical theory is compatible with the absence of consciousness" (Chalmers, 1995: 214). While Chalmers' position is novel in some respects, it is based upon an ambiguity so widespread that it is worth our while to examine it.

We do not know the premise of the Chalmers argument quoted above, and its author does not defend it. Instead, he defends a related claim: that the cognitive and behavioral *functions* of conscious experience are not identical with that experience:

> To see this, note that even when we have explained the performance of all the cognitive and behavioral functions in the vicinity of experience — perceptual discrimination, categorization, internal access, verbal report — there may still

remain a further unanswered question: *Why is the performance of these functions accompanied by experience?* A simple explanation of the functions leaves this question open. (Chalmers 1995: 208)

There is some confusing slippage between two ways Chalmers talks about explanation of functions. If by a 'simple explanation' Chalmers means an explanation at the functional level — an explanation of the causal role of the functions — then experience remains unexplained. But if he means instead what he states on the previous page — that the performance of a function is explained 'by specifying a mechanism that performs the function (1995: 207) — then it is not at all obvious that an explanation of the functions would not account for experience. It might well be that experience is a natural and predictable physical product of the *mechanism* that performs the function. Our functional-level understanding of experience might not reach down far enough to include that feature of the mechanism. So Chalmers' claim that everything in physical theory is compatible with the absence of consciousness is unsupported.

The mechanisms underlying the functions of conscious experience are not, of course, completely understood. Neuroscientific theories about categorization of environmental stimuli, integration of information (the 'binding problem'), and the focus of attention are in their early stages. Nevertheless, enough is now known that Mysterianism should no longer be an attractive option.

2.   Characterizing conscious experience

Before we can evaluate the likelihood of a physical explanation of conscious experience, we need a precise conception of the phenomenon. While in what follows I confine myself to the terminology of visual experience, the reader should keep in mind that my general descriptions of conscious experience apply not only to sensory modalities other than vision, but also to the experience of imagery in all modalities. The neural relations between imagery and sensory experience will be made explicit further on.

Four features of conscious perceptual experience can be distinguished. First, there is the *externality* of the entire content of experience. It is always experienced as 'out there,' not just as a component of the mind of the subject. This feature may not seem applicable to imagery, but only to novel sensory experience. Images, however, also possess an externality: imaging is having an experience like that of perceiving something in the external physical world. Having a visual image is seeming to see a real external object, not an imaginary object; imagining a headache is seeming to have a pain in one's *head*, not in one's *mind*.

Second, there is the *unity* of the objects of perceptual experience and their properties. We see, e.g., a red ball resting on a green surface, rather than redness, roundness, etc. as isolated elements.

To naive observers there may seem nothing remarkable in these features of externality and unity, simply because they appear not as features of experience but as actual properties of its *objects* — that is, of the external (real or imagined) world. But those who are scientifically literate know that these are not objective properties of external objects, but of the way these objects appear to us. Different brain cells respond to different features of objects, and process them independently at early stages. In spite of this knowledge, however, we are unable to experience properties like color and shape otherwise than as external, unitary properties. These features, therefore, are cognitively-impenetrable features of conscious experience itself.

Third, there is the self-awareness that accompanies conscious perceptual experience, the basis for Cartesian claims about the *reflexivity* of consciousness. Fourth, and unavoidably, there is the ineffability of *awareness itself.*

Externality and unity (and, I shall argue, the self) are experienced as features of the content of perceptual experience. But they are not properties that identify individual phenomena, as are the properties of colors described in theories like Churchland's; they are common to all phenomenal objects as phenomena, and hence belong to general descriptions of perceptual and imaginative consciousness (always consciousness of something), and not just of its objects considered in themselves. Awareness *itself*, unlike its content, has no describable phenomenology except for temporal duration. Nevertheless, it needs to be accounted for explicitly. In what follows I examine these features and describe neural processes that might explain them. Common to all these processes is the *blending,* by what Edelman calls 'reentrant signaling,' of the results of parallel perceptual and memory processes into a unified representation such that the components are phenomenologically indistinguishable. (The blending in the brain of individually processed components into one representation is analogous to distributed representation in connectionist systems, in which the activity of individual nodes contributes to a single state of the whole.) This blending accounts in various ways, I shall argue, for the apparent externality of phenomenal properties, for the unification of separately processed aspects of external objects, for the self-awareness in conscious perception, and ultimately for the presence of all of these features in a higher-order awareness.

3. Externality

Contrary to the hopes of Churchland and other reductionists, sensory phenomena seem incapable of being experienced as brain properties. Try to see the red of the book in front of you as a property of your brain! Colors are essentially visual phenomena, and we cannot (normally) see our brains with our own visual mechanisms. I can learn to think about my brain when I see red, but I cannot thereby affect the phenomenology of red. Sensory properties are *not like* brain properties.

Hardin argues that the colors we see are not objective properties of physical objects, nor are they reducible to brain states. They are illusions caused by brain states, to which our color *experiences* are reducible (Hardin 1988: 111). Hardin's approach is truer to the phenomenology of color than is Churchland's: if color *experience* is reducible, then we should not expect scientific knowledge to remove the illusion, as indeed it seems incapable of doing. Churchland thinks that the illusion that qualia are *not* brain states is caused by a false psychological theory. But if Hardin is right then the illusion is 'wired-in,' and hence can be explained but not abandoned.

Hardin has not explained it. He cannot, of course, be faulted for that. Here I point out something misleading in what his work may seem to imply: that explanation of the phenomenality of color experience will involve more detailed accounts of mechanisms underlying specifically *color* phenomena. The illusion involves more than just color.

Consider phenomenal properties in all modalities. All, say reductionists, are explicable in terms of brain states, but all involve some 'illusion' that they emanate from an external physical object — which may include parts of the subject's physical body accessible by proprioception as well as by the external senses. They differ in the ways in which they seem to be 'in' the object. Colors seem both to originate and to remain entirely in the surface of external objects; tastes and smells seem to come from objects but take form in our mouths and noses; sounds and textures seem to be both in the objects and in our bodies. Pain is entirely in our bodies (Newton 1989). We can explain these differences partly in terms of the amount of bodily information transmitted along with other data. In the case of taste, along with the qualities of sweet and sour we can distinguish changes in the state of the tongue. Sounds of different frequencies cause felt vibrations and can hurt our ears. Color is an extreme case: while color experience begins with an effect on the eyes, it does not make us directly aware of them; they feel the same no matter what color we see. Colors stay in the external world. Thus part of the illusory nature of color is its location. We can now see why color is such a prominent example of phenomenal mystery: in it, the illusion of externality is at its most extreme.

The other part of the illusion involves what it is that seems to be located in the external world. Color is a homogeneous expanse with an intrinsic nature not analyzable into relations or quantities of components of the expanse, nor reducible to relations among different expanses. The features of color experience known to be products of brain processing are the very ones that seem firmly attached to external objects. When the retinal cones are stimulated they respond with firing patterns that eventually 'become' the colors that we see. We are justified in saying, with Hardin, that red is the product of a higher brain process, when input from the cones is read together with other visual input to produce the final seen color. As such a product, *and* as the object of conscious awareness, red can be described as a mental entity. But what we inexorably see *as a property of the external world* is this product of internal processes. In other words, there is a sense in which, in seeing a red object we are *seeing a subjective, or mental,* state.

Colors are not always experienced as colors of external objects; viz. phosphenes or after images. Nevertheless, there is no color experience that is not a visual experience (Hardin 1988: 95). So while some color experiences are not *object* experiences, all constitute the illusion that we are looking at an external colored expanse. This remains true even when we know that we are not *actually* looking at such a thing.

The illusion of externality may account in part for the so-called 'reflexivity' of conscious experience, the feature that tempts philosophers like Nagel to speak as if we can be aware of subjective properties of our own experience. Since Descartes, self-consciousness has been justifiably described as the direct awareness of our own mental states. Most prominently in color, but notably in all sensory modalities (including proprioception) what we are aware of in conscious experience cannot be captured by accounts of the external (or bodily) conditions causing the experience since the object of awareness includes *the having of* the experience. But neither can accounts of the external conditions *plus* the direct neural responses to them, since these responses are always experienced *as* external conditions. So a reductionist account of this feature of experience must explain how the result of the neural response to external conditions is always experienced as if it itself is a feature of the external conditions.

Several groups of scientists have drawn attention to types of brain structure which might underlie the conscious experience of externality. They are interested in the multiple back projections or feedback loops carrying signals from higher to lower areas processing sensory input. Vernon Mountcastle (1978) and Gerald Edelman (1978, 1987) (see also Changeux, 1985) have made general proposals that such loops, or 'reentrant signals,' may underlie consciousness. Francis Crick (1984), Christof Koch (1985, 1987), and others (for discussion see P.S. Churchland, 1986: 474-478), focus on pathways from the visual cortex back to the lateral geniculate nucleus (LGN), which they suggest may explain visual attention, or the 'search-light' in Crick's phrase. My discussion will start with the more general approach.

> Reentrant signaling is a component of distributed neural systems, which are composed of large numbers of modular elements linked together in echeloned parallel and serial arrangements. Information flow through such a system may follow a number of different pathways, and the dominance of one path or another is a dynamic and changing property of the system. (Mountcastle 1978: 40)

Reentrant signaling is a mechanism allowing different processing units to exchange their results, thereby providing for continuity and updating of the representation of the world. Reentry occurs when an "internally generated signal is reentered [functions as input to another module] *as though it were an external signal*" (Edelman 1978: 76; italics in original). In hierarchical systems, results of higher-level processing are fed back into the system at a lower level, to be processed along with new external signals to update a representation or map of the external stimulus. In an early stage of perception external signals generate a map:

> The main function of such a map is to provide a reference for higher-order input-output relationships and successive mappings in a reentrant system. Inasmuch as other regions of the nervous system (and of the cortex in

> particular) must carry out routines involving multimodal input, abstractions, and map-free routines, a place must be maintained for continual reference to continuity properties. This place is the local map and its constituent domains within the primary receiving areas. (Edelman, 1987: 109-110)

Later processing creates higher-order functional maps. Updating and continuity is maintained in these maps by reentered input from other high-level maps; and the lower-level map in the primary receiving area is continually fed by input from all of these, as well as by new external signals. Mountcastle describes such a system as providing the basis for consciousness:

> Finally, distributed systems are by definition and observation both reentrant systems and linkages to inflow and outflow channels of the nervous system. This suggests that the large numbers of processing modules in the neocortex are accessible to both internally generated and externally induced neural activity. Phasic cycling of internally generated activity, accessing first primary sensory but then successively more general and abstract processing units of the homotypical cortex, should allow a continual updating of the perceptual image of self and self-in-the-world as well as a matching function between that perceptual image and impinging external events. This internal readout of internally stored information, and its match with the neural replication of the external continuum, is thought to provide an objective mechanism for conscious awareness. (Mountcastle 1978: 41)

My suggestion is that the combination of processed data with 'raw' data in a single input phase is part of what gives phenomenal experience in general the feature of externality. As with connectionist computational systems, in which the state of activation of a node is a function of its *total* input, a feature of distributed neural systems with extensive overlapping synaptic connections is that 'such synapses cannot be identified in terms of their cell of origin by the cell upon which they terminate' (Edelman 1987). If processed signals are joined with external signals as input to a primary sensory unit, then the subject will not distinguish between the two types of input. In psychological terms this means that if we are unaware that the 'new' input is composed in part of internally generated input, we will believe that the features of this input should be describable quantitatively as objective features of our environment; and when they cannot be so described we are mystified about their nature. In light of this ignorance, resorting to talk of privileged 'perspectives' is understandable.

A more specific proposal for the type of reentrant loop described by Edelman and Mountcastle is the mechanism for visual attention, discussed by

Christof Koch (1987), consisting of the connections between the thalamus and the cortex. Koch hypothesizes that attention to specific areas in the visual field is mediated by feedback from the visual cortex to certain receptors (NMDA receptors) of cells in the LGN, which intensifies the response of those cells to retinal input, the function of this feedback being to enhance "conspicuous or interesting features in sensory stimulus-space" (1987: 403). On this account, raw input passes from the retina through the thalamus to the cortex, to be processed for significant qualitative features. Signals from the cortex back to the original thalamic cells increase the gain of these cells, which then transmit enhanced signals back to the cortex as long as new retinal input continues. The enhanced signals constitute a primary representation of the qualitative aspects of external objects. Since the cortical cells cannot distinguish processed from unprocessed data, these enhanced or processed signals are received as though they were external input. Thus it is likely that this attentional mechanism also contributes to the illusion that qualitative properties are part of the external world.

4. Unity

The unity of phenomenal properties does not feel mysterious; naively we believe that the properties we perceive are ontologically bound together and appear directly as they are in the world. But scientifically we know that components of experience are processed separately in the brain, and that there is no known location where the results of this processing converge (Crick, 1984). Not only are different properties processed separately, but so are their different aspects: e.g. some cells respond to differences of hue between figure and ground, regardless of the specific hues involved; others respond to specific wavelengths regardless of surroundings (Hardin 1988: 52-58).

The phenomenon of unity is related to that of attention. When one is alert, certain features of experience present themselves as though bound together in a vivid picture; generally speaking, only when we are paying attention is our experience 'like' that (or 'like' *anything*) for us. Work by Anne Triesman (1986; see also Julesz, 1984) indicates a preattentive stage of visual processing when certain features (such as a square in a field of circles) automatically 'pop out' while others require a deliberate focus of attention. A significant finding is that the 'pop-out' features are not at this stage bound to other features with which they are actually associated, and errors of synthesis occur when subjects describe brief visual displays:

> It is as if the red color of the triangle were represented by an abstract code for red rather than being incorporated into a kind of analog of the triangle that also encodes the object's size and shape. (Treisman 1986: 117)

Thus it appears that objects in the visual field are decomposed in early vision and are somehow put back together again later. A major problem has been to explain how this resynthesis occurs without a homunculus (the 'binding problem'). We cannot hope for a group of contiguous neurons to represent the combined features of an object, given the number of different objects that can be recognized and greater number of ways they can appear. The representation of an object is distributed about the brain.

Francis Crick and Christof Koch (1990) have proposed a mechanism for unifying the different features of visual objects. They suggest that neurons responding to the separate features of an object are bound into temporary *cell assemblies* by semi-synchronous oscillations (in the 40-70 Hz range). The binding is brought about by means of attentional mechanisms such as the cortico-thalamic feedback loops described above. A hypothetical model of the process is as follows. External input is transmitted from the retina via the thalamus to the cortex, where distinct features of objects are processed in separate areas. When features processed in these areas are conspicuous, feedback to the LGN enhances the output of corresponding locations there. This enhanced output projects to a *saliency map* (Koch and Ullman, 1985) in the cortex, which codes the most conspicuous portions of the visual field. On the basis of this map, semi-synchronous oscillations of neural firing at various locations in the cortex are effected. These locations process features of significant objects, which are represented by the resulting unification of their features. As Crick puts it in an earlier paper.

> The content of the cell assembly — the 'meaning' of all the neurons so linked together — can in this way be impressed on the rest of the system in a manner that would not be possible at all if all of the neurons in it fired at random times, unless they were firing very rapidly indeed. (Crick 1984: 4589)

This binding mechanism together with reentrant signaling may explain how in perception we have a unified 'picture' of the external world, complete with already-processed 'qualitative' properties, *as though it had come in directly from the outside.* The (unconscious) processing stages before binding are the sources of the qualitative properties that we see; thus there is a sense in which in conscious visual perception we are seeing our own visual processes. Conscious perception of the external world is thus second-order perception, the first order being the cortical response to the same data before attentional selection and binding. In this sense we can say that conscious perceptual awareness is perception of a perception.

If so, David Armstrong's account is, to an extent, empirically supported. Armstrong distinguishes three states: minimal consciousness, in which there is some mental activity; perceptual consciousness, consisting of awareness of events in one's environment; and introspective consciousness, or "perception-like awareness of current states and activities in our own mind" (Armstrong 1981: 61). The latter two states are illustrated:

> My proposal is that [introspective] consciousness . . . is nothing but *perception or awareness of the state of our own mind.* The driver in a state of automatism perceives, or is aware of, the road. If he did not, the car would be in a ditch. But he is not currently aware of his awareness of the road. He perceives the road, but he does not perceive his perceiving. . . . He is not, as we normally are, conscious of what is going on in his mind. (1981: 61)

The driver in a state of automatism has only first order perception. Visual input arrives at the cortex but the attentional mechanism is not activated, or is activated only weakly. On coming-to, the driver has second-order perception; significant objects are strongly represented and he is aware of perceiving them.

The current model suggests that rather than Armstrong's three distinct levels there is a spectrum, along which is ranged the degree of activation of the attentional mechanism, and hence the unity and significance of the objects of perception. But it also suggests that critics who attack Armstrong for holding a perceptual model of introspection are too hasty. Shoemaker has argued that introspection cannot be the perception of a perception since there are no sense impressions of mental states (Shoemaker 1985: 23). But given the neural structures described above, there is a (very broad) sense of 'sense impression' in which we do have sense impressions of mental states: when, due to the functioning of the attentional mechanism, external input is processed for enhancement, and enhanced signals then enter the cortex to be perceived as raw input.

5. Self-awareness

Some claim that all consciousness is self-consciousness, and that in conscious perception our own perceiving self is always part of the content of our awareness. I will argue that there is a sense in which that is true.

Unlike features describable as belonging to *objects* of awareness, the feature of experience which is one's own awareness is not easily conceptualized. While being in a state of awareness is a property of oneself, it is not experienced as a property of oneself (or of anything else) in the way that red is experienced as a property of a tomato. But if we are guided by Armstrong's distinction between the automatistic and the introspectively conscious truck driver, we can say that perhaps the most striking thing about conscious awareness of objects is the *immediate experiential apprehension* of oneself aware of them. Even when our attention is not on ourselves but on what we perceive, conscious perceptual awareness includes awareness of our own perceiving.

It has been thought that there is a special nature to consciousness of one's own subjective states. If, like the truck driver, I suddenly become aware that I have been seeing a red object, my awareness of the red quale becomes reflexive. *Without any addition of new data into the content of my awareness,* it is thought to alter from being an awareness of an object to being an awareness of itself aware of an object. This new awareness, the 'reflexivity' of consciousness, is a completely mysterious property.

It need not, however, be so mysterious. Awareness of oneself as either perceiving or imaging is not a special kind of awareness, I suggest, but simply ordinary perceptual awareness occurring when somatic data is added to the content of the attentional focus in the awareness of other input, either internally- or externally-generated. Self-awareness, as Damasio argues, is awareness of bodily responses to sensory input, of movements and adjustments which covary with alterations in the input.

When I am consciously aware of a quale I am aware that I am aware of it. This awareness is not the knowledge of self implicit in the nature of qualia. While a qualitative experience is, I have argued, in effect a perceiving of one's own perceiving (or imaging), we have not seen why it should seem that way to the perceiver. The felt reflexivity of conscious perception must be due, not to an experience of the internal origin of the qualia, but to additional data: to proprioceptive and other somatically-generated input.

In any perceptual experience there is a constant background of bodily input which provides a framework for perceived objects. I perceive the orientation of my eyes and the edges of my eye sockets framing the visual field, my posture and the positions of limbs, visceral states, etc. I also perceive a correlation between bodily motions and alterations in the appearances of objects. This input may not be prominent in attention, but its absence can be dramatic (see Churchland 1988: 281-282).

James claims that awareness of self is just awareness of bodily events:

> Whenever my introspective glance succeeds in turning around quickly enough to catch one of these manifestations of spontaneity in the act, all it can ever feel distinctly is some bodily process, for the most part taking place within the head. . . .The 'Self of selves,' when carefully examined, is found to consist mainly of the collection of these peculiar motions in the head or between the head and throat. It would follow that our entire feeling of spiritual activity, or what commonly passes by that name, is really a feeling of bodily activities whose exact nature is by most men overlooked. (James 1890, Vol. 1: 300-302)

Bodily awareness, James notes, is present not only when we try expressly to focus on our selves, but also during sensory imagery, or simply thinking about sensory objects: 'I cannot think in visual terms . . . without feeling a fluctuating play of pressures, convergences, divergences, and accommodations in my eyeballs' (1890: 300). In this case what is true of imagery seems also true of actual visual experience. The externality of perceptual objects supports the inference: objects are seen as external *to me*; in the case of physical objects in the world, that means external to my body. They could not appear that way in the absence of any bodily awareness. Since objects are seen as located at a particular distance and orientation with respect to my body in space, a sense of my location and orientation must form part of my experience of the object: I see it as it looks *from here*. Evans sees a necessary connection between perceiving objects in space and having *an idea* of one's body:

> Any thinker who has an idea of an objective spatial world — an idea of a world of objects and phenomena which can be perceived but which are not dependent on being perceived for their existence — must be able to think of his perception of the world as being simultaneously due to his position in the world, and to the condition of the world at that position. The very idea of a perceivable, objective, spatial world brings with it the idea of the subject as being in the world, with the course of his perceptions due to his changing position in the world and to the more or less stable way the world is. (Evans 1982: 222)

Strawson (1959) also emphasizes the role of the body in perceptual experiences, but argues that we still need to know why perceptual experiences should be ascribed to any subject at all, and why they and the corporeal experiences should be ascribed to the same subject (1959: 93). In noting that bodily experience accompanies all perceptual experience haven't I simply multiplied the experiences which still, unaccountably, are ascribed to the self? And how do I know it is *my body* I experience?

Bodily and mental self-ascription is a difficult problem for epistemology and philosophy of language, not strictly germane to this chapter on the reduction of the phenomenology of consciousness. But something must be said here on the subject since I have claimed that what seems to be an awareness of self as subject is really perceptual input from the body. Why should that seem like the *self?*

One way to avoid both a direct awareness of an inner Cartesian self and an infinite regress is to say that bodily sensations are originally, in infancy, *constitutive* of 'self.' This seems to be James' view. There is no identification of these experiences as 'mine;' they are simply the most familiar and most imbued with interest and value. Learning that these experiences are 'mine' is learning that they provide information about a public object; that they are experiences or sensations from *this object, this person*, which I am to refer to in the first-person. As a public object in the world with other objects and as a source of sensations from these other objects, 'my' body is the source of information about their location, size, etc., which I exploit with varying degrees of consciousness. I may also, under the influence of folk theories, speak as though there is another, deeper self to which this body and these sensations belong. But thoughts of this self continue to be (unrecognized) thoughts of bodily sensations.

There is a long-standing objection to my claim that bodily information is the source of the sense of self; many have held that we can imagine ourselves completely disembodied while retaining self-consciousness. Anscombe's version is the best-known:

> And now imagine that I get into a state of 'sensory deprivation.' Sight is cut off, and I am locally anaesthetized everywhere, perhaps floated in a tank of tepid water; I am unable to speak, or touch any part of my body with any other. Now I tell myself, 'I won't let this happen again!' If the object meant by 'I' is this body, this human being, then in these circumstances it won't be present to my senses; and how else can it be 'present to' me? But have I lost what I mean

by 'I'? Is that not present to me? Am I reduced to, as it were, 'referring in absence?' I have not lost my 'self-consciousness;' nor can what I mean by 'I' be an object no longer present to me. This both seems right in itself, and will be required by the 'guaranteed reference' we are considering. (Anscombe 1981: 31)

Anscombe is arguing against the view, later defended by Evans (1982), that self-reference is dependent upon information from one's body. Recently, Lucy O'Brien (1995) has revived this issue, arguing that Evans has not refuted Anscombe's claim. On my view of consciousness, disembodied thought would not be possible, and Anscombe's description must be incorrect. Let us look at it more closely.

Anscombe claims that one can 'tell oneself' something in the absence of all bodily information. Her wording invites the following objection. If one can consciously and literally 'tell oneself' something with specific content, such as 'I won't let this happen again,' one must represent the statement to oneself somehow. No discussion of the hypothetical situation, as far as I am aware, addresses the way this is done. Thus we must speculate. It seems that there are only two general types of representations of specific propositional content of which one could be conscious: representations of words of natural language, or sensory images.

It might be held that there is a third type of representation: some kind of 'mentalese' or language of thought, consisting of syntactically-interacting representations. But such representations, if they exist, would not be accessible to introspective consciousness. Telling oneself something in the current example must be a conscious act, since it is part of what one imagines doing. If it were not conscious, one could not imagine it. Thus we are left with natural language and sensory representations. While these are superficially different, they reduce to the same thing. Imagining words requires imagining them in some medium: e.g. as read, heard, or spoken by oneself. In any one of these cases, one must imagine input: visual, auditory, or motor sensations. Imagining such input, the current objection holds, entails reference to one's body.

Imagining these sensations is imagining *having* them, through one's eyes or ears, or through feedback from the vocal system. When one does this, recent neuroscientific work suggests, one activates stored representations — traces of past sensory events (Roland and Gulyas 1994; Damasio 1994). Thus if telling oneself something entails at least imagining sensations, then it entails a reference to one's own body, even if only as remembered.

It can be objected that Anscombe did not attempt to rule out remembered sensations. Her claim is that self-consciousness in the absence of actual bodily input is imaginable, and hence that 'I' does not mean 'this body,' since one's body might, so far as one knows in the absence of current input, no longer exist. But while she may not rule this out, Evans seems to try to do so; his subject is amnesiac as well as anaesthetized (Evans 1982: 215). Evans accepts Anscombe's claim that self-reference is possible in the absence of any actual bodily information. His position is that all that is required for self-reference is a *disposition* to "have such thinking controlled by [such] information" (Evans 1982: 216). That is, if such information were available, which it may not be, a subject would be disposed to accept it "as germane to the thoughts we regard as manifesting self-consciousness" (1982: 249). It is only in this way, according to Evans, that self-reference is not independent of bodily information.

It is not clear how we are to understand the amnesia of Evans's subject. If the subject has lost specific episodic memories but not basic cognitive skills such as language use, then the amnesia does not remove the bodily reference that I have argued is required for telling oneself something. If the amnesia wipes the mental slate completely clean, on the other hand, then it is not at all obvious that the subject could have a self-referring thought, any more than could a newborn infant. He would have forgotten not only language, but all acquired concepts. Under those circumstances, Anscombe's description is incoherent. Since Evans describes his subject as "wondering . . . why he is *not* receiving information in the usual way" (1982: 215), he must be remembering the usual way, and thus a clean slate is ruled out. But then so is the absence of bodily reference apparently required for the independence thesis. Thus it seems that Evans could have maintained a stronger view than the dispositional one regarding the dependence of self-reference upon bodily information.

This possibility is resisted by O'Brien (1995), who points out that "it is not clear what use a conception based on past experience will be if we have no way of assuring ourselves in the tank that we have not lost track of the object our conception applied to" (O'Brien 1995: 239). In other words, remembering reading, hearing or speaking the words 'I won't let this happen again' may be remembering only that the sensations occurred in some body. Applied to my claim that telling oneself something is imagining, which means remembering, sensations of words, O'Brien's point might be that memories of perceiving or saying the words would not suffice to make those words refer to me now; they need only refer to some past object. But if all I can now know about the word

'I' as I am currently (remembering) thinking it is that it was once heard or
uttered, then I am not using it now to refer to myself, and hence am not really
thinking 'I will not . . . ;' that is, I am not using the sentence to refer to my
actual self. I am simply thinking about earlier occasions on which those words
were used.

It might be suggested that the fact that I remember *my own perception or
use* of the words is what makes the words refer to me now. But that would
presuppose self-reference, since the memories would have to be recognized as
being one's own by means of a prior or distinct concept.

It appears that if I can think self-referentially by means of imagining the
use of natural language, then current sensory or motor input *must* be involved,
and not just remembered input. How is that possible if I am not actually seeing,
hearing or speaking the words, but only thinking them? In other words, if
thinking about or in language is activating traces of past linguistic experiences,
then how is such thought ever tied to one's current body (whether or not one is
not in a sensory-deprivation vat)? The most plausible way is if memories of
linguistic events are superposed on some current bodily experiences or feelings. These current experiences, as we have suggested, are *constitutive* of
one's (present) self. Judgments about the self could then be made by means of
linguistic images in combination with the self-constituting experiences.

Let us set aside for a moment the hypothesis that disembodied thought is
imaginable, and look at recent views among cognitive scientists (e.g. Damasio
1994; Edelman 1989, 1992; Jackendoff 1987) that the sense of self is provided
by a combining of novel with internally-generated sensorimotor input. In
Damasio's words, "that experience of what your body is doing while thoughts
about specific contents roll by, is the essence of what I call a feeling" (1994:
145). Damasio's account of emotional feelings is particularly relevant to the
present topic:

> If an emotion is a collection of changes in body state connected to particular
> mental images that have activated a specific brain system, *the essence of
> feeling an emotion is the experience of such changes in juxtaposition to the
> mental images that initiated the cycle.* In other words, a feeling depends on the
> juxtaposition of an image of the body proper to an image of something else,
> such as the visual image of a face or the auditory image of a melody.
> (Damasio 1994: 145; italics in original)

Feeling an emotion in connection with a thought is juxtaposing an image (the
thought) to the experience of current bodily response to the image. If it is

objected that for the subject in the tank, no emotion has been posited, one need only note that the thought 'I won't let this happen again!' *presupposes a negative emotion*; if the subject were emotionally neutral with respect to his situation such a decision would be inexplicable.

Of course it would be question-begging to accept Damasio's theory as a counter to Anscombe's thesis without explaining away the intuition that her description is coherent. But we can explain it away. The intuition is the result of the prior belief, inherited from Descartes, that disembodied thought is possible. But once it is asked how a specific thought, particularly a self-referential, emotion-laden thought, is actually accomplished, Damasio's account seems a very plausible one. One can then realize that in imagining being in the tank, one is still imagining being aware of one's body. The awareness is in the background and is easy to overlook in a description of what one imagines.

But could one not be anaesthetized in such a way that no bodily input at all is received? This would mean no internal bodily sensations: no feelings of muscle tensions, of breath, of the pull of internal organs on connective tissue. I see no reason why one could not lack all these sensations, but it is also not clear that we can *imagine* lacking them, in the sense of mentally experiencing what it would be like to lack them. It is quite possible that it would be *like nothing at all*. Trying to imagine this would certainly involve a vastly greater mental effort than the normal understanding of Anscombe's description requires. It might well be that in such a state one would lose touch with one's actual circumstances, and would hallucinate (as one does when dreaming). Note that *believing* that one has imagined the situation is not necessarily the same thing as *actually* imagining it; one may wrongly believe that one has imagined it if one has overlooked and hence failed to imagine away any internal bodily sensations required for thinking. Therefore the view that disembodied consciousness is possible remains unsupported.

Finally, one might argue that telling oneself something does not require the imagining of any words or sentences. Normally, however, those who hold that conscious thought without language is possible (the present author is one of these) argue that thought can occur by means of nonlinguistic sensorimotor imagery. That, for example, is Damasio's view (Damasio 1994: 94f). Such imagery would involve bodily reference just as much as would linguistic imagery. Thus defending the independence thesis from the present objection would require positing some other form of conscious thought, involving no sensory images of any kind, and it is quite mysterious what that form could be.

I now turn to a second proposal concerning the possibility of disembodied self-consciousness. While it is not an especially compelling one, refuting it will illustrate points that have been made earlier in this chapter about conscious experience. In her 1995 article, O'Brien discusses the possibility of referring to oneself solely by means of information that one *wrongly believes* to come from oneself. I might be wired up so that

> I take my legs to be crossed when — and because — someone else's are . . . 'My legs are crossed,' I might say. How are we to understand such an utterance? Well we will, surely, understand the utterance as saying something false about me whose legs are not crossed, and not something true about the subject from whose position the information actually derives. (O'Brien 1995: 240)

O'Brien takes this situation to be a problem for Evans's dispositional account of self-reference, for the following reason. Here the subject is disposed to take the information received as relating to her own position. That means that the information should determine reference. If it did, however, we would not take the subject to refer to herself when she says 'My legs are crossed;' but we do take her that way.

This type of case leads, I believe, to the same kind of mistake as does the sensory deprivation one. When our intuitions tell us that the subject is referring to herself but that *all* of her information is derived from another, we are forgetting the experiences involved in making a judgment about something that is perceived. Making a judgment is an action that itself produces experiences. These experiences enable the thinker to self-refer, even if the judgment also makes use of sensory information that is derived from another.

There are two ways to show this. The first way is indirect. Notice that while our intuitions clearly tell us that the judgment 'My legs are crossed' refers to the subject, they do *not* tell us that the judgment refers to the subject's *legs*. Imagine that the subject has always lacked legs, but is unaware of that fact. 'My legs' refers to the legs that she senses; but 'my' refers to herself. She mistakenly assigns the legs that she senses to herself; she does not mistakenly assign herself to the legs. (If Evans' position entailed the latter, and if *all* the subject's information came from the legs, the position would entail that she believed herself to be identical to the legs themselves, not to some unseen other owner of the legs). Thus it seems that Evans's dispositional account, or even a stronger dependence thesis, may still hold for objects about which we receive information, and that there is or could be some *additional* information the thinker receives from the self that enables her thoughts to self-refer. This information might be any of the ongoing internal bodily sensations mentioned in the first section.

The direct way to show that some information derives from the one who thinks about the legs is to look even more closely at what happens when we think about something that is perceived. When we think about something perceived, we attend to sensations from that thing. Once again, recent work in the neurosciences has something relevant to tell us, this time about attentional processes in the brain. Recall Crick's hypothesis that mechanisms of attention involve reverberating cortico-thalamic circuits constituting very short-term memory (Crick 1994: 241). If a subject is thinking about what she takes to be her legs, then the relevant sensory input (even if, as we are supposing, it comes somehow from another person) is being processed by some such mechanism in the subject's brain. Now, when such a process is occurring, the subject is aware of it; we can tell when we are paying attention to something. Thus *the prominence of the leg sensations in short-term memory* can itself be taken as information from the subject — that is, from the attentional mechanisms in the subject's brain — even though the informational *content* that is being processed is derived from another person. In other words, just consciously thinking about a thing is generating information about myself, and it is bodily information.

Other recent work on focal attention emphasizes an executive function in the frontal lobes (Posner and Dehaene 1994):

> . . . an executive is informed about the processes taking place within the organization. A system that would be related to our subjective experience of focal attention would clearly play this function for a subset of current (sensory) and stored (memory) information. There are reasons for relating anterior cingulate function to focal awareness of the target. The strongest reason is that the intensity of cingulate activity tends to increase with the number of targets in a set of stimuli and decreases with practice on any single stimulus set. (Posner and Dehaene 1994: 79)

While the authors discuss data based on target search experiments, and by hypothesis no search is involved in the legs example (on the stipulation that no other information is provided), focal attention is clearly involved. The subject is thinking specifically about the perceived legs rather than, for example, other remembered events. There is a conscious experience, as the authors note, associated with such focal attention, which appears to be derived from the cingulate cortex. Thus on this hypothesis, as on the previous one, the subject *is* receiving information from her own body in the very act of thinking about the perceived legs.

Perhaps, however, we are intended by stipulation to take the subject as receiving *no* information at all other than that from the real owner of the legs. If so, information from the subject's attentional mechanisms is ruled out. But so, in that case, is the plausibility of the example. If the legs are being attended to on this stipulation, the attention is being paid by the legs' actual owner. Whatever attentional experiences accompany the thought 'My legs are crossed,' they are due to the legs' owner thinking that thought, rather than our subject. If so, it is hard to know what it means to say that nevertheless the 'subject' is thinking that her legs are crossed (or anything at all). 'My legs' in this case would seem to assign the legs to their rightful owner.

The two cases discussed by O'Brien are both examples of a trap noted by Bernard Williams, who warns that "at least with regard to the self, the imagination is too tricky a thing to provide a reliable road to the comprehension of what is logically possible" (Williams 1973: 45; see also Tye 1983 for related arguments). Intuitions are fed by traditions, in ways that are often very hard to see; arguments based on them are thus prone to circularity. In this 'decade of the brain,' new opportunities to rethink these traditions arise almost daily. There are many empirical reasons for thinking that Evans is on the right track in linking self-reference to bodily information. Presuppositions about the possibility of disembodied thought should be examined in the light of these, before being allowed to deflect sound philosophical reasoning.

The fact that much bodily sensation is unconscious (or preattentive) explains why 'out-of-body' experiences seem like coherent possibilities. Custom may be one reason bodily input is overlooked; another may be the attentional mechanisms described above. Normally we are interested in objects in the external world, and the attentional mechanism tends to favor these except when drawn to bodily states, as with a sudden pain. It is thus plausible that the appearance of introspective consciousness in the midst of (mere) perceptual consciousness is due simply to the spotlighting of bodily input along with significant features of the external world.

This proposal parallels an account by Carol Rovane (1987) concerning first-person reference. She supports a Fregean account according to which we use 'I' as we use other referring terms: by means of individuating descriptive beliefs about the referent (Frege's *sense*), and not by means of some unmediated self-consciousness, a "direct awareness of the *activity* of thinking [which] includes a direct awareness of *oneself* thinking" (1987: 158). Special features of self-reference thought to set it apart, such as immunity from error through misidentification, exist, she argues, because:

> speakers have enough true beliefs about themselves in virtue of which they are quite clear about their identities even though they have some false beliefs about themselves as well. . . . The kind of knowledge I mean here does not amount to some ineffable understanding that 'I am me,' but, rather, to genuinely descriptive knowledge about which thing in the world I am, knowledge about my past, my spatial location, my relations to others, etc. (Rovane 1987: 154)

Rovane argues that we refer to ourselves by the same mechanism that we use to refer to other things; I argue that we are aware of ourselves by the same mechanism that we use to be aware of other things. In her account the mechanism is descriptive beliefs; in mine it is sensory input. The mechanisms in my account can be seen as underlying the ones in hers. Sensory input from my body (along with that from external objects) is one way I acquire "knowledge about which thing in the world I am . . ." This knowledge provides the sense for the use of the first person.

For a simple model of the neural underpinnings of self-awareness, the binding mechanism proposed by Crick and Koch can be extended to include not just input from the visual field, but somatic input as well. The binding mechanism can operate across sensory modalities as well as within them. Recall that this mechanism operates after the attentional mechanism has selected significant features from the sensory input and increased the activity of cells responding to that input. These cells are caused to fire in synch, thereby unifying the features they represent. If bodily events associated with perception (eye orientation etc.) are included in the data available to this mechanism, then their binding along with nonbodily input would result in a sense of unity of perceiver and perceived: perceived objects are *united in being perceived by me*.

6.   Awareness itself

Traditionally conscious awareness has seemed to involve a duality between subject and object of awareness. A difficulty is that the subject (the conscious self) is supposed to be self-aware, and hence also part of the object; such awareness is hard to envisage as a brain state. Another difficulty is that from Hume on it has been widely held that the self is no perceptual object; what sort of object of awareness the self is has been mysterious. In the preceding section I argued that the (bodily) self is an object of awareness like any other, and consciousness has no special (nonperceptual) access to it. If so then the above two difficulties may evaporate. But with them seems to evaporate any intuitive way of describing awareness — describing what it is like to be aware of something — separately from the content. Perhaps there is nothing to describe. But there is something still to understand: how can there be awareness of this perceptual content? *What* is aware, and how do objects present themselves to it?

I suggest that the apparent subject-object duality is in reality simply temporal extension. In conscious perception new input is linked with the active representation, in short-term memory (STM) or iconic memory, of the immediately preceding phase of input. The superposition of the two levels of response to signals from the same perceptual object could yield the effect of the present perception of the just-past. The past, in effect, lingers in the present, producing a temporal perspective analogous to visual spatial perspective in which both near and far are presented in a unified space. If the response to new input is precategorical or not fully categorized, while the content in STM is postcategorical, we can understand how highly processed, meaningful phenomenal content can appear to be immediately present in awareness. Once again, the *blend* of results of lower-level processing with the content of memory is what produces the effect of a present perception of past, already-perceived objects.

James calls this effect the 'specious present' (after E. R. Clay):

> If the constitution of consciousness were that of a string of bead-like sensations and images, all separate . . . [o]ur consciousness would be like a glow-worm spark, illuminating the point it immediately covered, but leaving all beyond in total darkness. [The actual situation is otherwise.] *The knowledge of some other part of the stream, past or future, near or remote, is always mixed in with our knowledge of the present thing.* (James 1890, Vol. I: 605-606)

When we are consciously aware, the present moment lingers; there is a constant renewal, while at the same time the phenomenal properties remain to be savored. We can attend to ourselves (our bodily sensations) and to external objects in turn, without losing our place in the present by these shifts. I think it is plausible (although I do not know how to prove it) that the truly ineffable aspect of conscious awareness is the result of the unification of past and present externally and internally generated (bodily) input to sensory processors. With these elements consciousness "seems like a light switched on, illuminating utter darkness" (Armstrong 1981: 63). Unification means that the components of experience cannot easily be distinguished by experience; thus without scientific knowledge it might be impossible, simply by having conscious experience, to understand the structure of perceptual consciousness. The blended experience thus lends itself to various interpretations consistent with prevailing folk theories, such as the perception of internal states by a Cartesian ego. Conscious experience can feel like that, if you think about it in a certain way.

There is much scientific support for the involvement of memory in conscious experience. The most explicit recent theory of the connection is given by Edelman in *The Remembered Present* (1989). He postulates special memory repertoires which store both internally and externally generated data, such that the distinction between self (in the biological sense) and nonself, and associated values, are represented. This memory interacts with current perceptual (partially categorized) processes:

> The functioning of the memory repertoires depends upon connecting interoceptive signals (which are primary and relate to value but cannot be categorized in spatio-temporal detail) to those exteroceptive signals that can be categorized in great detail and that happen to be temporally correlated with those interoceptive signals. This results in a value-dominated memory system that associates sensorimotor perceptual categories with value states. (1989: 98-99)
>
> . . . In effect, primary consciousness results from the interaction in real time between memories of past value-category correlations and present world input as it is categorized by global mappings (but before the components of these mappings are altered by internal states). (1989: 155)

Edelman's account needs no homunculus to unify the components since unification is effected by correlation of signals brought about by reentry:

> Since reentry to and from mapped receiving areas correlates the various
> signals emerging from an object, and since previous categorizations in
> memory can interact with the outputs of these reentrant paths, there is no
> homunculus 'looking at the image.' It is the discriminative comparison be-
> tween a value-dominated memory involving the conceptual system and cur-
> rent ongoing perceptual categorization that generates primary consciousness
> of objects and events. (1989: 155)

The special memory involved in Edelman's theory is not short-term memory.
My reason for favoring STM rather than long-term memory (LTM) as essential
to perceptual consciousness is that while LTM appears to be central to a full
conscious awareness of who one is, where one has been and where one is
heading, it is not essential for having a *present.* Tulving (1985) describes a
case, N.N., with severe amnesia, who:

> seems to have no capability of experiencing extended subjective time . . . even
> if he feels that he has a personal identity, it does not include the past or the
> future; . . . He seems to be living in a 'permanent *present.*' (1985: 4)

N.N., like other amnesiacs such as H.M. (Scoville and Milner, 1957), had a
normal digit span and could describe what his memory loss felt like to him. His
short-term memory seemed unaffected. Such patients have been an important
source of evidence for the STM/LTM distinction (Squire 1987: 142). Since
they appear to have retained the sort of consciousness in which I am interested
— immediate perceptual consciousness as distinct from higher-level states
with more extensive conceptual awareness — I conclude that STM is sufficient. Edelman's theory is significant, however, in his support for the view that
it is the *overlapping* of a current perceptual state with an activated memory of
similar but more highly categorized content that produces consciousness.

In the account of Crick and Koch (1990) STM or *working memory* is
specified. Working memory, a form of STM, is a system for temporarily
holding information involved in various tasks (see Baddeley 1986: 34). It is
post-categorical, as distinct from iconic memory, which is a pre-categorical
form of STM:

> *We further postulate that objects for which the binding problem has been*
> *solved are placed into working memory.* In other words, some (or all) of the
> properties associated with the attended location would automatically be re-
> membered for a short time. One very attractive possibility, with no
> experimental support, is that it is the 40 Hz oscillations themselves that
> preferentially activate the mechanisms underlying working memory and pos-
> sibly other longer forms of memory as well. . . . A striking feature of our visual

awareness (and of consciousness in general) is that it is very rich in information. . . . Not only can the system switch rapidly from one object to another,
but in addition it can handle a very large amount of information in a coherent
way *at a single moment*. We believe it is mainly these two abilities, combined
with the very transient memory systems involved, that has made it appear so
strange. (Crick and Koch 1990: 272-274)

Crick and Koch do not specify the exact contribution of working memory to
conscious experience; their focus is the binding mechanisms unifying
experiential content. However, their account is useful in that their suggested
mechanism by which perceptual content is placed into working memory would
explain the relation among memory, attention and consciousness: we are
perceptually conscious of objects to the extent that we attend to them, and only
if we can attend to them are they stored in memory.

The relation between STM and consciousness is important also in theories
of cognitive psychologists such as Johnson-Laird (1988: Ch. 19) and Jackendoff (1987). Jackendoff's approach is particularly compatible with mine. He
argues for an 'intermediate level' theory of consciousness, rather than a
central-level theory according to which conceptual structure is the essential
content of consciousness (1987: 286), and he stresses the 'top-down' influence
of higher-level on lower-level representations in STM. In vision, the intermediate level corresponds to Marr's 2 1/2D sketch, which represents the surface
appearance of objects in the visual field, distinct from the 3D model which
represents the unseen surfaces and interiors of the objects (Marr 1982). On
Jackendoff's account the 2 1/2D sketch ('the way things *look* ') and the 3D
model (the 'content' or 'meaning' of visual awareness) are activated together
when there is conceptual understanding of what is seen (1987: 294-295).
While Jackendoff focuses on the blend in STM of different levels of representation, rather than on the blend of the material in STM with new input, he
makes clear that activation of STM along with new input is required for
perceptual awareness:

> STVM [short-term visual memory] should be seen as a device that creates and
> maintains several levels of visually relevant representation — at least 2 1/2D
> sketch, 3D model, and conceptual structure. STVM can be activated by input
> from lower levels in the case of perception, or by conceptual input in the case
> of imagery; whichever is the source of activation, a full set of levels is created.
> Moreover, these levels are kept *in registration* with each other . . . this is
> suggested by the perceptual stability of the world in the face of constant eye
> movements. (Jackendoff 1987: 188-189)

Jackendoff argues that STVM, while central to perception and imagery, is activated differently in each. I argue, in effect, that the phenomenological difference between perceiving and imaging is explained by the difference in source of activation of STVM. When lower-level input is kept in registration with higher levels (by what Jackendoff calls 'integrative processors,' 1987: 187) the content of STVM is experienced as present and actual; when lower-level input is lacking, the content is experienced as imagery.

In spite of the empirical support for the connection between consciousness and memory, my proposal concerning awareness itself may seem the weakest of the four. That is because a phenomenal description of the feature I want to reduce is not predictable from the reducing structures in the same way as are descriptions of the other features. The synchrony of parallel processors of sensory input, for example, implies phenomenal unity. But it is not similarly obvious that continued activity in memory of sensory traces, combined with new sensing of the same stimuli, would produce awareness itself 'as we know it.' Unlike the other features which as features of structured content are essentially relational and hence describable, awareness itself can be called an 'intrinsic property' of our experience. It has seemed otherwise because of the assumption that the primary feature of conscious awareness is reflexivity and that awareness is a relation between the self and objects. But if the self is simply part of the content, then awareness is non-relational. The apparent duality is conceptual, not experiential. It is sense perception that requires a subject and an object, not the awareness which is an aspect of sense perception.

If awareness is nonrelational in the above sense, then no phenomenal description of it follows from its neural nature. Awareness requires, if I am right, a superposition of past and present perception; but the experience is not analyzable into these two moments. (It is tempting to call awareness an emergent property of the union of STM and immediate sensation, in somewhat the way that the experience of depth perception is an emergent property of binocular vision: the experience of visual depth is not analyzable into two two-dimensional fields, although unlike the specious present it can be reduced to its components by the subject (closing alternate eyes recaptures the two-dimensional fields). The union of past and present produces an extended attentional state in which sensory qualities develop and inform the response to new stimuli. The result is clearly describable only with reference to the content of the state. The only thing awareness is like is what its content is like; awareness is the state in which perceptual content is like something. Awareness itself is unique; it is not comparable to any other state, since (my apologies for stating the obvious) it is the only state with which we are acquainted. For these reasons, the requirements on a reduction of awareness itself are actually less demanding than those on a reduction of describable content. There the phenomenology must be predictable from the reducing account. But with awareness itself, since there is no phenomenology distinct from that of its content, all that is required is that the reducing account be scientifically sound on its own terms. We are not yet at that point, but the work on STM is promising.

CHAPTER NINE

Conclusion

1. Summary

The traditional goal of philosophical analysis has been to illuminate the structures of the conceptual frameworks with which we organize our conscious experience. My focus has been a different one. While I am interested in explaining features of the framework through which we view mentality, my primary subject has been the conscious experience itself as the basis upon which that framework has been erected. Thus much of my discussion has involved phenomenology. Almost as much emphasis, however, has been upon the mentalistic concepts that we understand by means of that phenomenology. The result, I hope, is an account of the concept of intentionality in terms of the experience of conscious understanding.

I have presented and defended a view of intentionality and consciousness which departs radically from the linguistic approach to human mentality, currently the dominant view. I have argued that the intentionality of goal-directed physical actions and of mental states is a single natural phenomenon, completely analyzable in biological, nonintentional terms. This means that the intentionality of a mental state cannot be understood in terms of its propositional content (conceived as expressible linguistically in a 'that'-clause). Instead, the intentionality of a mental state, considered as a response to an environmental stimulus, consists in the understanding the subject has of that stimulus and of her goals in responding to it, just as the intentionality (the *meaning*) of a fragment of physical behavior consists in its being part of a goal-directed action, understood by the agent.

There are two ways in which language has been used to explain human mentality. First, the property of intentionality, viewed by many philosophers as the defining characteristic of mental states, is commonly explained in terms of language. Intentional mental states are characterized as relations to content with the semantic properties of meaning and truth value. Thus entertaining a thought is treated as analogous to expressing a statement. Second, language is thought to constitute an autonomous representational medium in which all higher human mental activities are carried out. The descriptionalist theory of mental imagery holds that even forming a mental image is a linguistic process. I have argued that the linguistic view of intentionality has failed to explain intentional understanding, and that the linguistic view of the representation used in thought has failed to account for known properties of human reasoning. I have also discussed evidence from neuroscience, cognitive psychology and cognitive ethology against the linguistic view of mental representation.

Characterizing intentional mental states in terms of our understanding of actions is a more fruitful approach to intentionality and representation. Physical and mental actions share a structure: they consist of stages or components which are adjusted toward the achievement of some end-state. The common physical bond between the two forms of intentionality consists in the stored and reactivated traces of sensorimotor experience, which are used both to plan and execute physical actions, and to construct the mental representations by which mental actions are performed. It is here that language has its role: like any other behavior, it can be represented in thought as a type of goal-directed action. In intentional mental actions, sensorimotor experience is the basis both of linguistic understanding and of the phenomenal self-consciousness that normally accompanies intentional states in human beings.

In Chapters Two and Eight we looked at recent work in the neurosciences and in cognitive psychology that supports this view of the role of sensorimotor experience in human psychology. This empirical evidence allows us to draw conclusions that go beyond the psychology of human beings. Much of the work supporting the sensorimotor basis of mind has consisted of evidence of types of brain structures and mechanisms that humans share with other animals. If human intentionality and consciousness are explainable in terms of these, rather than in terms of language, then there is no longer any basis for viewing humans as unique possessors of these mental properties. A primitive form of intentionality exists in any animal capable of purposeful action. Intentional mental states, moreover, exist in any animal using a sensorimotor representation in the pursuit of a goal, and consciousness exists in any animal with the memory and reentrant structures discussed in the previous chapter.

2.   The preeminence of the linguistic paradigm

Viewing intentionality in terms of action relegates language to a position of secondary importance in mental activity. But is it plausible that (as many others have suggested) our traditional view of the centrality of language to mind could be so mistaken? Two points make the claim easier to accept.

First, language has enjoyed its glory in large part because it is the one feature that sets us decisively apart from other animals. As long as humans insist on a position of unique superiority within the animal kingdom, the qualities that distinguish us must be granted a special importance. It is true that while other animals use language-like signs for communication, and in ways that may be more sophisticated than is currently appreciated (see Griffin 1992, and Cheney and Seyfarth 1988), it appears that only natural human language has the combinatorial productivity that allows the elaboration of concepts on which civilization depends. But just as cooking and other refinements of food preparation have not changed the workings of our digestive mechanisms from their animal origins, so the hyperdevelopment of our communication tools need not have changed the thinking mechanisms that make use of them. Our digestive and thinking mechanisms, however, are normally invisible; food and language behavior are highly visible. Thus it makes sense that language would be viewed as more significant than it really is for understanding the nature of our mental life.

The second reason for the longevity of the linguistic paradigm is that language has made possible the creation of truly unique domains of intellectual activity. Philosophy, science, literature, etc., all are developments for which language is necessary, both genetically and constitutively. Those for whom these activities are primary concerns naturally find that linguistic behavior is represented in their thinking. This is true not, I have argued, because reasoning takes place by means of language, but because language is the primary tool by means of which activities in these domains are conducted, and thinking uses representations of common sensorimotor activities (of which language behavior is just one). We continually review in our minds what we have read, what we will write, what we will say.

In view of the tradition of human superiority and the importance of language-based cultural institutions, therefore, the strength of the linguistic paradigm is not surprising. If language, as urged in this book, proves not to be an autonomous representational medium uniquely responsible for intentionality and consciousness, then it becomes difficult to deny those attributes to other animals.

3.   Understanding and semantic structure: iceberg and tip

If language as traditionally studied is of secondary importance in human cognitive activity, then exposure of that status might paradoxically appear to restore language to primary importance in the study of the mind. It is not the syntactic structure of language that reveals thought processes, but the semantic structure. As has been pointed out by Johnson-Laird, Lakoff, Johnson, and Langacker, semantic structures are identical to the mental models and image schemata created in language use; in Langacker's words, "Semantic structure is conceptualization tailored to the specifications of linguistic convention. . . . I believe that mental experience is real, that it is susceptible to empirical investigation, and that it constitutes the natural subject matter of semantics" (Langacker 1987: 99). If semantic structure is indeed indistinguishable from mental experience, then why is the study of this feature of language not sufficient for understanding the representational abilities of the human mind?

An important argument for the preeminence of semantics in studying cognition is that, unlike much of the experience associated with nonlinguistic understanding, semantic experience is directly tied to a set of fixed and public behavioral patterns. The objective nature of linguistic behavior conferred respectability upon the study of cognition during a period still influenced by behaviorism, and now allows researchers to substantiate claims with the help of computer models of language behavior, such as neural nets that simulate language learning (Pinker and Mehler, 1988). I have argued, moreover, that the mechanisms of language understanding underlie all understanding. Thus, one might hold, the direct and systematic link to of semantic understanding to observable behavior not only provides the study of semantic experience with a welcome objectivity, but also ensures that nothing of fundamental importance to cognition is overlooked if semantic experience is taken as paradigmatic of the representational capacities of the mind. Semantic structures, we might say, are the tip of the iceberg of human cognitive abilities, and one can learn as much about the structure of ice by studying the tip as by studying the rest of the iceberg.

It is true that all of our cognitive abilities are involved in semantic understanding. This follows from the foundational theory of understanding urged in this book. It may also follow that once the relations between semantic understanding and its nonlinguistic foundations have been fully illuminated, then the study of semantic structures could proceed independently. The study of semantic structures by themselves is, however, like the tip of the iceberg, *dangerous when approached in ignorance of what is below the surface.*

The 'danger' in the case of semantics is that the mechanisms of understanding will appear to be essentially linguistic. Understanding will seem, as it has to so many philosophers, to be a matter of language competence, and reasoning itself will appear as nothing but a succession of propositional attitudes. We have seen that this approach explains nothing, however, about how human beings consciously understand not only the content of the language they use, but also what they are trying to achieve when using language. Once the tip of the iceberg is known for what it is, then it can be safely and profitably studied. Thus I conclude with the hope that the unified view of body and mind in human beings offered here may help lead toward a more adequate account of human cognitive abilities in both linguistic and nonlinguistic activities.

References

Adams, F. and Mele, A. 1989. The role of intention in intentional action. *Canadian Journal of Philosophy* 19, 511-31.

Anscombe, G.E.M. 1981. The first person. In *Metaphysics and Philosophy of Mind: Collected Philosophical Papers Volume II*, 21-36. Oxford: Blackwell.

Armstrong, D.M. 1973. *Belief, Truth and Knowledge*. Cambridge: Cambridge University Press.

Baars, B.J. 1988. *A Cognitive Theory of Consciousness*. Cambridge: Cambridge University Press.

Baddeley, A. 1986. *Working Memory*. Oxford: Clarendon Press.

Baddeley, A. 1992 (a). Working memory. *Science* 255, 556-559.

Baddeley, A. 1992 (b). Working memory: the interface between memory and cognition. *Journal of Cognitive Neuroscience* 4, 3, 281-288.

Ballim, A., Wilks, Y. and Barnden, J. 1991. Belief ascription, metaphor, and intensional identification. *Cognitive Science* 15, 133-171.

Baron-Cohen, S. 1991. Precursors to a theory of mind: Understanding attention in others. In *Natural Theories of Mind,* A. Whiten (ed.), 233-251. Oxford: Blackwell.

Berndt, R. and Caramazza, A. 1980. A redefinition of the syndrome of Broca's aphasia: Implications for a neuropsychological model of language. *Applied Psycholinguistics* 1:225-78

Bisiach, E. 1988. Language without thought. In *Thought Without Language,* L. Weiskrantz (ed.), 464-484. Oxford: Oxford University Press.

Block, N. 1980. What is functionalism? In *Readings in Philosophy of Psychology* v. 1. Block, N. (ed.), 171-184. Cambridge, Mass.: Harvard University Press.

Boden, M. 1982. Implications of language studies for human nature. In *Language, Mind and Brain,* Simon, T.W. and Scholes, R.J. (eds), 129-143. Hillsdale, N.J.: Lawrence Erlbaum.

Boden, M. 1990. Escaping from the chinese room. In *The Philosophy of Artificial Intelligence*, Boden, M. (ed.), 89-104. Oxford: Oxford University Press.

Brand, M. 1986. Intentional actions and plans. In *Midwest Studies in Philosophy,* French, P., Uehling, T. Jr., and Wettstein, H. (eds), 213-230. Minneapolis: University of Minesota Press.

Bransford, J. and McCarrell, N. 1977. A cognitive approach to comprehension. In *Thinking*, Johnson-Laird, P.N. and Wason, P.C., (eds), 377-399. Cambridge: Cambridge University Press.

Brentano, F. 1960. The distinction between mental and physical phenomena. In *Realism and the Background of Phenomenology,* Chisolm, R.M. (ed), 164-176. Glencoe, IL: Free Press.

Brown, R. 1958. *Words and Things* . New York: Free Press.

Canseco-Gonzalez, E., Shapiro, L., Zurif, E. and Baker, E. 1990. Predicate-argument structure as a link between linguistic and nonlinguistic representations. *Brain and Language* 39, 391-404.

Chalmers, D. 1995. Facing up to the problem of consciousness. *Journal of Consciousness Studies* 2, 200-219.

Cheney, D.L., and Seyfarth, R.M. 1990. *How Monkeys See the World.* Chicago: University of Chicago Press.

Chomsky N. 1980. Rules and representations. *Behavioral and Brain Sciences* 3, 1-61.

Churchland, P.M. 1985. Reduction, qualia, and the direct introspection of brain states. *Journal of Philosophy* 82, 2, 2-28.

Churchland, P.M. 1984. *Matter and Consciousness.* Cambridge, Mass.: MIT Press.

Churchland, P.S. 1986. *Neurophilosophy.* Cambridge, Mass.: MIT Press.

Cussins, A. 1993. Nonconceptual content and the elimination of misconceived composites. *Mind and Language* 8, 2, 234-252.

Cussins, A. 1992. Content, embodiment and objectivity: The theory of cognitive trails. *Mind* 101, 404, 651-688.

Cussins, A. 1990. The connectionist construction of concepts. In *The Philosophy of Artificial Intelligence*, Boden, M. (ed), 368-440. Oxford: Oxford University Press.

Damasio, A.R. 1989. Time-locked multiregional retroactivation: A systems-level proposal for the neural substrates of recall and recognition. In *Neurobiology of Cognition*, Eimas, P.D. and Galaburda, A.M. (eds), 25-62. Cambridge, Mass.: MIT Press.

Damasio, A. R. 1992. Aphasia. *The New England Journal of Medicine* 326, 8, 531-539.

Damasio, A. R. 1994. *Descartes' Error.* New York: Putnam & Sons.

Damasio, A. and Damasio, H. 1992. Brain and language. *Scientific American*, September, 88-109.

Dascal, M. 1985. Language use in jokes and dreams: Sociopragmatics vs psychopragmatics. *Language and Communication* 5, 2, 95-106.

Dascal, M. 1987. Language and reasoning: Sorting out sociopragmatic and psychopragmatic factors'. In *The Role of Language In Problem-Solving 2* , Boudreaux, J.C., Hamill, B.W., and Jernigan, R. (eds), 183-197. Dordrecht,: Elsevier Science Publishers.

Dascal, M. and Berenstein, I. 1987. Two modes of understanding: Comprehending and grasping. *Language and Communication* 7, 2, 139-151.

Davidson, D. 1984. *Inquiries into Truth and Interpretation.* Oxford: Clarendon Press.

Dennett, D. 1969. *Content and Consciousness.* London: Routledge and Kegan Paul.

Dennett, D. 1987. *The Intentional Stance.* Cambridge, Mass: MIT Press.

Dennett, D. 1988. Quining qualia. *Consciousness in Contemporary Science,* Marcel, A. and Bisiach, E. (eds.), 42-77. Oxford: Clarendon Press.

Dennett, D. 1991. *Consciousness Explained.* Boston: Little, Brown and Co.

Dinsmore, J. 1987. Mental spaces from a functional perspective. *Cognitive Science* 11, 1-21.

Edelman, G.M. 1978. Group selection and phasic reentrant signalling. In Edelman and Mountcastle, 1978, 51-100.

Edelman, G.M. 1987. *Neural Darwinism.* New York: Basic Books.

Edelman, G.M. 1989. *The Remembered Present.* New York: Basic Books.

Edelman, G.M. 1992. *Bright Air, Brilliant Fire.* New York: Basic Books.

Edelman, G.M. and Mountcastle, V. B. 1978. *The Mindful Brain.* Cambridge: The MIT Press.

Ellis, R. D. 1995a. The imagist approach to inferential thought patterns: The crucial role of rhythm pattern recognition. *Pragmatics and Cognition* 3, 1, 75-110.

Ellis, R.D. 1995b. *Questioning Consciousness.* Amsterdam, Philadelphia John Benjamins.

Evans, G. 1982. *Varieties of Reference.* New York: Oxford University Press.

Farah, M. 1989. The neural basis of mental imagery. *Trends in Neuroscience* 12, 395-399.

Fauconnier, G. 1985. *Mental Spaces: Aspects of Meaning Construction in Natural Language.* Cambridge: The MIT Press.

Fodor, J. 1973. *The Language of Thought.* Cambridge: Harvard Univ. Press.

Fodor, J. 1983. *The Modularity of Mind.* Cambridge, Mass.: MIT Press.

Fodor, J. 1987. *Psychosemantics.* Cambridge: MIT Press.

Fox, P., Peterson, S., Posner, M., and Raichle, M. 1988. Is Broca's area language specific? *Neurology* 38 (Supplement 1): 172.

Freud, S. 1900. *The Interpretation of Dreams.* (Trans. Strachey, J.). London: The Hogarth Press.

Freud, S. 1957. *A General Selection from the Works of Sigmund Freud,* (John Rickman, M.D., ed.). New York: Liveright Publishing Corp.

Geach, P. 1957. *Mental Acts: Their Content and Their Objects.* New York: Humanities Press.

Gendlin, E. 1973. Experiential phenomenology. In *Phenomenology and the Social Sciences,* Natanson, M. (ed), 281-319. Evanston: Northwestern University Press.

Gentner, D. 1983. Structure mapping: A theoretical framework for analogy. *Cognitive Science* 7, 155-170.

Goldman, A. 1970. *A Theory of Human Action.* Englewood Cliffs, N.J.: Prentice-Hall.

Goldman, A. 1976. The volitional theory revisited. In *Action Theory,* Brand, M. and Walton, D. (eds), 67-83. Dordrecht: D. Reidel.

Goldman, A. 1986. *Epistemology and Cognition.* Cambridge: Harvard University Press.

Goldman, A. 1990. Action and free will. In *Visual Cognition and Action,* Vol. 2, Osherson, D.N., Kosslyn, S.M., and Hollerbach, J.M. (eds), 317-340. Cambridge, Mass.: MIT Press.

Goldman, A. 1993. The psychology of folk psychology. *Behavioral and Brain Sciences* 16, 15-28.

Goldman-Rakic, P. 1987. Circuitry of the prefrontal cortex and the regulation of behavior by representational memory. *Handbook of Physiology* 5 (Part 1, Ch. 9): 373-417.

Goldman-Rakic, P. 1988. Topography of cognition: Parallel distributed networks in primate association cortex. *Annual Review of Neuroscience* 11: 137-156.

Goldman-Rakic, P. 1992. Working memory and the mind. *Scientific American,* September, 110-117.

Gopnik, A. 1993. How do we know our minds? *Behavioral and Brain Sciences* 16, 1-14.

Gordon, R. 1986. Folk psychology as simulation. *Mind and Language* 1, 2, 158-171.

Greenfield, P. 1991. Language, tools and brain: The ontogeny and phylogeny of hierarchically organized sequential behavior. *Behavioral and Brain Sciences,* 14, 4, 531-551.

Griffin, D. 1992. *Animal Minds* . Chicago: University of Chicago Press.

Harman, G. 1986. *Change in View*. Cambridge, Mass.: MIT Press.

Harman, G. 1990. The intrinsic quality of experience. In *Philosophical Perspectives, 4, Action Theory and Philosophy of Mind*, Tomberlin, J. (ed), 31-52.

Haugeland, J. 1979. Understanding natural language. *The Journal of Philosophy* 76, 619-632.

Haugeland, J. 1985. *Artificial Intelligence: The Very Idea*. Cambridge: MIT.

Huttenlocher, J. 1968. Constructing spatial images: A strategy in reasoning. *Psychological Review* 75, 286-298.

Ito, M. 1993. Movement and thought: Identical control mechanisms by the cerebellum. *Trends in the Neurosciences* 16, 11: 448-450.

Jackendoff, R. 1983. *Semantics and Cognition.* Cambridge, Mass.: MIT Press.

Jackendoff, R. 1987. *Consciousness and the Computational Mind*. Cambridge: MIT.

Jeannerod, M. 1988. *The Neural and Behavioral Organization of Goal-Directed Movements*. Oxford: Clarendon Press.

Jeannerod, M. 1994. The representing brain: Neural correlates of motor intention and imagery. *Behavioral and Brain Sciences* 17:2, 187-244.

Johnson, M. 1987. *The Body in the Mind*. Chicago: University of Chicago Press.

Johnson-Laird, P. 1983. *Mental Models*. Cambridge: Harvard University Press.

Julesz, B. 1984. A brief outline of the texton theory of human vision. *Trends in Neuroscience*. February.

Kandel, E.R. and Schwartz, J.H. 1985. *Principles of Neural Science*. New York: Elsevier.

Kersetz, A. 1988. Cognitive fuction in severe aphasia. In *Thought Without Language,* Weiskrantz, L. (ed), 451-463. Oxford: Clarendon Press.

Kimura, D. 1979. Neuromotor mechanisms in the evolution of human communication. In *Neurobiology of Social Communication in Primates*, Steklis, H. and Raleigh, M.J. (eds), 197-219. New York: Academic Press.

Kurata, K. 1992. Somatotopy in the human supplementary motor area. *Trends In Neurosciences* 15, 5, 159-161.

Lakoff, G. and Johnson, M. 1980. *Metaphors We Live By*. Chicago: The University of Chicago Press.

Lakoff, G. and Johnson, M. 1987. *Women, Fire and Dangerous Things*. Chicago: University of Chicago Press.

Langacker, R.W. 1987. *The Foundations of Cognitive Grammar*, Vol. I. Stanford: Stanford University Press.

LeDoux, J. E. 1992. Brain mechanisms of emotion and emotional learning. *Current Opinion in Neurobiology* 2:191-197.

Leiner, H.C., Leiner, A.L. and Dow, R.S. 1993. Cognitive and language functions of the human cerebellum. *Trends in the Neurosciences* 16, 11: 444-447.

Leslie, A. and Roth, D. 1992. What autism teaches us about metarepresentation. In *Understanding Other Minds: Perspectives from Autism,* Baron-Cohen, S., Tager-Flusberg, H. and Cohen, D. (eds). Oxford: Oxford University Press.

Lieberman, P. 1991. *Uniquely Human: The Evolution of Speech, Thought, and Selfless Behavior.* Cambridge: Harvard University Press.

Livingston, M. and Hubel, D. 1988. Segregation of form, color, movement and depth: Anatomy, physiology, and perception. *Science* 240, 740-749.

MacLane, S. 1981. Mathematical models: A sketch for the philosophy of mathematics. *American Mathematical Monthly,* Aug.-Sept., 462-72.

McClelland, J.L., Rumelhart, D. E., and the PDP Research Group 1986. *Parallel Distributed Processing.* Cambridge, Mass.: MIT Press.

McNeil, D. 1979. *The Conceptual Basis of Language.* Hillsdale, N.J.: Lawrence Erlbaum Associates.

McNeil, D. 1985. So you think gestures are nonverbal? *Psychological Review* 92, 3, 350-371.

McNeil, D. 1992. *Hand and Mind.* Chicago: University of Chicago Press.

Marr, D. 1976. Early processing of visual information. *Philosophical Transactions of the Royal Society of London B,* 275, 483-524.

Mele, A. 1992. *Springs of Action.* Oxford: Oxford University Press.

Meltzoff, A. and Gopnik, A. 1993. The role of imitation in understanding persons and developing theories of mind. In *Understanding Other Minds: Perspectives from Autism,* Baron-Cohen, S., Tager-Flusberg, H., and Cohen, D. (eds), 335-366. Oxford: Oxford University Press.

Merleau-Ponty, M. 1962. *Phenomenology of Perception.* London: Routledge and Kegan Paul.

Metcalfe, J. and Shimamura, A. P. 1994. *Metacognition.* Cambridge: MIT Press.

Millikam, R.G. 1984. *Language, Thought, and other Bilological Categories.* Cambridge, Mass.: MIT Press.

Nemirow, L.E. 1995. Understanding rules. *Journal of Philosophy* XCII, 1, 28-43.

Newton, N. 1982. Experience and imagery. *Southern Journal of Philosophy* 20, 4, 475-487.

Newton, N. 1985. Acting and perceiving in body and mind. *Philosophy Research Archives,* vol. XI, 407-429.

Newton, N. 1988. Machine understanding and the chinese room. *Philosophical Psychology* 1, 2, 207-215.

Newton, N. 1992. Dennett on intrinsic intentionality. *Analysis ,* 52, 1, 18-23.

Nisbett, R. and Ross, L. 1980. *Human Inference: Strategies and Shortcomings of Social Judgement.* Englewood Cliffs, N.J.: Prentiss-Hall.

Nisbett, R. and Wilson, T. 1977. Telling more than we can know. *Psychological Review* 84:231-259.

Norman, D. 1981. Categorization of action slips. *Psychological Review* 88, 1-15.

Norman, D. and Shallice, T. 1986. Attention to action. In *Consciousness and Self-Regulation,* vol. 4, 1-18. New York: Plenum Press.

Nute, D. (ed) 1991. *Defeasible Reasoning*: special issue of *Minds and Machines,* 1, 4.

O'Brien, L. F. 1995. Evans on self-identification. *NOUS* 29:2, 232-247.

Pandya, D. and Yeterian, E. 1985. Architecture and connections of cortical connection areas. In *Principles of Behavioral Neurology,* Mesulam, M-M. (ed), 3-61. Philadelphia: Davis Co.

Pardo, J., Pardo, P., Janer, K., and Raichle, M. 1990. The anterior cingulate cortex mediates processing selection in the stroop attentional conflict paradigm. *Proceedings of the National Academy of Sciences* 87, 256-259.

Penrose, R. 1989. *The Emporer's New Mind.* Oxford: Oxford University Press.

Perry, J. 1979. The problem of the essential indexical. *Nous* 13: 3-21.

Piaget, J. 1954. *The Construction of Reality in the Child.* New York: Basic Books.

Pinker, S. and Mehler, J. 1988. *Connections and Symbols.* Cambridge, Mass.: MIT Press.

Pinker, S. 1994. *The Language Instinct.* New York: William Morrow and Company.

Polanyi, M. 1958. *Personal Knowledge: Towards a Post-Critical Philosophy.* Chicago: University of Chicago Press.

Posner, M. and Dehaene, S. 1994. Attentional networks. *Trends in the Neurosciences* 17, 2, 75-79.

Posner, M. and Rothbart, S. 1991. Attentional mechanisms and conscious experience. In *The Neuropsychology of Consciousness.* Milner, A.D. and Rugg, M.D. (eds), 91-111. Academic Press.

Premack, D. 1988. Minds with and without language. In *Thought Without Language,* Weiskrantz, L. (ed), 46-65. Oxford: Clarandon Press.

Pribram, K. 1976. Problems concerning the structure of consciousness. In *Consciousness and the Brain,* Globus, G., Maxwell, G., and Savodnik, I., (eds), 295-313. New York: Plenum Press.

Putnam, H. 1960. Minds and machines. In *Dimensions of Mind*, Hook, S. (ed), 148-179. New York: Barnes and Noble.

Putnam, H. 1988. *Representation and Reality.* Cambridge, Mass.: MIT Press.

Pylyshyn, Z. 1973. What the mind's eye tells the mind's brain, *Psychological Bulletin* 80, 1-23.

Quine, Willard V.O. 1960. *Word and Object.* Cambridge, Mass.: MIT Press.

Reason, J. 1984. Lapses of attention in everyday life. In *Varieties of Attention,* Parasuraman, R. and Davies, D.R. (eds), 515-549. New York: Academic Press.

Roland, P.E. and Friberg, L. 1985. Localization of cortical areas activated by thinking. *Journal of Neurophysiology*, 53, 5, 1219-1243.

Roland, P. E. and Gulyas, B. 1994. Visual imagery and visual representation. *Trends in the Neurosciences* 17, 7, 281-287.

Ryle, G, 1949. *The Concept of Mind.* New York: Barnes and Noble.

Saussure, F de 1966. *Course in General Linguistics,* Bally, C. and Sechehaye, A. (eds). New York: McGraw-Hill Book Co. [1st French edn, 1916.]

Schank, R.C. and Abelson, R.P. 1977. *Scripts, Plans, Goals and Understanding.* Hillsdale, NJ: Lawrence Erlbaum.

Schiffer, S. 1987. *Remnants of Meaning.* Cambridge: MIT Press.

Schmidt, R. 1982. *Motor Control and Learning: A Behavioral Emphasis.* Champaign, Ill.: Human Kinetics Publishers.

Scoville, W.B. and Milner, B. 1957. Loss of recent memory after bilateral hippocampal lesions. *Journal of Neurology, Neurosurgery, and Psychiatry* 23, 589-599.

Searle, J. 1969. *Speech Acts*. Cambridge: Cambridge University Press.

Searle, J. 1980. Minds, brains and programs. *The Behavioral and Brain Sciences* 3, 417-424.

Searle, J. 1983. *Intentionality*. Cambridge: Cambridge University Press.

Searle, J. 1984. *Minds, Brains and Science*. Cambridge: Harvard University Press.

Shallice, T. 1988. *From Neuropsychology to Mental Structure*. Cambridge: Cambridge University Press.

Sloman, A. 1985. What enables a machine to understand? In *Proceedings of the 9th International Joint Conference on Artificial Intelligence*, v. 2, 995-1001.

Spiegelberg, H. 1960. *The Phenomenological Movement: A Historical Introduction*. The Hague: Martinus Nijhoff.

Strawson, P. 1959. *Individuals: An Essay in Descriptive Metaphysics*. London: Methuen & Co, Ltd.

Stuss, D.T. and Benson, D.F. 1986. *The Frontal Lobes*. New York: Raven Press.

Tranel, D. and Damasio, A.R. 1985. Knowledge without awareness: An autonomic index of facial recognation in prosopagnosics. *Science* 228, 1453-4.

Treisman, A. 1986. Features and objects in visual processing. *Scientific American* 255, 144-125.

Tulving, E. 1983. *Elements of Episodic Memory*. Oxford: Oxford University Press.

Tulving, E. 1985. Memory and consciousness. *Canadian Psychology* 26: 1-12

Tversky, A., and Kahneman, D. 1983. Extensional versus intuitive reasoning: The conjunction fallacy in probability judgement. *Psychological Review* 90, 4: 293-315.

Tye, M. 1983. On the possibility of disembodied existence. *Australasian Journal of Philosophy* 61, 3, 275-282.

Tye, M. 1992. Naturalism and the mental. *Mind* 101, 403, 421-441.

Washburn, M.F. 1916. *Movement and Mental Imagery*. Boston: Houghton Mifflin.

Weiskrantz, L. 1988. *Thought Without Language*. Oxford: Clarendon Press.

Werner, H., and Kaplan, E. 1952. *The Acquisition of Word Meanings: A Developmental Study*. Evanston, Ill.: Child Development Publications

Whorf, B. 1956. Science and Linguistics. In *Language, Thought and Reality: Selected Writings of Benjamin Lee Whorf*, Carroll, J.B.(ed.) Cambridge, Mass.: MIT Press.

Williams, B. 1973. Imagination and the self. In *Problems of the Self*, Cambridge: Cambridge University Press, 26-45.

Winograd, T. 1972. *Understanding Natural Language*. New York: Academic Press.

Wittgenstein, L. 1953. *Philosophical Investigations*. New York: MacMillan.

Wright, C. 1990. Controlling sequential motor activity. In *Visual Cognition and Action*, vol. 2, Osherson, D., Kosslyn, S., and Hollerbach, J. (eds). Cambridge: MIT Press. 285-316.

Zeki, S. 1980. The representation of colors in the cerebral cortex. *Nature,* 284, 412-418.

Index

9161